Conference of the North American Chapter of the Association for Computational Linguistics: Human Language Technologies (NAACL HLT 2015)

Demonstrations

Denver, Colorado, USA
31 May – 5 June 2015

ISBN: 978-1-5108-0448-7

Printed from e-media with permission by:

Curran Associates, Inc.
57 Morehouse Lane
Red Hook, NY 12571

CURRAN ASSOCIATES INC.
proceedings.com

Some format issues inherent in the e-media version may also appear in this print version.

Printed by Curran Associates, Inc. (2015)

Association for Computational Linguistics
209 N. Eighth Street
Stroudsburg, Pennsylvania 18360

Phone: 1-570-476-8006
Fax: 1-570-476-0860

acl@aclweb.org

Additional copies of this publication are available from:

Curran Associates, Inc.
57 Morehouse Lane
Red Hook, NY 12571 USA
Phone: 845-758-0400
Fax: 845-758-2634
Email: curran@proceedings.com
Web: www.proceedings.com

Introduction (TODO)

Welcome to the ACL Workshop on Unresolved Matters. We received 17 submissions, and due to a rigerous review process, we rejected 16.

Organizers:

Matthew Gerber, University of Virginia
Catherine Havasi, Luminoso
Finley Lacatusu, Language Computer Corporation

Reviewers:

Zeljko Agic, University of Zagreb
Omar Alonso, Microsoft Research
Tyler Baldwin, IBM Research
Georgeta Bordea, NUI Galway
Kevin Cohen, University of Colorado School of Medicine
Montse Cuadros, Universitat Politecnica de Catalunya
Thierry Declerck, DFK
Karthik Dinakar, MIT Media Lab
Mark Dras, Macquarie University
Michele Filannino, University of Manchester
Marek Krawczyk, Hokkaido University
Brigitte Krenn, Qustrian Research Institute for Artificial Intelligence (OFAI)
Changsong Liu, Michigan State University
Clare Llewellyn, University of Edinburgh
Marie-Jean Meurs, Concordia University
Tsuyoshi Okita, Dublin City University
Arzucan Ozgur, Bogazici University
Stelios Piperidis, National Technical University of Athens
Zahar Prasov, Michigan State University
Kirk Roberts, University of Texas
Melissa Roemmele, ICT, USC
Masoud Rouhizadeh, Oregon Health & Science University
Irene Russo, Istituto di Linguistica Computazionale, CNR
Le Sun, Chinese Academy of Sciences
Maarten van Gompel, Radboud University
Marc Vilain, MITRE
Liang-Chih Yu, Yuan Ze University
Guodong Zhou, Soochow University

Table of Contents

Conference Program

Tuesday, June 2, 2015

17:00–18:30 ***NAACL Demo Session A***

Two Practical Rhetorical Structure Theory Parsers
Mihai Surdeanu, Tom Hicks and Marco Antonio Valenzuela-Escarcega

Analyzing and Visualizing Coreference Resolution Errors
Sebastian Martschat, Thierry Göckel and Michael Strube

hyp: A Toolkit for Representing, Manipulating, and Optimizing Hypergraphs
Markus Dreyer and Jonathan Graehl

Enhancing Instructor-Student and Student-Student Interactions with Mobile Interfaces and Summarization
Wencan Luo, Xiangmin Fan, Muhsin Menekse, Jingtao Wang and Diane Litman

RExtractor: a Robust Information Extractor
Vincent Kríž and Barbora Hladka

An AMR parser for English, French, German, Spanish and Japanese and a new AMR-annotated corpus
Lucy Vanderwende, Arul Menezes and Chris Quirk

ICE: Rapid Information Extraction Customization for NLP Novices
Yifan He and Ralph Grishman

AMRICA: an AMR Inspector for Cross-language Alignments
Naomi Saphra and Adam Lopez

Ckylark: A More Robust PCFG-LA Parser
Yusuke Oda, Graham Neubig, Sakriani Sakti, Tomoki Toda and Satoshi Nakamura

ELCO3: Entity Linking with Corpus Coherence Combining Open Source Annotators
Pablo Ruiz, Thierry Poibeau and Fréderique Mélanie

SETS: Scalable and Efficient Tree Search in Dependency Graphs
Juhani Luotolahti, Jenna Kanerva, Sampo Pyysalo and Filip Ginter

Visualizing Deep-Syntactic Parser Output
Juan Soler-Company, Miguel Ballesteros, Bernd Bohnet, Simon Mille and Leo Wanner

WOLFE: An NLP-friendly Declarative Machine Learning Stack
Sameer Singh, Tim Rocktäschel, Luke Hewitt, Jason Naradowsky and Sebastian Riedel

17:00–18:30 ***NAACL Demo Session B***

Lean Question Answering over Freebase from Scratch
Xuchen Yao

A Web Application for Automated Dialect Analysis
Sravana Reddy and James Stanford

An Open-source Framework for Multi-level Semantic Similarity Measurement
Mohammad Taher Pilehvar and Roberto Navigli

Brahmi-Net: A transliteration and script conversion system for languages of the Indian subcontinent
Anoop Kunchukuttan, Ratish Puduppully and Pushpak Bhattacharyya

A Concrete Chinese NLP Pipeline
Nanyun Peng, Francis Ferraro, Mo Yu, Nicholas Andrews, Jay DeYoung, Max Thomas, Matthew R. Gormley, Travis Wolfe, Craig Harman, Benjamin Van Durme and Mark Dredze

CroVeWA: Crosslingual Vector-Based Writing Assistance
Hubert Soyer, Goran Topić, Pontus Stenetorp and Akiko Aizawa

Online Readability and Text Complexity Analysis with TextEvaluator
Diane Napolitano, Kathleen Sheehan and Robert Mundkowsky

Natural Language Question Answering and Analytics for Diverse and Interlinked Datasets
Dezhao Song, Frank Schilder, Charese Smiley and Chris Brew

WriteAhead2: Mining Lexical Grammar Patterns for Assisted Writing
Jim Chang and Jason Chang

Question Answering System using Multiple Information Source and Open Type Answer Merge
Seonyeong Park, Soonchoul Kwon, Byungsoo Kim, Sangdo Han, Hyosup Shim and Gary Geunbae Lee

Tuesday, June 2, 2015 (continued)

Two Practical Rhetorical Structure Theory Parsers

Mihai Surdeanu, Thomas Hicks, and Marco A. Valenzuela-Escárcega
University of Arizona, Tucson, AZ, USA
{msurdeanu, hickst, marcov}@email.arizona.edu

Abstract

We describe the design, development, and API for two discourse parsers for Rhetorical Structure Theory. The two parsers use the same underlying framework, but one uses features that rely on dependency syntax, produced by a fast shift-reduce parser, whereas the other uses a richer feature space, including both constituent- and dependency-syntax and coreference information, produced by the Stanford CoreNLP toolkit. Both parsers obtain state-of-the-art performance, and use a very simple API consisting of, minimally, two lines of Scala code. We accompany this code with a visualization library that runs the two parsers in parallel, and displays the two generated discourse trees side by side, which provides an intuitive way of comparing the two parsers.

1 Introduction

This paper describes the design and development of two practical parsers for Rhetorical Structure Theory (RST) discourse (Mann and Thompson, 1988). This work contributes to the already vast body of research on RST parsing (see, inter alia, Soricut and Marcu, 2003; Feng and Hirst, 2012; Joty et al., 2013, Joty et al., 2014) with the following:

1. We propose two parsers that use constituent-based and dependency-based syntax, respectively. The underlying framework, other than the syntax-based features, is identical between the parsers, which permits a rigorous analysis of the impact of constituent and dependency syntax to RST parsing. We describe the parsers in Section 2 and empirically compare the impact of the two syntactic representations in Section 3. Our analysis indicates that both parsers achieve state-of-the-art performance. The parser based on dependency syntax performs marginally worse (by 0.1 F_1 points) but runs approximately 2.5 times faster than the parser based on constituent syntax. On average, the faster parser processes one document from the RST corpus in 2.3 seconds.

2. Both parsers have been released as open-source Scala code with a very simple API; consisting of, minimally, two lines of code. We discuss this API in Section 4.

3. We also introduce a visualization tool that runs the two parsers in parallel, and displays the two generated discourse structures side by side. This allows users to directly compare the runtimes and outputs of the two parsers. This visualization tool will be the centerpiece of the proposed demo session. We summarize this tool in Section 5.

2 The Two Parsers

The proposed parsing approach follows the architecture introduced by Hernault et al. (2010), and Feng and Hirst (2012). The parser first segments the text into elementary discourse units (EDUs) using an i.i.d. classifier that identifies which tokens end an EDU. Then the parser iteratively constructs the discourse tree (consisting of binary relations between discourse units) using a greedy bottom-up approach that interleaves two classifiers: the first de-

Proceedings of NAACL-HLT 2015, pages 1–5,
Denver, Colorado, May 31 – June 5, 2015. ©2015 Association for Computational Linguistics

tects which two adjacent discourse units are most likely to be connected given the current sequence of units; and the second labels the corresponding relation. The resulting discourse unit produced by the new relation replaces its two children. The process repeats until there is a single discourse unit spanning the text.[1]

We chose this algorithm rather than other recent proposed approaches (Joty et al., 2013; Joty and Moschitti, 2014) because: (a) it promotes a simple, modular architecture; (b) it is fast, and (c) as we show later, it performs well. For classification, we experimented with Support Vector Machines (SVM), Perceptron, and Logistic Regression (LR). The results reported here use Perceptron for EDU segmentation and relation detection, and LR for relation labeling, thus offering a good balance between performance and quick training.

With respect to features, our approach builds on previous work (Hernault et al., 2010; Feng and Hirst, 2012; Joty et al., 2013) and extends it in two ways. First, we implement all syntactic features using both constituent and dependency syntax. For example, a crucial feature used by the relation detection/labeling classifiers is the *dominance relations* of Soricut and Marcu (2003), which capture syntactic dominance between discourse units located in the same sentence. While originally these dominance relations were implemented using constituent syntax, we provide an equivalent implementation that relies on dependency syntax. There are two advantages to this approach: (a) we can now implement a full RST discourse parser using a (much faster) dependency parser; (b) when using a parser that produces both constituent and dependency syntax, such as Stanford's CoreNLP[2], our experiments show that using both these feature sets increases the performance of the model.

Our second contribution is adding features based on coreference links. We currently use coreference information in two of the latter classifiers (relation detection and labeling) by counting the number of coreference links crossing between the two discourse units under consideration. The intuition behind this feature is that the more coreferential relations exist between two discourse units, the more likely they are to be directly connected.

Using the above framework, we implemented two discourse parsers. The first uses CoreNLP for syntactic parsing and coreference resolution. This parser uses both constituent- and dependency-based features generated using the parser of Manning and Klein (2003). The second discourse parser uses either Malt[3] or the recent neural-network-based parser of Chen and Manning (2014) for dependency parsing. The second discourse parser does not use constituent- nor coreference-based features. For all syntactic parsers, we used the "basic" Stanford dependency representation (de Marneffe et al., 2006). Empirically, we found that this representation yields better discourse parsing performance than any of the "collapsed" representations.

3 Analysis

We analyze the performance of the two discourse parsers in Table 1. For conciseness, we identify the parser that uses both constituent- and dependency-based syntax and coreference resolution (all produced using CoreNLP) as C, and the parser that uses only dependency-based features as D. The latter one is subclassed as D_{malt}, if the syntactic analysis is performed with the Malt parser, or $D_{stanford}$, if syntactic parsing is performed with the parser of Chen and Manning (2014). Because we are interested in end-to-end performance, we report solely end-to-end performance on the RST test corpus (Carlson et al., 2003). This analysis yields several observations:

- The overall performance of the proposed parsers compares favorably with the state of the art. Both the C and D parsers outperform the parser of Hernault et al. (2010), and perform comparably to the parser of Joty et al. (2013). The recent work of Joty et al. (2014), which uses a considerably more complex architecture based on reranking, outperforms our parsers by 1.8 F_1 points.

- In general, the C parser performs better than D on all metrics. This is to be expected

[1]Interleaving the two classifiers in this iterative procedure guarantees that the classifiers have access to features extracted from the discourse subtrees constructed in previous iterations.

[2]http://nlp.stanford.edu/software/corenlp.shtml

[3]http://www.maltparser.org

	Manual EDUs	Predicted EDUs		
	F_1	P	R	F_1
D_{malt}	54.3	48.3	47.5	47.9
$D_{stanford}$	55.2	49.1	48.5	48.8
C	55.5	**49.2**	**48.5**	**48.9**
C – dep	55.5	47.9	47.6	47.7
C – const	53.7	47.7	47.0	47.3
C – coref	55.2	49.0	48.3	48.7
C – const – coref	53.9	47.9	47.2	47.5
Hernault 2010	54.8	47.7	46.9	47.3
Joty 2013	55.8	–	–	–
Joty 2014	**57.3**	–	–	–

Table 1: Performance of the two discourse parsers: one relying on constituent-based syntactic parsing (C), and another using a dependency parser (D). We report end-to-end results on the 18 relations with nuclearity information used by (Hernault et al., 2010; Feng and Hirst, 2012), using both manual segmentation of text into EDUs (left table block), and EDUs predicted by the parser (right block). We used the Precision/Recall/F_1 metrics introduced by Marcu (2000). The ablation test removes various feature groups: features extracted from the dependency representation (dep), features from constituent syntax (const), and coreference features (coref). We compare against previous work that reported end-to-end performance of their corresponding approaches (Hernault et al., 2010; Joty et al., 2013; Joty and Moschitti, 2014).

considering that C uses both constituent- and dependency-based features, and coreference information. However, the improvement is small (e.g., 0.2 F_1 points when gold EDUs are used) and the D parser is faster: it processes the entire test dataset in 88 seconds (at an average of 2.3 seconds/document) vs. 224 seconds for C.[4] For comparison, the (Feng and Hirst, 2012) discourse parser processes the same dataset in 605 seconds.

- The comparison of the two configurations of the dependency-based parser ("D_{malt}" vs. "$D_{stanford}$") indicates that the parser of Chen and Manning (2014) yields better RST parsing performance than the Malt parser, e.g., by 0.9 F_1 points when predicted EDUs are used.

- The ablation test in rows 4–5 of the table indicate that the two syntactic representations complement each other well: removing dependency-based features (the "C – dep" row) drops the F_1 score for predicted EDUs by 1.2 points (because of the worse EDU segmentation); removing constituent-based features ("C – const") drops performance by 1.6 F_1 points.

- Feature wise, the "C – const – coref" system is equivalent to D, but with dependency parsing performed by converting the constituent trees produced by the Stanford parser to dependencies, rather than direct dependency parsing. It is interesting to note that the performance of this system is lower than both configurations of the D parser, suggesting that direct dependency parsing with a dedicated model is beneficial.

- The "C – coref" ablation experiment indicates that coreference information has a small contribution to the overall performance (0.3 F_1 points when gold EDUs are used). Nevertheless, we find this result exciting, considering that this is a first attempt at using coreference information for discourse parsing.

4 Usage

With respect to usage, we adhere to the simplicity principles promoted by Stanford's CoreNLP, which introduced a simple, concrete Java API rather than relying on heavier frameworks, such as UIMA (Ferrucci and Lally, 2004). This guarantees that a user is "up and running in ten minutes or less", by "doing one thing well" and "avoiding over-design" (Manning et al., 2014). Following this idea, our API contains two `Processor` objects, one for each discourse parser, and a single method call, `annotate()`, which implements the complete analysis of a document (represented as a `String`), from tokenization to discourse parsing.[5] Figure 1 shows sample API usage. The `annotate()` method produces a `Document` object, which stores all NLP annotations: tokens, part-of-speech tags, constituent trees, dependency graphs, coreference relations, and discourse trees.

[4]These times were measured on a laptop with an i7 Intel CPU and 16GB of RAM. The times include end-to-end execution, including model loading and complete preprocessing of text, from tokenization to syntactic parsing and coreference resolution.

[5]Additional methods are provided for pre-existing tokenization and/or sentence segmentation.

```
import edu.arizona.sista.processors.corenlp._
import edu.arizona.sista.processors.fastnlp._
//
// CoreNLPProcessor:
// - syntax/coref with CoreNLP;
// - constituent-based RST parser.
// FastNLPProcessor:
// - syntax with Malt or CoreNLP.
// - dependency-based RST parser.
//
val processor = new CoreNLPProcessor()
val document = processor.annotate(
  "Tandy Corp. said it won't join U.S.
   Memories, the group that seeks to battle
   the Japanese in the market for computer
   memory chips.")
println(document.discourseTree.get)
```

Figure 1: Minimal (but complete) code for using the discourse parser. Use `CoreNLPProcessor` for the constituent-based RST parser, and `FastNLPProcessor` for the dependency-based discourse parser. Other than the different constructors, the APIs are identical.

The `DiscourseTree` class is summarized in Figure 2.

The code for the two parsers is available on GitHub, and is also packaged as two JAR files in the Maven Central Repository (one JAR file for code, and another for the pre-trained models), which guarantees that others can install and use it with minimal effort. For code and more information, please see the project's GitHub page: `https://github.com/sistanlp/processors`.

5 Visualization of Discourse Trees

We accompany the above Scala library with a web-based visualization tool that runs the two parsers in parallel and visualizes the two outputs for the same text side by side. This allows the users to: (a) directly compare the runtimes of the two systems in realtime for arbitrary texts; (b) analyze the qualitative difference in the outputs of two parsers; and (c) debug incorrect outputs (e.g., is the constituent tree correct?). Figure 3 shows a screenshot of this visualization tool.

The visualization tool is implemented as a client-server Grails[6] web application which runs the parsers (on the server) and collects and displays the results (on the client side). The application's client-side code displays both the discourse trees and syntactic information using Dagre-d3[7], a D3-based[8] renderer for the Dagre graph layout engine.

[6] `https://grails.org`

```
class DiscourseTree (
  /** Label of this tree, if non-terminal */
  var relationLabel:String,
  /** Direction of the relation,
    * if non-terminal. It can be:
    * LeftToRight, RightToLeft,
    * or None. */
  var relationDir:RelationDirection.Value,
  /** Children of this non-terminal node */
  var children:Array[DiscourseTree],
  /** Raw text attached to this node */
  val rawText:String,
  /** Position of the first token in the
    * text covered by this discourse tree */
  var firstToken: TokenOffset,
  /** Position of the last token in the
    * text covered by this discourse tree;
    * this is inclusive! */
  var lastToken: TokenOffset
)
```

Figure 2: Relevant fields in the `DiscourseTree` class, which stores the RST tree produced by the parsers for a given document. The token offsets point to tokens stored in the `Document` class returned by the `annotate()` method above.

6 Conclusions

This work described the design, development and the resulting open-source software for a parsing framework for Rhetorical Structure Theory. Within this framework, we offer two parsers, one built on top of constituent-based syntax, and the other that uses dependency-based syntax. Both parsers obtain state-of-the-art performance, are fast, and are easy to use through a simple API.

In future work, we will aim at improving the performance of the parsers using joint parsing models. Nevertheless, it is important to note that RST parsers have already demonstrated their potential to improve natural language processing applications. For example, in our previous work we used features extracted from RST discourse relations to enhance a non-factoid question answering system (Jansen et al., 2014). In recent work, we showed how to use discourse relations to generate artificial training data for mono-lingual alignment models for question answering (Sharp et al., 2015).

[7] `https://github.com/cpettitt/dagre-d3`
[8] `http://d3js.org`

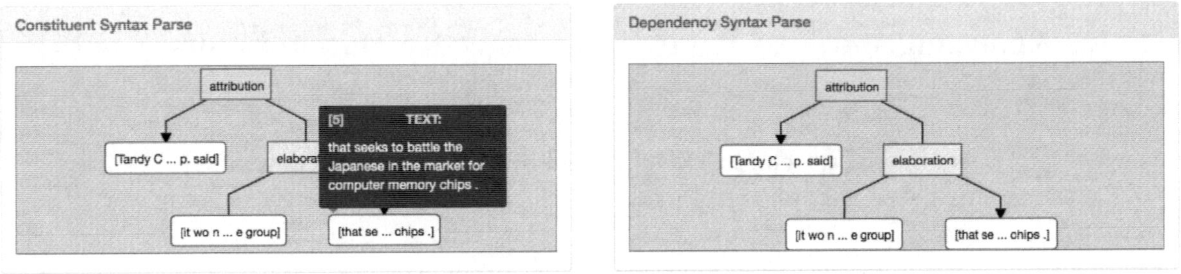

Figure 3: Screenshot of the discourse parser visualization tool for the input: *"Tandy Corp. said it won't join U.S. Memories, the group that seeks to battle the Japanese in the market for computer memory chips."* The left pane shows the output of the C parser; the right one shows the output of the D parser. Hovering with the cursor over a tree node shows its full content. Not shown here but included in the visualization: syntactic analyses used by the two parses and runtimes for each component (from tokenization to syntactic analysis).

Acknowledgments

This work was funded by the DARPA Big Mechanism program under ARO contract W911NF-14-1-0395.

References

L. Carlson, D. Marcu, and M. E. Okurowski. 2003. Building a Discourse-Tagged Corpus in the Framework of Rhetorical Structure Theory. In Jan van Kuppevelt and Ronnie Smith, editors, *Current Directions in Discourse and Dialogue*, pages 85–112. Kluwer Academic Publishers.

D. Chen and C. D. Manning. 2014. A fast and accurate dependency parser using neural networks. In *Proceedings of the Conference on Empirical Methods in Natural Language Processing (EMNLP)*.

M.-C. de Marneffe, B. MacCartney, and C. D. Manning. 2006. Generating typed dependency parses from phrase structure parses. In *Proceedings of the International Conference on Language Resources and Evaluation (LREC)*.

V. W. Feng and G. Hirst. 2012. Text-level discourse parsing with rich linguistic features. In *Proceedings of the Association for Computational Linguistics*.

D. Ferrucci and A. Lally. 2004. UIMA: an architectural approach to unstructured information processing in the corporate research environment. *Natural Language Engineering*, 10:327–348.

H. Hernault, H. Prendinger, D. duVerle, and M. Ishizuka. 2010. HILDA: A discourse parser using support vector machine classification. *Dialogue and Discourse*, 1(3):1–33.

P. Jansen, M. Surdeanu, and P. Clark. 2014. Discourse complements lexical semantics for non-factoid answer reranking. In *Proceedings of the 52nd Annual Meeting of the Association for Computational Linguistics*.

S. Joty and A. Moschitti. 2014. Discriminative reranking of discourse parses using tree kernels. In *Proceedings of the Conference on Empirical Methods in Natural Language Processing*.

S. Joty, G. Carenini, R. Ng, and Y. Mehdad. 2013. Combining intra- and multi-sentential rhetorical parsing for document-level discourse analysis. In *Proceedings of the 51st Annual Meeting of the Association for Computational Linguistics*.

D. Klein and C. D. Manning. 2003. Accurate unlexicalized parsing. In *Proceedings of the 41st Annual Meeting of the Association for Computational Linguistics (ACL)*.

W. C. Mann and S. A. Thompson. 1988. Rhetorical structure theory: Toward a functional theory of text organization. *Text*, 8(3):243–281.

C. D. Manning, M. Surdeanu, J. Bauer, J. Finkel, S. J. Bethard, and D. McClosky. 2014. The Stanford CoreNLP natural language processing toolkit. In *Proceedings of the 52nd Annual Meeting of the Association for Computational Linguistics*.

D. Marcu. 2000. *The Theory and Practice of Discourse Parsing and Summarization*. MIT Press.

R. Sharp, P. Jansen, M. Surdeanu, and P. Clark. 2015. Spinning straw into gold: Using free text to train monolingual alignment models for non-factoid question answering. In *Proceedings of the Conference of the North American Chapter of the Association for Computational Linguistics - Human Language Technologies (NAACL HLT)*.

R. Soricut and D. Marcu. 2003. Sentence level discourse parsing using syntactic and lexical information. In *Proceedings of the Human Language Technology and North American Association for Computational Linguistics Conference*.

Analyzing and Visualizing Coreference Resolution Errors

Sebastian Martschat[1], **Thierry Göckel**[2] and **Michael Strube**[1]
[1]Heidelberg Institute for Theoretical Studies gGmbH, Heidelberg, Germany
(sebastian.martschat|michael.strube)@h-its.org
[2]iQser GmbH, Walldorf, Germany
thierry.goeckel@iqser.com

Abstract

We present a toolkit for coreference resolution error analysis. It implements a recently proposed analysis framework and contains rich components for analyzing and visualizing recall and precision errors.

1 Introduction

Coreference resolution is the task of determining which mentions in a text refer to the same entity. Both the natural language processing engineer (who needs a coreference resolution system for the problem at hand) and the coreference resolution researcher need tools to facilitate and support system development, comparison and analysis.

In Martschat and Strube (2014), we propose a framework for error analysis for coreference resolution. In this paper, we present *cort*[1], an implementation of this framework, and show how it can be useful for engineers and researchers. *cort* is released as open source and is available for download[2].

2 Error Analysis Framework

Due to the set-based nature of coreference resolution, it is not clear how to extract errors when an entity is not correctly identified. The idea underlying the analysis framework of Martschat and Strube (2014) is to employ spanning trees in a graph-based entity representation.

Figure 1 summarizes their approach. They represent reference and system entities as complete one-directional graphs (Figures 1a and 1b). To extract recall errors, they compute a spanning tree of the reference entity (Figure 1a). All edges in the spanning tree which do not appear in the system output are extracted as recall errors (Figure 1c). For extracting precision errors, the roles of reference and system entities are switched.

The analysis algorithm is parametrized only by the spanning tree algorithm employed: different algorithms lead to different notions of errors. In Martschat and Strube (2014), we propose an algorithm based on Ariel's accessibility theory (Ariel, 1990) for reference entities. For system entity spanning trees, we take each output pair as an edge.

3 Architecture

Our toolkit is available as a Python library. It consists of three modules: the `core` module provides mention extraction and preprocessing, the `coreference` module implements features for and approaches to coreference resolution, and the `analysis` module implements the error analysis framework described above and ships with other analysis and visualization utilities.

3.1 `core`

All input and output must conform to the format of the CoNLL-2012 shared task on coreference resolution (Pradhan et al., 2012). We employ a rule-based mention extractor, which also computes a rich set of mention attributes, including tokens, head, part-of-speech tags, named entity tags, gender, number, se-

[1]Short for **co**reference **r**esolution **t**oolkit.
[2]http://smartschat.de/software

Proceedings of NAACL-HLT 2015, pages 6–10,
Denver, Colorado, May 31 – June 5, 2015. ©2015 Association for Computational Linguistics

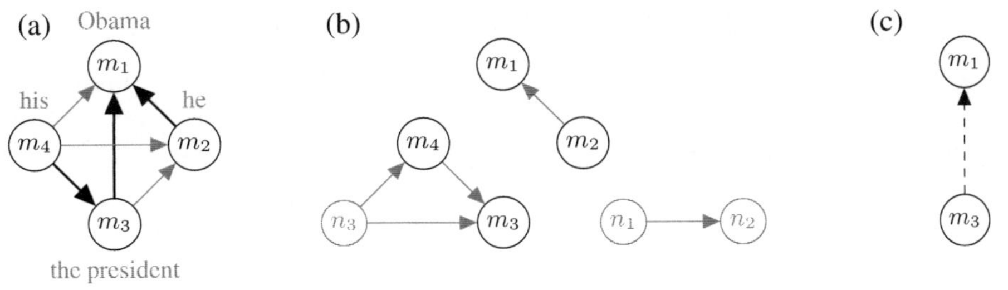

Figure 1: (a) a reference entity r (represented as a complete one-directional graph) and its spanning tree T_r, (b) a set S of three system entities, (c) the errors: all edges in T_r which are not in S.

mantic class, grammatical function, coarse mention type and fine-grained mention type.

3.2 `coreference`

cort ships with two coreference resolution approaches. First, it includes *multigraph*, which is a deterministic approach using a few strong features (Martschat and Strube, 2014). Second, it includes a mention-pair approach (Soon et al., 2001) with a large feature set, trained via a perceptron on the CoNLL'12 English training data.

System	MUC	B^3	$CEAF_e$	Average
StanfordSieve	64.96	54.49	51.24	56.90
BerkeleyCoref	70.27	59.29	56.11	61.89
multigraph	69.13	58.61	56.06	61.28
mention-pair	69.09	57.84	53.56	60.16

Table 1: Comparison of systems on CoNLL'12 English development data.

In Table 1, we compare both approaches with *StanfordSieve* (Lee et al., 2013), the winner of the CoNLL-2011 shared task, and *BerkeleyCoref* (Durrett and Klein, 2013), a state-of-the-art structured machine learning approach. The systems are evaluated via the CoNLL scorer (Pradhan et al., 2014).

Both implemented approaches achieve competitive performance. Due to their modular implementation, both approaches are easily extensible with new features and with training or inference schemes. They therefore can serve as a good starting point for system development and analysis.

3.3 `analysis`

The core of this module is the `ErrorAnalysis` class, which extracts and manages errors extracted from one or more systems. The user can define own spanning tree algorithms to extract errors. We already implemented the algorithms discussed in Martschat and Strube (2014). Furthermore, this module provides functionality to

- categorize and filter sets of errors,
- visualize these sets,
- compare errors of different systems, and
- display errors in document context.

Which of these features is interesting to the user depends on the use case. In the following, we will describe the popular use case of improving a coreference system in detail. Our system also supports other use cases, such as the cross-system analysis described in Martschat and Strube (2014).

4 Use Case: Improving a Coreference Resolution System

A natural language processing engineer might be interested in improving the performance of a coreference resolution system since it is necessary for another task. The needs may differ depending on the task at hand: for some tasks proper name coreference may be of utmost importance, while other tasks need mostly pronoun coreference. Through model and feature redesign, the engineer wants to improve the system with respect to a certain error class.

The user will start with a baseline system, which can be one of the implemented systems in our toolkit or a third-party system. We now describe how *cort* facilitates improving the system.

4.1 Initial Analysis

To get an initial assessment, the user can extract all errors made by the system and then make use of the plotting component to compare these errors with the maximum possible number of errors[3].

For a meaningful analysis, we have to find a suitable error categorization. Suppose the user is interested in improving recall for non-pronominal coreference. Hence, following Martschat and Strube (2014), we categorize all errors by coarse mention type of anaphor and antecedent (proper name, noun, pronoun, demonstrative pronoun or verb)[4].

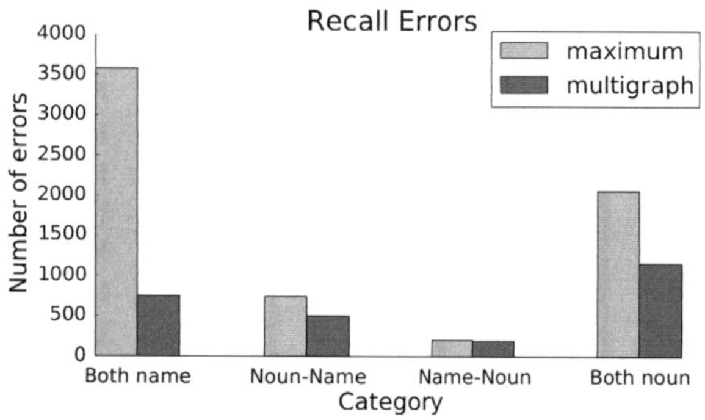

Figure 2: Recall errors of the *multigraph* baseline.

Figure 2 compares the recall error numbers of the *multigraph* system with the maximum possible number of errors for the categories of interest to the engineer. The plot was created by our toolkit via *matplotlib* (Hunter, 2007). We can see that the model performs very well for proper name pairs. Relative to the maximum number of errors, there are much more recall errors in the other categories. A plot for precision errors shows that the system makes only relatively few precision errors, especially for proper name pairs.

After studying these plots the user decides to improve recall for pairs where the anaphor is a noun and the antecedent is a name. This is a frequent category which is handled poorly by the system.

[3]For recall, the maximum number of errors are the errors made by a system which puts each mention in its own cluster. For precision, we take all pairwise decisions of a model.

[4]For a pair of mentions constituting an error, we call the mention appearing later in the text the *anaphor*, the other mention *antecedent*.

4.2 Detailed Analysis

In order to determine how to improve the system, the user needs to perform a detailed analysis of the noun-name errors. Our toolkit provides several methods to do so. First of all, one can browse through the pairwise error representations. This suggests further subcategorization (for example by the presence of token overlap). An iteration of this process leads to a fine-grained categorization of errors.

However, this approach does not provide any document context, which is necessary to understand some errors. Maybe context features can help in resolving the error, or the error results from multiple competing antecedents. We therefore include a visualization component, which also allows to study the interplay between recall and precision.

Figure 3 shows a screenshot of this visualization component, which runs in a web browser using JavaScript. The header displays the identifier of the document in focus. The left bar contains the navigation panel, which includes

- a list of all documents in the corpus,
- a summary of all errors for the document in focus, and
- lists of reference and system entities for the document in focus.

To the right of the navigation panel, the document in focus is shown. When the user picks a reference or system entity from the corresponding list, *cort* displays all recall and precision errors for all mentions which are contained in the entity (as labeled red arrows between mentions). Alternatively, the user can choose an error category from the error summary. In that case, all errors of that category are displayed.

We use color to distinguish between entities: mentions in different entities have different background colors. Additionally mentions in reference entities have a yellow border, while mentions in system entities have a blue border (for example, the mention *the U.S.-backed rebels* is in a reference entity and in a system entity). The user can choose to color the background of mentions either depending on their gold entity or depending on their system entity.

These visualization capabilities allow for a detailed analysis of errors and enable the user to take all document information into account.

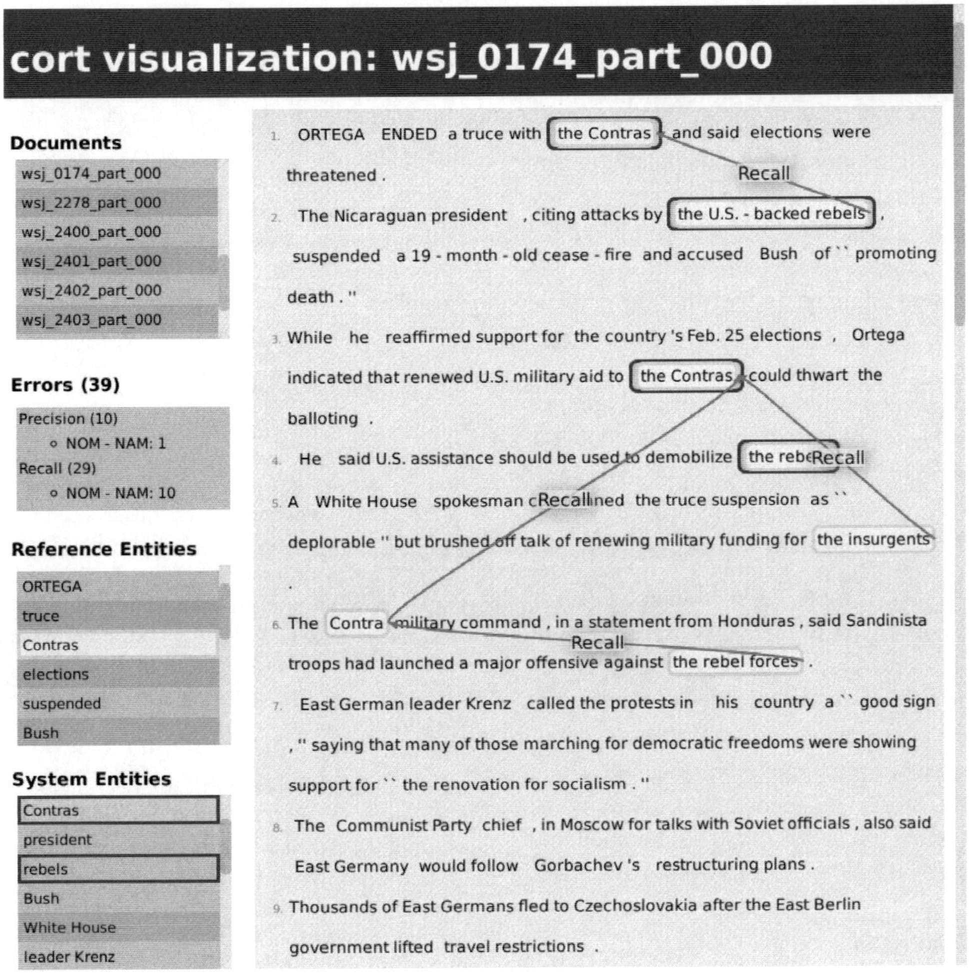

Figure 3: Screenshot of the visualization component.

The result of the analysis is that almost all errors are missed is-a relations, such as in the examples in Figure 3 (*the U.S.-backed rebels* and *the Contras*).

4.3 Error Comparison

Motivated by this, the user can add features to the system, for example incorporating world knowledge from Wikipedia. The output of the changed model can be loaded into the `ErrorAnalysis` object which already manages the errors made by the baseline system.

To compare the errors, *cort* implements various functions. In particular, the user can access common errors and errors which are unique to one or more systems. This allows for an assessment of the qualitative usefulness of the new feature. Depending on the results of the comparison, the user can decide between discarding, retaining and improving the feature.

5 Related Work

Compared to our original implementation of the error analysis framework (Martschat and Strube, 2014), we made the analysis interface more user-friendly and provide more analysis functionality. Furthermore, while our original implementation did not include any visualization capabilities, we now allow for both data visualization and document visualization.

We are aware of two other software packages for coreference resolution error analysis. Our toolkit complements these. Kummerfeld and Klein (2013) present a toolkit which extracts errors from transformation of reference to system entities. Hence, their definition of what an error is not rooted in a pairwise representation, and is therefore conceptually different from our definition. They do not provide any visualization components.

ICE (Gärtner et al., 2014) is a toolkit for coreference visualization and corpus analysis. In particular, the toolkit visualizes recall and precision errors in a tree-based visualization of coreference clusters. Compared to ICE, we provide more extensive functionality for error analysis and can accommodate for different notions of errors.

6 Conclusions and Future Work

We presented *cort*, a toolkit for coreference resolution error analysis. It implements a graph-based analysis framework, ships with two strong coreference resolution baselines and provides extensive functionality for analysis and visualization.

We are currently investigating whether the analysis framework can also be applied to structurally related tasks, such as cross-document coreference resolution (Singh et al., 2011) or entity linking.

Acknowledgements

This work has been funded by the Klaus Tschira Foundation, Heidelberg, Germany. The first author has been supported by a HITS PhD scholarship.

References

Mira Ariel. 1990. *Accessing Noun Phrase Antecedents.* Routledge, London, U.K.; New York, N.Y.

Greg Durrett and Dan Klein. 2013. Easy victories and uphill battles in coreference resolution. In *Proceedings of the 2013 Conference on Empirical Methods in Natural Language Processing,* Seattle, Wash., 18–21 October 2013, pages 1971–1982.

Markus Gärtner, Anders Björkelund, Gregor Thiele, Wolfgang Seeker, and Jonas Kuhn. 2014. Visualization, search, and error analysis for coreference annotations. In *Proceedings of 52nd Annual Meeting of the Association for Computational Linguistics: System Demonstrations,* Baltimore, Md., 22–27 June 2014, pages 7–12.

John D. Hunter. 2007. Matplotlib: A 2D graphics environment. *Computing in Science & Engineering,* 9(3):90–95.

Jonathan K. Kummerfeld and Dan Klein. 2013. Error-driven analysis of challenges in coreference resolution. In *Proceedings of the 2013 Conference on Empirical Methods in Natural Language Processing,* Seattle, Wash., 18–21 October 2013, pages 265–277.

Heeyoung Lee, Angel Chang, Yves Peirsman, Nathanael Chambers, Mihai Surdeanu, and Dan Jurafsky. 2013. Deterministic coreference resolution based on entity-centric, precision-ranked rules. *Computational Linguistics,* 39(4):885–916.

Sebastian Martschat and Michael Strube. 2014. Recall error analysis for coreference resolution. In *Proceedings of the 2014 Conference on Empirical Methods in Natural Language Processing,* Doha, Qatar, 25–29 October 2014, pages 2070–2081.

Sameer Pradhan, Alessandro Moschitti, Nianwen Xue, Olga Uryupina, and Yuchen Zhang. 2012. CoNLL-2012 Shared Task: Modeling multilingual unrestricted coreference in OntoNotes. In *Proceedings of the Shared Task of the 16th Conference on Computational Natural Language Learning,* Jeju Island, Korea, 12–14 July 2012, pages 1–40.

Sameer Pradhan, Xiaoqiang Luo, Marta Recasens, Eduard Hovy, Vincent Ng, and Michael Strube. 2014. Scoring coreference partitions of predicted mentions: A reference implementation. In *Proceedings of the 52nd Annual Meeting of the Association for Computational Linguistics (Volume 2: Short Papers),* Baltimore, Md., 22–27 June 2014, pages 30–35.

Sameer Singh, Amarnag Subramanya, Fernando Pereira, and Andrew McCallum. 2011. Large-scale cross-document coreference using distributed inference and hierarchical models. In *Proceedings of the 49th Annual Meeting of the Association for Computational Linguistics (Volume 1: Long Papers),* Portland, Oreg., 19–24 June 2011, pages 793–803.

Wee Meng Soon, Hwee Tou Ng, and Daniel Chung Yong Lim. 2001. A machine learning approach to coreference resolution of noun phrases. *Computational Linguistics,* 27(4):521–544.

hyp: A Toolkit for Representing, Manipulating, and Optimizing Hypergraphs

Markus Dreyer*
SDL Research
6060 Center Drive Suite 150
Los Angeles, CA 90045
markus.dreyer@gmail.com

Jonathan Graehl
SDL Research
6060 Center Drive Suite 150
Los Angeles, CA 90045
graehl@sdl.com

Abstract

We present hyp, an open-source toolkit for the representation, manipulation, and optimization of weighted directed hypergraphs. hyp provides compose, project, invert functionality, k-best path algorithms, the inside and outside algorithms, and more. Finite-state machines are modeled as a special case of directed hypergraphs. hyp consists of a C++ API, as well as a command line tool, and is available for download at github.com/sdl-research/hyp.

1 Introduction

We present hyp, an open-source toolkit that provides data structures and algorithms to process weighted directed hypergraphs.

Such hypergraphs are important in natural language processing and machine learning, e.g., in parsing (Klein and Manning (2005), Huang and Chiang (2005)), machine translation (Kumar et al., 2009), as well as in logic (Gallo et al., 1993) and weighted logic programming (Eisner and Filardo, 2011).

The hyp toolkit enables representing and manipulating weighted directed hypergraphs, providing compose, project, invert functionality, k-best path algorithms, the inside and outside algorithms, and more. hyp also implements a framework for estimating hypergraph feature weights by optimization on forests derived from training data.

*Markus Dreyer is now at Amazon, Inc., Seattle, WA.

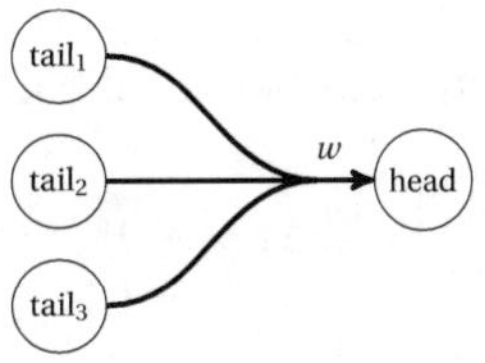

Figure 1: An arc leading from three tail states to a head state, with weight w.

2 Definitions

A weighted directed hypergraph (hereinafter *hypergraph*) is a pair $\mathrm{H} = \langle \mathrm{V}, \mathrm{E} \rangle$, where V is a set of vertices and E a set of edges. Each edge (also called *hyperedge*) is a triple $e = \langle \mathrm{T}(e), h(e), w(e) \rangle$, where $\mathrm{T}(e)$ is an ordered list of tails (i.e., source vertices), $h(e)$ is the head (i.e., target vertex) and $w(e)$ is the semiring weight (see Section 3.4) of the edge (see Figure 1).

We regard hypergraphs as *automata* and call the vertices *states* and edges *arcs*. We add an optional start state $\mathrm{S} \in \mathrm{V}$ and a final state $\mathrm{F} \in \mathrm{V}$.

Each state s has an input label $i(s) \in (\Sigma \cup \{\varnothing\})$ and output label $o(s) \in (\Sigma \cup \{\varnothing\})$; if $o(s) = \varnothing$ then we treat the state as having $o(s) = i(s)$. The label alphabet Σ is divided into disjoint sets of nonterminal, lexical, and special $\{\epsilon, \phi, \rho, \sigma\}$ labels. The input and output labels are analogous to those of a finite-state transducer in some hyp operations (Section 3.3).

The set of incoming arcs into a state s is called the *Backward Star* of s, or short, $\mathrm{BS}(s)$. Formally, $\mathrm{BS}(s) = \{a \in \mathrm{E} : h(a) = s\}$. A *path* π is a sequence of arcs $\pi = (a_1 \ldots a_k) \in \mathrm{E}^*$ such that $\forall a \in \pi, \forall t \in \mathrm{T}(a), (\exists a' \in \pi : h(a') = t) \vee \mathrm{BS}(t) = \emptyset$. Each tail state

Proceedings of NAACL-HLT 2015, pages 11–15,
Denver, Colorado, May 31 – June 5, 2015. ©2015 Association for Computational Linguistics

t of each arc on the path must be the head of some arc on the path, unless *t* is the start state or has no incoming arcs and a terminal (lexical or special) input label, in which case we call *t* an *axiom*. The rationale is that each tail state of each arc on the path must be *derived*, by traveling an arc that leads to it, or given as an *axiom*. If the hypergraph has a start state, the first tail of the first arc of any path must be the start state. The head of the last arc must always be the final state, $h(a_k) = \mathrm{F}$. Paths correspond to trees, or proofs that the final state may be reached from axioms.

Hypergraph arcs have exactly one head; some authors permit multiple heads and would call our hypergraphs *B-hypergraphs* (Gallo et al., 1993).

3 Representing hypergraphs

Text representation. hyp uses a simple human-readable text format for hypergraphs. For example, see the first two lines in Figure 2. Each hypergraph arc has the following format:

```
head <- tail1 tail2 ... tailn / weight
```

Head and tail states are non-negative integers followed by an optional label in parentheses (or a pair of (input output) labels). If it is lexical (i.e., a word), then it is double-quoted with the usual backslash-escapes; nonterminal and special symbols are unquoted. Special symbols like ϵ, ϕ, ρ, σ are written with brackets, as <eps>, <phi>, <rho>, <sigma>. Each arc may optionally have a slash followed by a weight, which is typically a negative log probability (i.e., the cost of the arc). A final state n is marked as FINAL <- n. Figure 2 shows the text and visual representation of a hypergraph with only one arc; it represents and accepts the string *he eats rice*.

Visual representation. A provided Draw command can render hypergraphs using Graphviz (Gansner and North, 2000). Small gray numbers indicate the order of arc tails. Axiom nodes are filled gray.[1] The final state is drawn as a double circle, following finite-state convention.

[1]Gray is used analogously in graphical models for *observed* nodes.

```
0(S) <- 1("he") 2("eats") 3("rice") / 0.693
FINAL <- 0(S)
```

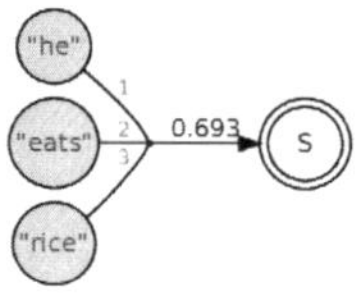

Figure 2: The text and visual representation of a hypergraph with a single arc, similar to Figure 1. The visual representation leaves out the state IDs of labeled states.

```
0(S) <- 1(NP) 2(VP)
1(NP) <- 3(PRON)
2(VP) <- 4(V) 5(NP) 6(PP)
3(PRON) <- 10("He")
4(V) <- 11("eats")
5(NP) <- 7(N)
6(PP) <- 8(PREP) 9(N)
7(N) <- 12("rice")
8(PREP) <- 13("with")
9(N) <- 14("sticks")
FINAL <- 0(S)
# These added arcs
# make it into a forest:
15(NP) <- 7(N) 6(PP)
2(VP) <- 4(V) 15(NP)
```

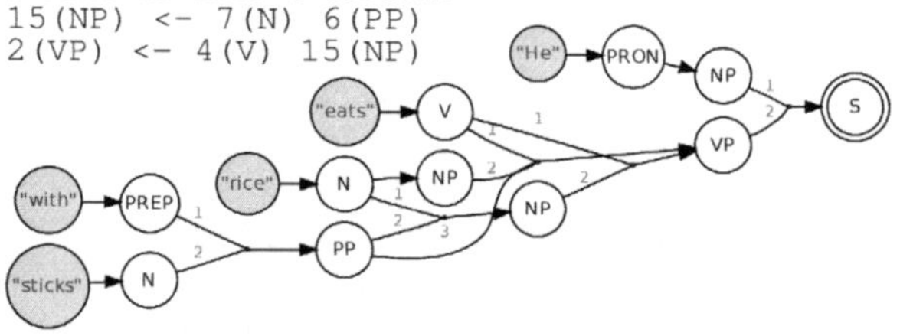

Figure 3: A packed forest.

Reducing redundancy. State labels need not be repeated at every mention of that state's ID; if a state has a label anywhere it has it always. For example, we write the label S for state 0 in Figure 2 only once:

```
0(S) <- 1("he") 2("eats") 3("rice") / 0.693
FINAL <- 0
```

Similarly, state IDs may be left out wherever a label uniquely identifies a particular state:

```
0(S) <- ("he") ("eats") ("rice") / 0.693
FINAL <- 0
```

hyp generates state IDs for these states automatically.

3.1 Trees and forests

A forest is a hypergraph that contains a set of trees. A forest may be *packed*, in which case its trees share substructure, like strings in a lattice. An example forest in hyp format is shown in Figure 3. Any two or more arcs pointing into one state have OR semantics; the depicted forest compactly rep-

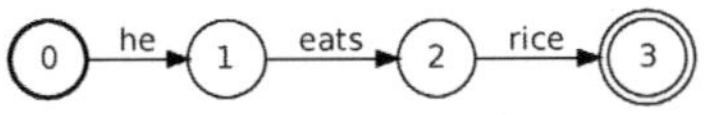

Figure 4: A one-sentence finite-state machine in OpenFst.

```
START <- 0
1 <- 0 4("he")
2 <- 1 5("eats")
3 <- 2 6("rice")
FINAL <- 3
```

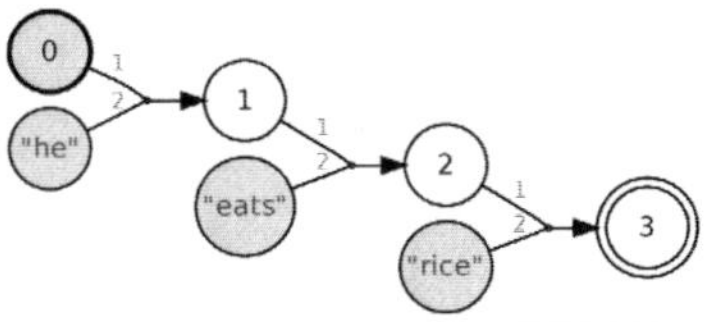

Figure 5: A one-sentence finite-state hypergraph in hyp.

resents two interpretations of one sentence: (1) he eats rice using sticks OR he eats rice that has sticks. Hypergraphs can represent any context-free grammar, where the strings in the grammar are the lexical yield (i.e., leaves in order) of the hypergraph trees.

3.2 Strings, lattices, and general FSMs

In addition to trees and forests, hypergraphs can represent strings, lattices, and general finite-state machines (FSMs) as a special case. A standard finite-state representation of a string would look like Figure 4, which shows a left-recursive bracketing as (((he) eats) rice), i.e., we read "he", combine it with "eats", then combine the result with "rice" to accept the whole string (Allauzen et al., 2007).

We can do something similar in hyp using hypergraphs—see Figure 5. The hypergraph can be traversed bottom-up by first reading start state 0 and the "he" axiom state, reaching state 1, then reading the following words until finally arriving at the final state 3. The visual representation of this left-recursive hypergraph can be understood as an unusual way to draw an FSM, where each arc has an auxiliary label state. If a hypergraph has a start state and all its arcs are *finite-state arcs*, hyp recognizes it as an FSM; some operations may require or optimize for an FSM rather than a general hypergraph. A finite-state arc has two tails, where the first one is a structural state and the second one a terminal label state.[2] Adding additional arcs to the simple sentence hypergraph of Figure 5, we could arrive at a more interesting lattice or even an FSM with cycles and so infinitely many paths.

3.3 Transducers

A leaf state s with an output label $o(s) \neq i(s)$ rewrites the input label. This applies to finite-state as well as general hypergraphs. The following arc, for example, reads "eats" and an NP and derives a VP; it also rewrites "eats" to "ate":

```
(V) <- ("eats" "ate") (NP)
```

If a state has an output label, it must then have an input label, though it may be <eps>. The start state conventionally has no label.

3.4 Semirings and features

Each hypergraph uses a particular semiring, which specifies the type of weights and defines how weights are added and multiplied. hyp provides the standard semirings (Mohri, 2009), as well as the expectation semiring (Eisner, 2002), and a new "feature" semiring. The feature semiring pairs with tropical semiring elements a sparse feature vector that adds componentwise in the semiring product and follows the winning tropical element in the semiring sum. Features 0 and 8 fire with different strengths on this arc:

```
(V) <- 11("eats" "ate") / 3.2[0=1.3,8=-0.5]
```

By using the expectation or the feature semiring, we can keep track of what features fire on what arcs when we perform compositions or other operations. Using standard algorithms that are implemented in hyp (e.g., the inside-outside algorithm, see below), it is possible to train arc feature weights from data (see Section 6).

4 Using the hyp executable

The hyp toolkit provides an executable that implements several commands to process and manipulate hypergraphs. It is generally called as hyp <command> <options> <input-files>, where <command> may be Compose, Best, or others. We now describe some of these commands.

[2] Some operations may efficiently transform a generalization of FSM that we call a "graph", where there are zero or more label states following the structural or "source" state, rather than exactly one.

Compose `hyp Compose` composes two semiring-weighted hypergraphs. Composition is used to parse an input into a structure and/or rewrite its labels. Composition can also rescore a weighted hypergraph by composing with a finite-state machine, e.g., a language model.

Example call:

```
$ hyp Compose cfg.hyp fsa.hyp
```

Since context-free grammars are not closed under composition, one of the two composition arguments must be finite-state (Section 3.2). If both structures are finite-state, hyp uses a fast finite-state composition algorithm (Mohri, 2009).[3] Otherwise, we use a generalization of the Earley algorithm (Earley (1970), Eisner et al. (2005), Dyer (2010)).[4]

Best and PruneToBest. `hyp Best` prints the k-best entries from any hypergraph. `hyp PruneToBest` removes structure not needed for the best path.

Example calls:

```
$ hyp Best --num-best=2 h.hyp > k.txt
$ hyp PruneToBest h.hyp > best.hyp
```

For acyclic finite-state hypergraphs, hyp uses the Viterbi algorithm to find the best path; otherwise it uses a general best-tree algorithm for CFGs (Knuth (1977), Graehl (2005)).

Other executables. Overall, hyp provides more than 20 commands that perform hypergraph operations. They can be used to concatenate, invert, project, reverse, draw, sample paths, create unions, run the inside algorithm, etc. A detailed description is provided in the 25-page hyp tutorial document (Dreyer and Graehl, 2015).

5 Using the hyp C++ API

In addition to the command line tools described, hyp includes an open-source C++ API for constructing and processing hypergraphs, for maximum flexibility and performance.[5] The following code snippet creates the hypergraph shown in Figure 2:

```
typedef ViterbiWeight Weight;
typedef ArcTpl<Weight> Arc;
MutableHypergraph<Arc> hyp;
StateId s = hyp.addState(S);
hyp.setFinal(s);
hyp.addArc(new Arc(Head(s),
                   Tails(hyp.addState(he),
                         hyp.addState(eats),
                         hyp.addState(rice)),
                   Weight(0.693)));
```

The code defines weight and arc types, then constructs a hypergraph and adds the final state, then adds an arc by specifying the head, tails, and the weight. The variables `S`, `he`, `eats`, `rice` are symbol IDs obtained from a vocabulary (not shown here). The constructed hypergraph `hyp` can then be manipulated using provided C++ functions. For example, calling

```
reverse(hyp);
```

reverses all paths in the hypergraph. All other operations described in Section 4 can be called from C++ as well.

The hyp distribution includes additional C++ example code and doxygen API documentation.

6 Optimizing hypergraph feature weights

hyp provides functionality to optimize hypergraph feature weights from training data. It trains a regularized conditional log-linear model, also known as conditional random field (CRF), with optional hidden derivations (Lafferty et al. (2001), Quattoni et al. (2007)). The training data consist of observed input-output hypergraph pairs (x, y). x and y are non-loopy hypergraphs and so may represent string, lattice, tree, or forest. A user-defined function, which is compiled and loaded as a shared object, defines the search space of all possible outputs given any input x, with their features. hyp then computes the CRF function value, feature expectations and gradients, and calls gradient-based optimization methods like L-BFGS or Adagrad (Duchi et al., 2010). This may be used to experiment with and train sequence or tree-based models. For details, we refer to the hyp tutorial (Dreyer and Graehl, 2015).

[3] If the best path rather than the full composition is requested, that composition is lazy best-first and may, weights depending, avoid creating most of the composition.

[4] In the current hyp version, the Earley-inspired algorithm computes the full composition and should therefore be used with smaller grammars.

[5] Using the C++ API to perform a sequence of operations, one can keep intermediate hypergraphs in memory and so avoid the cost of disk write and read operations.

7 Conclusions

We have presented hyp, an open-source toolkit for representing and manipulating weighted directed hypergraphs, including functionality for learning arc feature weights from data. The hyp toolkit provides a C++ library and a command line executable. Since hyp seamlessly handles trees, forests, strings, lattices and finite-state transducers and acceptors, it is well-suited for a wide range of practical problems in NLP (e.g., for implementing a parser or a machine translation pipeline) and related areas. hyp is available for download at github.com/sdl-research/hyp.

Acknowledgments

We thank Daniel Marcu and Mark Hopkins for guidance and advice; Kevin Knight for encouraging an open-source release; Bill Byrne, Abdessamad Echihabi, Steve DeNeefe, Adria de Gispert, Gonzalo Iglesias, Jonathan May, and many others at SDL Research for contributions and early feedback; the anonymous reviewers for comments and suggestions.

References

Cyril Allauzen, Michael Riley, Johan Schalkwyk, Wojciech Skut, and Mehryar Mohri. 2007. OpenFst: A general and efficient weighted finite-state transducer library. In *Proceedings of the Ninth International Conference on Implementation and Application of Automata, (CIAA 2007)*, volume 4783 of *Lecture Notes in Computer Science*, pages 11–23. Springer.

Markus Dreyer and Jonathan Graehl. 2015. Tutorial: The hyp hypergraph toolkit. http://goo.gl/O2qpi2.

J. Duchi, E. Hazan, and Y. Singer. 2010. Adaptive subgradient methods for online learning and stochastic optimization. *Journal of Machine Learning Research*, 12:2121–2159.

Christopher Dyer. 2010. *A formal model of ambiguity and its applications in machine translation.* Ph.D. thesis, University of Maryland.

Jay Earley. 1970. An efficient context-free parsing algorithm. *Communications of the ACM*, 13(2):94–102.

Jason Eisner and Nathaniel W. Filardo. 2011. Dyna: Extending datalog for modern AI. In *Datalog Reloaded*, pages 181–220. Springer.

Jason Eisner, Eric Goldlust, and Noah A. Smith. 2005. Compiling comp ling: Practical weighted dynamic programming and the Dyna language. In *In Advances in Probabilistic and Other Parsing.*

Jason Eisner. 2002. Parameter estimation for probabilistic finite-state transducers. In *Proceedings of the 40th Annual Meeting of the Association for Computational Linguistics (ACL)*, pages 1–8, Philadelphia, July.

Giorgio Gallo, Giustino Longo, and Stefano Pallottino. 1993. Directed hypergraphs and applications. *Discrete Applied Mathematics*, 42(2):177–201.

Emden R. Gansner and Stephen C. North. 2000. An open graph visualization system and its applications to software engineering. *Software: Practice and Experience*, 30(11):1203–1233.

Jonathan Graehl. 2005. Context-free algorithms. arXiv:1502.02328 [cs.FL].

Liang Huang and David Chiang. 2005. Better k-best parsing. In *Proceedings of the Ninth International Workshop on Parsing Technology*, pages 53–64. Association for Computational Linguistics.

Dan Klein and Christopher D. Manning. 2005. Parsing and hypergraphs. In *New developments in parsing technology*, pages 351–372. Springer.

Donald E. Knuth. 1977. A generalization of Dijkstra's algorithm. *Information Processing Letters*, 6(1):1–5.

Shankar Kumar, Wolfgang Macherey, Chris Dyer, and Franz Och. 2009. Efficient minimum error rate training and minimum bayes-risk decoding for translation hypergraphs and lattices. In *Proceedings of the Joint Conference of the 47th Annual Meeting of the ACL and the 4th International Joint Conference on Natural Language Processing of the AFNLP: Volume 1*, pages 163–171. Association for Computational Linguistics.

John Lafferty, Andrew McCallum, and Fernando Pereira. 2001. Conditional random fields: Probabilistic models for segmenting and labeling sequence data. In *Proceedings of the 18th International Conference on Machine Learning*, pages 282–289. Morgan Kaufmann, San Francisco, CA.

Mehryar Mohri. 2009. Weighted automata algorithms. In *Handbook of weighted automata*, pages 213–254. Springer.

A. Quattoni, S. Wang, L. P. Morency, M. Collins, and T. Darrell. 2007. Hidden conditional random fields. *IEEE Transactions on Pattern Analysis and Machine Intelligence*, 29(10):1848–1852.

Enhancing Instructor-Student and Student-Student Interactions with Mobile Interfaces and Summarization

Wencan Luo, Xiangmin Fan, Muhsin Menekse, Jingtao Wang, Diane Litman
University of Pittsburgh
Pittsburgh, PA 15260 USA
{wel55, xif14, muhsin, jingtaow, dlitman}@pitt.edu

Abstract

Educational research has demonstrated that asking students to respond to reflection prompts can increase interaction between instructors and students, which in turn can improve both teaching and learning especially in large classrooms. However, administering an instructor's prompts, collecting the students' responses, and summarizing these responses for both instructors and students is challenging and expensive. To address these challenges, we have developed an application called CourseMIRROR (**M**obile **I**n-situ **R**eflections and **R**eview with **O**ptimized **R**ubrics). CourseMIRROR uses a mobile interface to administer prompts and collect reflective responses for a set of instructor-assigned course lectures. After collection, CourseMIRROR automatically summarizes the reflections with an extractive phrase summarization method, using a clustering algorithm to rank extracted phrases by student coverage. Finally, CourseMIRROR presents the phrase summary to both instructors and students to help them understand the difficulties and misunderstandings encountered.

1 Introduction

In recent years, researchers in education have demonstrated the effectiveness of using reflection prompts to improve both instructors' teaching quality and students' learning outcomes in domains such as teacher and science education (Boud et al., 2013; Menekse et al., 2011). However, administrating an instructor's prompts, collecting the students' reflective responses, and summarizing these responses for instructors and students is challenging and expensive, especially for large (e.g., introductory STEM) and online courses (e.g., MOOCs). To address these challenges, we have developed CourseMIRROR, a mobile application[1] for collecting and sharing learners' in-situ reflections in large classrooms. The instant on, always connected ability of mobile devices makes the administration and collection of reflections much easier compared to the use of traditional paper-based methods, while the use of an automatic summarization algorithm provides more timely feedback compared to the use of manual summarization by the course instructor or TA.

From a natural language processing (NLP) perspective, the need in aggregating and displaying reflections in a mobile application has led us to modify traditional summarization methods in two primary ways. First, since the linguistic units of student inputs range from single words to multiple sentences, our summaries are created from extracted phrases rather than from sentences. Phrases are also easy to read and browse, and fit better on small devices when compared to sentences. Second, based on the assumption that concepts (represented as phrases) mentioned by more students should get more instructor attention, the phrase summarization algorithm estimates the number of students semantically covered by each phrase in a summary. The set of phrases in a summary and the associated student coverage estimates are presented to both the instruc-

[1] CourseMIRROR homepage: http://www.coursemirror.com; free download link in Google Play Store: https://play.google.com/store/apps/details?id=edu.pitt.cs.mips.coursemirror

Proceedings of NAACL-HLT 2015, pages 16–20,
Denver, Colorado, May 31 – June 5, 2015.

tors and the students to help them understand the difficulties and misunderstandings encountered from lectures.

2 Demonstration

One key challenge for both instructors and students in large classes is how to become aware of the difficulties and misunderstandings that students are encountering during lectures. Our demonstration will show how CourseMIRROR can be used to address this problem. First, instructors use the server side interface to configure a set of reflection prompts for an associated lecture schedule. Next, students use the mobile client to submit reflective responses to each assigned prompt according to the schedule. Finally, after each submission deadline, both students and instructors use CourseMIRROR to review an automatically generated summary of the student responses submitted for each prompt. The whole functionality of CourseMIRROR will be demonstrated using the scenario described below. In this scenario, Alice is an instructor teaching an introduction to engineering class and Bob is one of her students.

In order to use CourseMIRROR, Alice first logs in to the server and sets up the lecture schedule and a collection of reflection prompts.

Bob can see all the courses he enrolled in after logging into the CourseMIRROR client application[2]. After selecting a course, he can view all the lectures of that course (Fig. 1.a).

After each lecture, Bob writes and submits reflections through the reflection writing interface (Fig. 1.b). These reflections are transmitted to the server and stored in the database. In order to collect timely and in-situ feedback, CourseMIRROR imposes submission time windows synchronized with the lecture schedule (from the beginning of one lecture to the beginning of the next lecture, indicated by an edit icon shown in Fig. 1.a). In addition, to encourage the students to submit feedback on time, instructors can send reminders via mobile push notifications to the students' devices.

After the reflection collection phase for a given lecture, CourseMIRROR runs a phrase summarization algorithm on the server side to generate a summary of the reflections for each prompt. In the CourseMIRROR interface, the reflection prompts are highlighted using a green background, and are followed by the set of extracted phrases constituting the summary. The summary algorithm is described in Section 3; the summary length is controlled by a user-defined parameter and was 4 phrases for the example in Fig. 1.c.

For Bob, reading these summaries (Fig. 1.c) is assumed to remind him to recapture the learning content and rethink about it. It allows him to get an overview of the peers' interesting points and confusion points for each lecture. To motivate the students to read the summaries, CourseMIRROR highlights the phrases (by using light-yellow background) that were included or mentioned by the current user. This functionality is enabled by the proposed summarization technique which tracks the source of each phrase in the summary (who delivers it). We hypothesize that highlighting the presence of one's own reflections in the summaries can trigger the students' curiosity to some extent; thus they would be more likely to spend some time on reading the summaries.

For Alice, seeing both text and student coverage estimates in the summaries can help her quickly identify the type and extent of students' misunderstandings and tailor future lectures to meet the needs of students.

3 Phrase Summarization

When designing CourseMIRROR's summarization algorithm, we evaluated different alternatives on an engineering course corpus consisting of handwritten student reflections generated in response to instructor prompts at the end of each lecture, along with associated summaries manually generated by the course TA (Menekse et al., 2011). The phrase summarization method that we incorporated into CourseMIRROR achieved significantly better ROUGE scores than baselines including MEAD (Radev et al., 2004), LexRank (Erkan and Radev, 2004), and MMR (Carbonell and Goldstein, 1998). The algorithm involves three stages: candidate phrase extraction, phrase clustering, and phrase ranking by student coverage (i.e., how many students are associated with those phrases).

[2]Only Android client is provided. The iOS version is under development. Non-Android users now can use an isomorphic web client, optimized for mobile browsers.

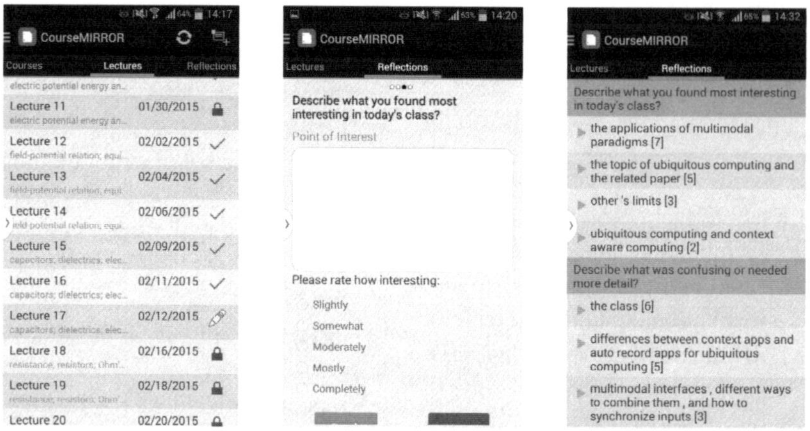

(a) (b) (c)

Figure 1: CourseMIRROR main interfaces; a) Lecture list; b) Reflection writing; c) Summary display: the numbers shown in square brackets are the estimated number of students semantically covered by a phrase and a student's own phrase is highlighted in yellow.

3.1 Candidate Phrase Extraction

To normalize the student reflections, we use a parser from the Senna toolkit (Collobert, 2011) to extract noun phrases (NPs) as candidate phrases for summarization. Only NP is considered because all reflection prompts used in our task are asking about "what", and knowledge concepts are usually represented as NPs. This could be extended to include other phrases if future tasks suggested such a need.

Malformed phrases are excluded based on Marujo et al. (2013) due to the noisy parsers, including single stop words (e.g. "it", "I", "we", "there") and phrases starting with a punctuation mark (e.g. "'t", "+ indexing", "?").

3.2 Phrase Clustering

We use a clustering paradigm to estimate the number of students who mention a phrase (Fig. 1.c), which is challenging since different words can be used for the same meaning (i.e. synonym, different word order). We use K-Medoids (Kaufman and Rousseeuw, 1987) for two reasons. First, it works with an arbitrary distance matrix between datapoints. This gives us a chance to try different distance matrices. Since phrases in student responses are sparse (e.g., many appear only once), instead of using frequency-based similarity like cosine, we found it more useful to leverage semantic similarity based on SEMILAR (Rus et al., 2013). Second, it is robust to noise and outliers because it minimizes a sum of pairwise dissimilarities instead of squared Euclidean distances. Since K-Medoids picks a random set of seeds to initialize as the cluster centers and we prefer phrases in the same cluster are similar to each other, the clustering algorithm runs 100 times and the result with the minimal within-cluster sum of the distances is retained.

For setting the number of clusters without tuning, we adapted the method used in Wan and Yang (2008), by letting $K = \sqrt{V}$, where K is the number of clusters and V is the number of candidate phrases instead of the number of sentences.

3.3 Phrase Ranking

The phrase summaries in CourseMIRROR are ranked by student coverage, with each phrase itself associated with the students who mention it (this enables CourseMIRROR to highlight the phrases that were mentioned by the current user (Fig. 1.c)). In order to estimate the student coverage number, phrases are clustered and phrases possessed by the same cluster tend to be similar. We assume any phrase in a cluster can represent it as a whole and therefore the coverage of a phrase is assumed to be the same as the coverage of a cluster, which is a union of the students covered by each phrase in the cluster. Within a cluster, LexRank (Erkan and Radev, 2004) is used to score the extracted candidate phrases. Only the top ranked phrase in the cluster is added to the output. This process repeats for the next cluster according to the student coverage until the length limit of the summary is reached.

4 Pilot Study

In order to investigate the overall usability and efficacy of CourseMIRROR, we conducted a semester-long deployment in two graduate-level courses (i.e., CS2001 and CS2610) during Fall 2014. These are introductory courses on research methods in Computer Science and on Human Computer Interaction, respectively. 20 participants volunteered for our study; they received \$10 for signing up and installing the application and another \$20 for completing the study. Both courses had 21 lectures open for reflections; 344 reflections were collected overall. We used the same reflection prompts as the study by Menekse et al. (2011), so as to investigate the impact of mobile devices and NLP on experimental results. Here we only focus on interesting findings from an NLP perspective. Findings from a human-computer interaction perspective are reported elsewhere (Fan et al., 2015).

Reflection Length. *Students type more words than they write.* The number of words per reflection in both courses using CourseMIRROR is significantly higher compared to the handwritten reflections in Menekse's study (11.6 vs. 9.7, $p < 0.0001$ for one course; 10.9 vs. 9.7, $p < 0.0001$ for the other course) and there is no significant difference between the two CourseMIRROR courses. This result runs counter to our expectation because typing is often slow on small screens. A potential confounding factor might be that participants in our study are Computer Science graduate students while Menekse's participants are Engineering undergraduates at a different university who had to submit the reflection within a few minutes after the lecture. We are conducting a larger scale controlled experiment (200+ participants) to further verify this finding.[3]

Questionnaire Ratings. *Students have positive experiences with CourseMIRROR.* In the closing lecture of each course, participants were given a Likert-scale questionnaire that included two questions related to summarization (*"I often read reflection summaries"* and *"I benefited from reading the reflection summaries"*). Participants reported positive experiences on both their quantitative and qualitative responses. Both questions had modes of 3.7 (on a scale of 1-5, $\sigma = 0.2$). In general, participants felt that they benefited from writing reflections and they enjoyed reading summaries of reflections from classmates. For example, one comment from a free text answer in the questionnaire is *"It's interesting to see what other people say and that can teach me something that I didn't pay attention to."* The participants also like the idea of highlighting their own viewpoints in the summaries (Fig. 1.c). Two example comments are *"I feel excited when I see my words appear in the summary."* and *"Just curious about whether my points are accepted or not."*

[3]Due to a currently low response rate, we are also deploying CourseMIRROR in another engineering class where about 50 out of 68 students regularly submit the reflection feedback.

5 Conclusion

Our live demo will introduce CourseMIRROR, a mobile application that leverages mobile interfaces and a phrase summarization technique to facilitate the use of reflection prompts in large classrooms. CourseMIRROR automatically produces and presents summaries of student reflections to both students and instructors, to help them capture the difficulties and misunderstandings encountered from lectures. Summaries are produced using a combination of phrase extraction, phrase clustering and phrase ranking based on student coverage, with the mobile interface highlighting the students' own viewpoint in the summaries and noting the student coverage of each extracted phrase. A pilot deployment yielded positive quantitative as well as qualitative user feedback across two courses, suggesting the promise of CourseMIRROR for enhancing the instructor-student and student-student interactions. In the future, we will examine how the students' responses (e.g., response rate, length, quality) relate to student learning performance.

Acknowledgments

This research is in-part supported by an RDF from the Learning Research and Development Center at the University of Pittsburgh. We also thank all the participants and anonymous reviewers for insightful comments and suggestions.

References

David Boud, Rosemary Keogh, David Walker, et al. 2013. *Reflection: Turning experience into learning*. Routledge.

Jaime Carbonell and Jade Goldstein. 1998. The use of mmr, diversity-based reranking for reordering documents and producing summaries. In *Proceedings of the 21st Annual International ACM SIGIR Conference on Research and Development in Information Retrieval*, SIGIR '98, pages 335–336.

Ronan Collobert. 2011. Deep learning for efficient discriminative parsing. In *International Conference on Artificial Intelligence and Statistics*, number EPFL-CONF-192374.

Günes Erkan and Dragomir R. Radev. 2004. Lexrank: Graph-based lexical centrality as salience in text summarization. *J. Artif. Int. Res.*, 22(1):457–479.

Xiangmin Fan, Wencan Luo, Muhsin Menekse, Diane Litman, and Jingtao Wang. 2015. CourseMIRROR: Enhancing large classroom instructor-student interactions via mobile interfaces and natural language processing. In *Works-In-Progress of ACM Conference on Human Factors in Computing Systems*. ACM.

Leonard Kaufman and Peter Rousseeuw. 1987. Clustering by means of medoids. *Statistical Data Analysis Based on the $L1$-Norm and Related Method*, pages 405–416.

Luis Marujo, Márcio Viveiros, and João Paulo da Silva Neto. 2013. Keyphrase cloud generation of broadcast news. *arXiv preprint arXiv:1306.4606*.

Muhsin Menekse, Glenda Stump, Stephen J. Krause, and Michelene T.H. Chi. 2011. The effectiveness of students daily reflections on learning in engineering context. In *Proceedings of the American Society for Engineering Education (ASEE) Annual Conference*.

Dragomir R. Radev, Hongyan Jing, Małgorzata Styś, and Daniel Tam. 2004. Centroid-based summarization of multiple documents. *Inf. Process. Manage.*, 40(6):919–938, November.

Vasile Rus, Mihai C Lintean, Rajendra Banjade, Nobal B Niraula, and Dan Stefanescu. 2013. Semilar: The semantic similarity toolkit. In *ACL (Conference System Demonstrations)*, pages 163–168.

Xiaojun Wan and Jianwu Yang. 2008. Multi-document summarization using cluster-based link analysis. In *Proceedings of the 31st Annual International ACM SIGIR Conference on Research and Development in Information Retrieval*, SIGIR '08.

RExtractor: a Robust Information Extractor

Vincent Kríž and Barbora Hladká
Charles University in Prague
Faculty of Mathematics and Physics
Institute of Formal and Applied Linguistics
{kriz, hladka}@ufal.mff.cuni.cz

Abstract

The RExtractor system is an information extractor that processes input documents by natural language processing tools and consequently queries the parsed sentences to extract a knowledge base of entities and their relations. The extraction queries are designed manually using a tool that enables natural graphical representation of queries over dependency trees. A workflow of the system is designed to be language and domain independent. We demonstrate RExtractor on Czech and English legal documents.

1 Introduction

In many domains, large collections of semi/unstructured documents form main sources of information. Their efficient browsing and querying present key aspects in many areas of human activities.

We have implemented an information extraction system, `RExtractor`, that extracts information from texts enriched with linguistic structures, namely syntactic dependency trees. This structure is represented as a rooted ordered tree with nodes and edges and the dependency relation between two nodes is captured by an edge between them. Namely, we work with the annotation framework designed in the Prague Dependency Treebank project.[1]

RExtractor forms an extraction unit of a complex system performing both information extraction and data publication according to the Linked Data Principles. More theoretical and practical details on the system are provided in (Kríž et al., 2014). The system focuses on processing Czech legal documents and has been implemented in an applied research project addressed by research and business partners.[2]

The extraction systems known from literature were evaluated against gold standard data, e.g. DKPro Keyphrases (Erbs et al., 2014), RelationFactory (Roth et al., 2014), KELVIN (McNamee et al., 2013), Propminer (Akbik et al., 2013), OLLIE (Mausam et al., 2012). We name this type of evaluation as *academic* one. According to the statistics provided by International Data Corporation (Gantz and Reinsel, 2010), 90% of all available digital data is unstructured and its amount currently grows twice as fast as structured data. Naturally, there is no capacity to prepare gold standard data of statistically significant amount for each domain. When exploring domains without gold standard data, a developer can prepare a small set of gold standard data and do academic evaluation. He gets a rough idea about his extractor performance. But he builds a system that will be used by users/customers, not researchers serving as evaluators. So it is user/customer feedback what provides evidence of performance. This particular feature of information extraction systems is discussed in (Chiticariu et al., 2013) together with techniques they use academic systems and commercial systems.

We decided to do a very first RExtractor testing by experts in accountancy. It has not done yet so we have no evidence about its quality from their perspective. However, we know what performance the

[1] `http://ufal.mff.cuni.cz/pdt3.0`

[2] `http://ufal.mff.cuni.cz/intlib`

Proceedings of NAACL-HLT 2015, pages 21–25,
Denver, Colorado, May 31 – June 5, 2015.

system achieves on the gold standard data that we prepared in the given domain. We list it separately for entity extraction, where Precision = 57.4%, Recall = 91.7%, and relation extraction, where P = 80.6%, R = 63.2%. Details are provided in (Kríž et al., 2014).

2 RExtractor Description

RExtractor is an information extractor that processes input documents by natural language processing tools and consequently queries the parsed sentences to extract a knowledge base of entities and their relations. The parsed sentences are represented as dependency trees with nodes bearing morphological and syntactic attributes. The knowledge base has the form of *(subject, predicate, object)* triples where *subject* and *object* are entities and *predicate* represents their relation. One has to carefully distinguish subjects, predicates and objects in dependency trees from subjects, predicates and objects in entity-relation triples.

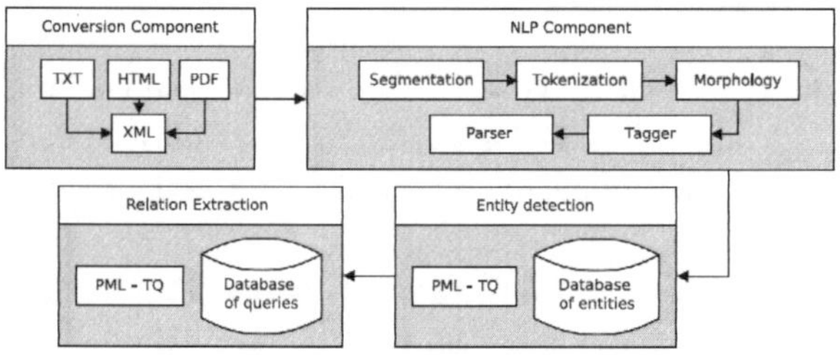

Figure 1: RExtractor workflow

RExtractor is designed as a four-component system displayed in Figure 1. The NLP component outputs a syntactic dependency tree for each sentence from the input documents using tools available in the Treex framework.[3] Then the dependency trees are queried in the Entity Detection and Relation Extraction components using the PML-TQ search tool (Pajas and Štěpánek, 2009). The Entity Detection component detects entities stored in Database of Entities (DBE). Usually, this database is built manually by a domain expert. The Relation Extraction component exploits dependency trees with detected entities using queries stored in Database of queries (DBQ). This database is built manually by a domain expert

[3] http://ufal.mff.cuni.cz/treex

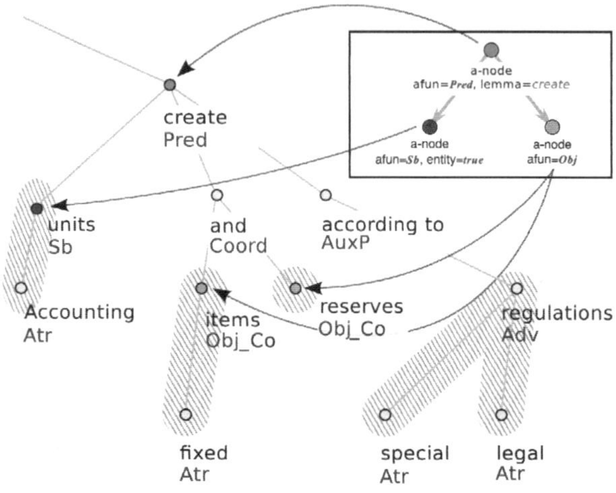

Figure 2: Extraction of *who creates what*

Subject	Predicate	Object
accounting unit	create	fixed item
accounting unit	create	reserve

Table 1: Data extracted by the query displayed in Figure 2

in cooperation with an NLP expert. Typically, domain experts describe what kind of information they are interested in and their requests are transformed into tree queries by NLP experts.

Illustration Let's assume this situation. A domain expert is browsing a law collection and is interested in the *to create something* responsibility of any body. In other words, he wants to learn *who creates what* as is specified in the collection. We illustrate the RExtractor approach for extracting such information using the sentence *Accounting units create fixed items and reserves according to special legal regulations.*

Firstly, the NLP component generates a dependency tree of the sentence, see Figure 2. Secondly, the Entity Detection component detects the entities from DBE in the tree: *accounting unit*, *fixed item*, *reserve*, *special legal regulation* (see the highlighted subtrees in Figure 2). Then an NLP expert formulates a tree query matching the domain expert's issue *who creates what*. See the query at the top-right corner of Figure 2: (1) he is searching for *creates*, i.e. for the predicate having lemma *create* (see the root node), (2) he is searching for *who*, i.e. the subject

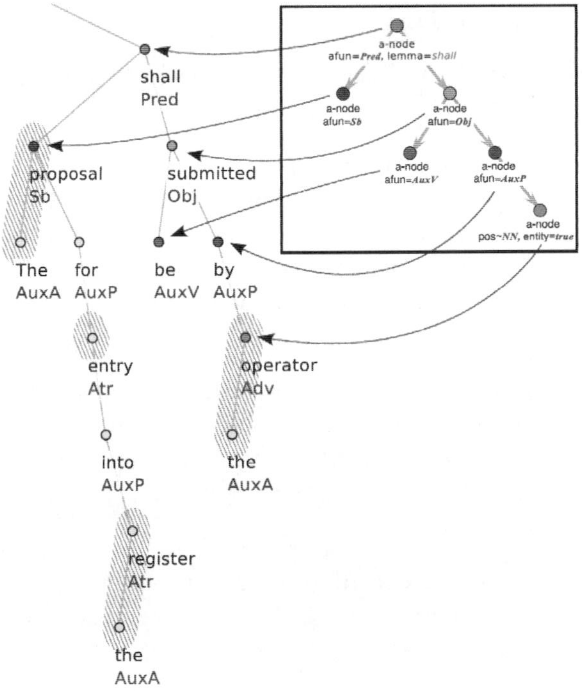

Figure 3: Extraction of *who should do what*

Subject	Predicate	Object
operator	submit	proposal

Table 2: Data extracted by the query displayed in Figure 3

(see the left son of the root and its syntactic function afun=`Sb`), and *what*, i.e. the object (see the right son of the root and its syntactic function afun=`Obj`). Even more, he restricts the subjects to those that are pre-specified in DBE (see the left son of the root and its restriction entity=`true`). Finally, the Relation Extraction component matches the query with the sentence and outputs the data presented in Table 1.

A domain expert could be interested in more general responsibility, namely he wants to learn *who should do what* where *who* is an entity in DBE. A tree query matching this issue is displayed in Figure 3. The query is designed to extract (*subject*, *predicate*, *object*) relations where the *subject* is the object in a sentence. We extract the data listed in Table 2 using this query for entity-relation extraction from the sentence *The proposal for entry into the register shall be submitted by the operator.*

Technical details RExtractor is conceptualized as a modular framework. It is implemented in Perl programming language and its code and technical details are available on Github:

`http://github.com/VincTheSecond/rextractor`

Each RExtractor component is implemented as a standalone server. The servers regularly check new documents waiting for processing. A document processing progress is characterized by a document processing status in the extraction pipeline, e.g. *520 – Entity detection finished.*

The system is designed to be domain independent. However, to achieve better performance, one would like to adapt the default components for a given domain. Modularity of the system allows adding, modifying or removing functionalities of existing components and creating new components. Each component has a configuration file to enable various settings of document processing.

A scenario with all settings for the whole extraction pipeline (set up in a configuration file) is called an *extraction strategy*. An extraction strategy sets a particular configuration for the extraction pipeline, e.g. paths to language models for NLP tools, paths to DBE and DBQ.

The RExtractor API enables easy integration into more complex systems, like search engines.

3 RExtractor Demonstration

The RExtractor architecture comprises two core components: (a) a background server processing submitted documents, and (b) a Web application to view a dynamic display of submitted document processing.

Web interface enables users to submit documents to be processed by RExtractor. In the submission window, users are asked to select one of the extraction strategies. Users can browse extraction strategies and view their detailed description. After successful document submission, the document waits in a queue to be processed according to the specified extraction strategy. Users can view a display of submitted document processing that is automatically updated, see Figure 4.

In Figure 5, the following information is visualized: (1) **Details** section contains metadata about document processing. (2) **Entities** section shows an

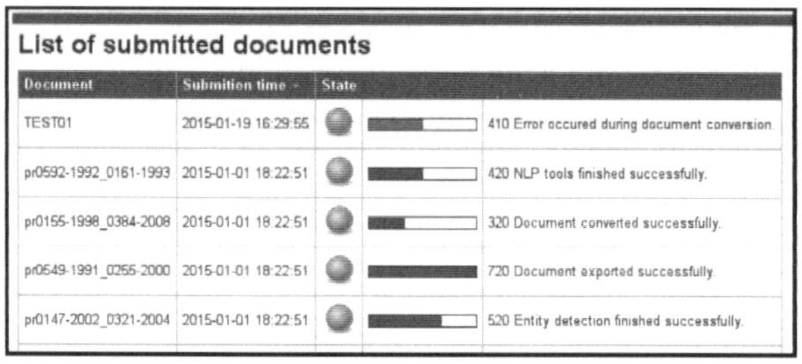

Figure 4: RExtractor web interface, part 1

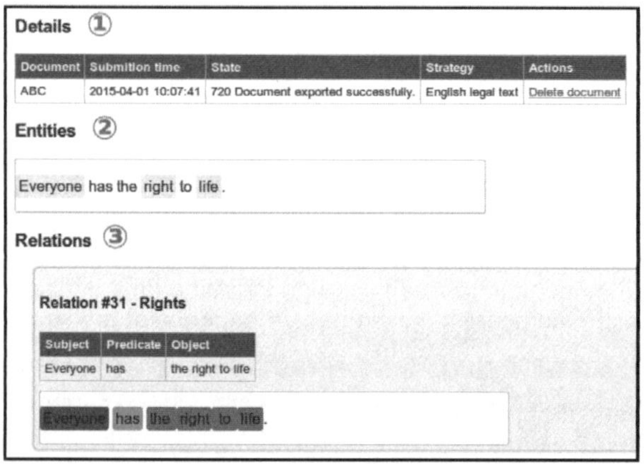

Figure 5: RExtractor web interface, part 2

input document with the highlighted entities that can be viewed interactively: by clicking on the entity, an additional information about the entity is uploaded and presented. (3) **Relations** section consists of tables where *(subject, predicate, object)* triples are listed. In addition, the relevant part of the document with the highlighted triples is presented as well.

Our demonstration enables users to submit texts from legal domain and process them according to two currently available extraction strategies, Czech and English. Once the document processing is finished, users can browse extracted entity-relation triples.

4 RExtractor Online

`http://odcs.xrg.cz/demo-rextractor`

5 Conclusion

We presented the RExtractor system with the following features:

- Our ambition is to provide users with an interactive and user-friendly information extraction system that enables submitting documents and browsing extracted data without spending time with understanding technical details.
- A workflow of RExtractor is language independent. Currently, two extraction strategies are available, for Czech and English. Creating strategies for other languages requires NLP tools, Database of entities (DBE) and Database of queries (DBQ) for a given language.
- A workflow of RExtractor is domain independent. Currently, the domain of legislation is covered. Creating strategies for other domains requires building DBE and DBQ. It is a joint work of domain and NLP experts.
- RExtractor extracts information from syntactic dependency trees. This linguistic structure enables to extract information even from complex sentences. Also, it enables to extract even complex relations.
- RExtractor has both user-friendly interface and API to address large-scale tasks. The system has already processed a collection of Czech legal documents consisting of almost 10,000 documents.
- RExtractor is an open source system but some language models used by NLP tools can be applied under a special license.

Our future plans concern the following tasks:

- experimenting with syntactic parsing procedures in the NLP component that are of a crucial importance for extraction
- evaluating RExtractor against the data that are available for various shared tasks and conferences on information retrieval, e.g. TAC[4], TRAC[5]

[4] `http://www.nist.gov/tac/`
[5] `http://trec.nist.gov/`

- making tree query design more user-friendly for domain experts
- getting feedback from customers
- incorporating automatic procedures for extraction of both entities and relations that are not pre-specified in Database of Entities and Database of Queries, resp.
- creating strategies for other languages and other domains

Through this system demonstration we hope to receive feedback on the general approach, explore its application to other domains and languages, and attract new users and possibly developers.

Acknowledgments

We gratefully acknowledge support from the Technology Agency of the Czech Republic (grant no. TA02010182), The Bernard Bolzano Foundation and SVV project no. 260 224. This work has been using language resources developed and/or stored and/or distributed by the LINDAT/CLARIN project. We highly appreciate RExtractor-related discussions with Martin Nečaský and colleagues from Sysnet, Ltd.

References

Alan Akbik, Oresti Konomi, and Michail Melnikov. 2013. Propminer: A workflow for interactive information extraction and exploration using dependency trees. In *Proceedings of the 51st Annual Meeting of the ACL: System Demonstrations*, pages 157–162. ACL.

Laura Chiticariu, Yunyao Li, and Frederick R. Reiss. 2013. Rule-based information extraction is dead! long live rule-based information extraction systems! In *EMNLP*, pages 827–832. ACL.

Nicolai Erbs, Bispo Pedro Santos, Iryna Gurevych, and Torsten Zesch. 2014. Dkpro keyphrases: Flexible and reusable keyphrase extraction experiments. In *Proceedings of 52nd Annual Meeting of the ACL: System Demonstrations*, pages 31–36. ACL.

John Gantz and David Reinsel. 2010. The digital universe decade – Are you ready?

Vincent Kríž, Barbora Hladká, Martin Nečaský, and Tomáš Knap. 2014. Data extraction using NLP techniques and its transformation to linked data. In *Human-Inspired Computing and Its Applications - 13th Mexican International Conference on Artificial Intelligence, MICAI 2014, Tuxtla Gutiérrez, Mexico, November 16-22, 2014. Proceedings, Part I*, pages 113–124.

Mausam, Michael Schmitz, Robert Bart, Stephen Soderland, and Oren Etzioni. 2012. Open language learning for information extraction. In *Proceedings of the 2012 Joint Conference on Empirical Methods in Natural Language Processing and Computational Natural Language Learning*, EMNLP-CoNLL '12, pages 523–534, Stroudsburg, PA, USA. ACL.

Paul McNamee, James Mayfield, Tim Finin, Tim Oates, Dawn Lawrie, Tan Xu, and Douglas Oard. 2013. Kelvin: a tool for automated knowledge base construction. In *Proceedings of the 2013 NAACL HLT Demonstration Session*, pages 32–35. ACL.

Petr Pajas and Jan Štěpánek. 2009. System for querying syntactically annotated corpora. In Gary Lee and Sabine Schulte im Walde, editors, *Proceedings of the ACL-IJCNLP 2009 Software Demonstrations*, pages 33–36, Suntec, Singapore. Association for Computational Linguistics.

Benjamin Roth, Tassilo Barth, Grzegorz Chrupała, Martin Gropp, and Dietrich Klakow. 2014. Relationfactory: A fast, modular and effective system for knowledge base population. In *Proceedings of the Demonstrations at the 14th Conference of the European Chapter of the ACL*, pages 89–92, Gothenburg, Sweden, April. ACL.

An AMR parser for English, French, German, Spanish and Japanese and a new AMR-annotated corpus

Lucy Vanderwende, Arul Menezes, Chris Quirk

Microsoft Research
One Microsoft Way
Redmond, WA 98052
{lucyv,arulm,chrisq}@microsoft.com

Abstract

In this demonstration, we will present our online parser[1] that allows users to submit any sentence and obtain an analysis following the specification of AMR (Banarescu et al., 2014) to a large extent. This AMR analysis is generated by a small set of rules that convert a native Logical Form analysis provided by a pre-existing parser (see Vanderwende, 2015) into the AMR format. While we demonstrate the performance of our AMR parser on data sets annotated by the LDC, we will focus attention in the demo on the following two areas: 1) we will make available AMR annotations for the data sets that were used to develop our parser, to serve as a supplement to the LDC data sets, and 2) we will demonstrate AMR parsers for German, French, Spanish and Japanese that make use of the same small set of LF-to-AMR conversion rules.

1 Introduction

Abstract Meaning Representation (AMR) (Banarescu et al., 2014) is a semantic representation for which a large amount of manually-annotated data is being created, with the intent of constructing and evaluating parsers that generate this level of semantic representation for previously unseen text. Already one method for training an AMR parser has appeared in (Flanigan et al., 2014), and we anticipate that more attempts to train parsers will follow. In this demonstration, we will present our AMR parser, which converts our existing semantic representation formalism, Logical Form (LF), into the AMR format. We do this with two goals: first, as our existing LF is close in design to AMR, we can now use the manually-annotated AMR datasets to measure the accuracy of our LF system, which may serve to provide a benchmark for parsers trained on the AMR corpus. We gratefully acknowledge the contributions made by Banarescu et al. (2014) towards defining a clear and interpretable semantic representation that enables this type of system comparison. Second, we wish to contribute new AMR data sets comprised of the AMR annotations by our AMR parser of the sentences we previously used to develop our LF system. These sentences were curated to cover a wide-range of syntactic-semantic phenomena, including those described in the AMR specification. We will also demonstrate the capabilities of our parser to generate AMR analyses for sentences in French, German, Spanish and Japanese, for which no manually-annotated AMR data is available at present.

2 Abstract Meaning Representation

Abstract Meaning Representation (AMR) is a semantic representation language which aims to assign the same representation to sentences that have

[1] Available at: http://research.microsoft.com/msrsplat

Proceedings of NAACL-HLT 2015, pages 26–30,
Denver, Colorado, May 31 – June 5, 2015.

the same basic meaning (Banarescu et al., 2014). Some of the basic principles are to use a graph representation, to abstract away from syntactic idiosyncrasies (such as active/passive alternation), to introduce variables corresponding to entities, properties and events, and to ground nodes to OntoNotes (Pradhan et al., 2007) wherever possible.

As a semantic representation, AMR describes the analysis of an input sentence at both the conceptual and the predicative level, as AMR does not annotate individual words in a sentence (see annotation guidelines, introduction). AMR, for example, provides a single representation for the constructions that are typically thought of as alternations: "it is tough to please the teacher" and "the teacher is tough to please" have the same representation in AMR, as do actives and their passive variant, e.g., "a girl read the book" and "the book was read by a girl". AMR also advocates the representation of nominative constructions in verbal form, so that "I read about the destruction of Rome by the Vandals" and "I read how the Vandals destroyed Rome" have the same representation in AMR, with the nominal "destruction" recognized as having the same basic meaning as the verbal "destroy". Such decisions are part-conceptual and part-predicative, and rely on the OntoNotes lexicon having entries for the nominalized forms. AMR annotators also can reach in to OntoNotes to represent "the soldier was afraid of battle" and "the soldier feared battle": linking "be afraid of" to "fear" depends on the OntoNotes frameset at annotation time.

3 Logical Form

The Logical Form (LF) which we convert to AMR via a small set of rules is one component in a broad-coverage grammar pipeline (see Vanderwende, 2015, for an overview). The goal of the LF is twofold: to compute the predicate-argument structure for each clause ("who did what to whom when where and how?") and to normalize differing syntactic realizations of what can be considered the same "meaning". In so doing, concepts that are possibly distant in the linear order of the sentence or distant in the constituent structure can be brought together, because the Logical Form is represented as a graph, where linear order is no longer primary. In addition to alternations and passive/active, other operations include: unbounded dependencies, functional control, indirect object paraphrase, and assigning modifiers.

As in AMR, the Logical Form is a directed, labeled graph. The nodes in this graph have labels that are either morphologically or derivationally related to the input tokens, and the arcs are labeled with those relations that are defined to be semantic. Surface words that convey syntactic information only (e.g. *by* in a passive construction, *do*-support, singular/passive, or (in)definite articles) are not part of the graph, their meaning, however is preserved as annotations on the conceptual nodes (similar to the Prague T-layer, Hajič et al., 2003).

```
have1 (+Pres +Proposition)
    Dsub   elephant1 (+Plur)
                  Attrib  African1 ()
                          hunt1 (+Pass +Perf ... )
                                 Dsub   _X1
                                 Dobj   elephant1
                                 for    decade1 (+Plur)
    Dobj   tusk1 (+Plur)
                  Attrib  large1 ()
```

Figure 1. The LF representation of "African elephants, which have been hunted for decades, have large tusks."

In Figure 1, we demonstrate that native LF uses reentrancy in graph notation, as does AMR, whenever an entity plays multiple roles in the graph. Note how the node elephant1 is both the Dsub of have1 and the Dobj of hunt1. The numerical identifiers on the leaf nodes are a unique label name, not a sense identification.

We also point out that LF attempts to interpret the syntactic relation as a general semantic relation to the degree possible, but when it lacks information for disambiguation, LF preserves the ambiguity. Thus, in Figure 1, the identified semantic relations are: Dsub ("deep subject"), Attrib (attributive), Dobj ("deep object"), but also the underspecified relation "for".

The canonical LF graph display proceeds from the root node and follows a depth first exploration of the nodes. When queried, however, the graph can be viewed with integrity from the perspective of any node, by making use of relation inversions. Thus, a query for the node elephant1 in Figure 1 returns elephant1 as the DsubOf have1 and also the DobjOf hunt1.

	Test without word sense annotations				Test with word sense annotations			
System	Proxy	DFA	Bolt	*Average*	Proxy	DFA	Bolt	*Average*
JAMR: proxy	**64.4**	40.4	44.2	*49.7*	**63.3**	38.1	42.6	*48.0*
JAMR: all	60.9	44.5	47.5	*51.0*	60.1	43.2	46.0	*49.8*
LF	59.0	**50.7**	**52.6**	***54.1***	55.2	**46.9**	**49.2**	***50.4***

Table 1. Evaluation results: balanced F-measure in percentage points. JAMR (proxy) is the system of Flanigan et al. (2014) trained on only the proxy corpus; JAMR (all) is the system trained on all data in LDC2014T12; and LF is the system described in this paper. We evaluate with and without sense annotations in three test corpora.

4 LF to AMR conversion

The description of LF in section 3 emphasized the close similarity of LF and AMR. Thus, conversion rules can be written to turn LF into AMR-similar output, thus creating an AMR parser. To convert the majority of the relations, only simple renaming is required; for example LF Dsub is typically AMR ARG0, LF Locn is AMR location, and so on.

We use simple representational transforms to convert named entities, dates, times, numbers and percentages, since the exact representation of these in AMR are slightly different from LF.

Some of the more interesting transforms to encourage similarity between LF and AMR are mapping modal verbs *can*, *may* and *must* to *possible* and *obligate* in AMR and adjusting how the copula is handled. In both AMR and LF the arguments of the copula are moved down to the object of the copula, but in LF the vestigial copula remains, whereas in AMR it is removed.

5 Evaluation

Using smatch (Cai and Knight, 2013), we compare the performance of our LF system to the JAMR system of Flanigan et al. (2014). Both systems rely on the Illinois Named Entity Tagger (Ratinov and Roth, 2009). LF strives to be a broad coverage parser without bias toward a particular domain. Therefore, we wanted to evaluate across a number of corpora. When trained on all available data, JAMR should be less domain dependent. However, the newswire data is both larger and important, so we also report numbers for JAMR trained on proxy data alone.

To explore the degree of domain dependence of these systems, we evaluate on several genres provided by the LDC: DFA (discussion forums data from English), Bolt (translated discussion forum data), and Proxy (newswire data). We did not experiment on the consensus, mt09sdl, or Xinhua subsets because the data was pre-tokenized. This tokenization must be undone before our parser is applied.

We evaluate in two conditions: "without word sense annotations" indicates that the specific sense numbers were discarded in both the gold standard and the system output; "with word sense annotations" leaves the sense annotations intact.

The AMR specification requires that concepts, wherever possible, be annotated with a sense ID referencing the OntoNotes sense inventory. Recall that the LF system intentionally does not have a word sense disambiguation component due to the inherent difficulty of defining and agreeing upon task-independent sense inventories (Palmer et al. 2004, i.a.). In order to evaluate in the standard evaluation setup, we therefore construct a word-sense disambiguation component for LF lemmas. Our approach is quite simple: for each lemma, we find the predominant sense in the training set (breaking ties in favor of the lowest sense ID), and use that sense for all occurrences of the lemma in test data. For those lemmas that occur in the test but not in the training data, we attempt to find a verb frame in OntoNotes. If found, we use the lowest verb sense ID not marked with DO NOT TAG; otherwise, the lemma is left unannotated for sense. Such a simple system should perform well because 95% of sense-annotated tokens in the proxy training set use the predominant sense. An obvious extension would be sensitive to parts-of-speech.

As shown in Table 1, the LF system outperforms JAMR in broad-domain semantic parsing, as measured by macro-averaged F1 across domains. This is primarily due to its better performance on discussion forum data. JAMR, when trained on newswire data, is clearly the best system on newswire data. Adding training data from other sources leads to improvements on the discussion forum data, but at the cost of accuracy on newswire. The lack of sophisticated sense disambiguation in LF causes a substantial degradation in performance on newswire.

6 Data Sets for LF development

The LF component was developed by authoring rules that access information from a rich lexicon consisting of several online dictionaries as well as information output by a rich grammar formalism. Authoring these LF rules is supported by a suite of tools that allow iterative development of an annotated test suite (Suzuki, 2002). We start by curating a sentence corpus that exemplifies the syntactic and semantic phenomena that the LF is designed to cover; one might view this sentence corpus as the LF specification. When, during development, the system outputs the desired representation, that LF is saved as "gold annotation". In this way, the gold annotations are produced by the LF system itself, automatically, and thus with good system internal consistency. We note that this method of system development is quite different from SemBanking AMR, but is similar to the method described in Flickinger et al. (2014).

As part of this demonstration, we share with participants the gold annotations for the curated sentence corpora used during LF development, currently 550 sentences that are vetted to produce correct LF analyses. Note that the example in Figure 2 requires a parser to handle both the passive/active alternation as well as control verbs. We believe that there is value in curated targeted datasets to supplement annotating natural data; e.g., AMR clearly includes control phenomena in its spec (the first example is "the boy wants to go") but in the data, there are only 3 instances of "persuade" in the amr-release-1.0-training-proxy, e.g., and no instances in the original AMR-bank.

7 AMR parsers for French, German, Spanish and Japanese

The demonstrated system includes not only a parser for English, but also parsers for French, German, Spanish and Japanese that produce analyses at the LF level. Thus, using the same set of conversion rules, we demonstrate AMR annotations generated by our parsers in these additional languages, for which there are currently no manually-annotated AMR SemBanks. Such annotations may be useful to the community as initial analyses that can be manually edited and corrected where their output does not conform to AMR-specifications already. Consider Figures 3-6 and the brief description of the type of alternation they are intended to demonstrate in each language.

```
# Pat was persuaded by Chris to eat the apple.
(p / persuade
      :ARG0 (p2 / person
            :name (c / name :op1 Chris))
      :ARG2 (e / eat
            :ARG0 (p4 / person
                  :name (p3 / name :op1 Pat))
            :ARG1 (a / apple))
      :ARG1 p3)
```

Figure 2. LF-AMR for the input sentence "Pat was persuaded by Chris to eat the apple", with both passive and control constructions.

Input: el reptil se volteó, quitándoselo de encima.
Gloss: the crocodile rolled over, throwing it off.

```
(v / voltear
      :ARG0 (r / reptil)
      :manner (q / quitar
            :ARG0 r
            :ARG1 (x / "él")
            :prep-de (e / encima)))
```

Figure 3 AMR in Spanish with clitic construction.

Input: Et j'ai vu un petit bonhomme tout à fait extraordinaire qui me considérait gravement.
Gloss: And I saw a small chap totally extraordinary who me looked seriously.

```
(e / et
 :op (v / voir
    :ARG0 (j / je)
    :ARG1 (b / bonhomme
          :ARG0-of (c / "considérer"
                :ARG1 j
                :mod (g / gravement))
          :mod (p / petit)
          :mod (e2 / extraordinaire
                :degree (t / "tout_à_fait")))))
```

Figure 4 AMR in French with re-entrant node "j"

Input: Die dem wirtschaftlichen Aufschwung zu verdankende sinkende Arbeitslosenquote führe zu höheren Steuereinnahmen.
Gloss: The the economic upturn to thank-for sinking unemployment rate led to higher tax-revenue

```
(f / "führen"
     :ARG0 (a / Arbeitslosenquote
           :ARG0-of (s / sinken)
           :ARG0-of (v / verdanken
                 :ARG2 (a2 / Aufschwung
                       :mod (w / wirtschaftlich))
                 :degree (z / zu)))
     :prep-zu (s2 / Steuereinnahme
           :mod (h / hoch)))
```

Figure 5 AMR in German for complex participial construction

Input: 東国 の 諸 藩主 に 勤王 を 誓わせた。
Gloss: eastern_lands various feudal_lords serve_monarchy swear-CAUS-PAST

```
東国の諸藩主に勤王を誓わせた。
(x / "させる" cause
   :ARG1 (x2 / "誓う"  swear
        :ARG0 (x3 / "藩主"  feudal lords
             :mod (x4 / "諸") various
             :prep-の (x5 / "東国")) Eastern lands
        :ARG1 (x6 / "勤王"))) serve monarchy
```

Figure 6. AMR in Japanese illustrating a causative construction

8 Conclusion

In the sections above, we have attempted to highlight those aspects of the system that will be demonstrated. To summarize, we show a system that:

- Produces AMR output that can be compared to the manually-annotated LDC resources. Available at: http://research.microsoft.com/msrsplat,
- Produces AMR output for a new data set comprised of the sentences selected for the development of our LF component. This curated data set was selected to represent a wide range of phenomena and representational challenges. These sentences and their AMR annotations are available at: http://research.microsoft.com/nlpwin-amr
- Produces AMR annotations for French, German, Spanish and Japanese input, which may be used to speed-up manual annotation/correction in these languages.

Acknowledgements

We are grateful to all our colleagues who worked on NLPwin. For this paper, we especially recognize Karen Jensen, Carmen Lozano, Jessie Pinkham, Michael Gamon and Hisami Suzuki for their work on Logical Form. We also acknowledge Jeffrey Flanigan and his co-authors for their contributions of making the JAMR models and code available.

References

Laura Banarescu, Claire Bonial, Shu Cai, Madalina Georgescu, Kira Griffitt, Ulf Hermjakob, Kevin Knight, Philipp Koehn, Martha Palmer, and Nathan Schneider. 2014. Abstract Meaning Representation (AMR) 1.2.1 Specification. Available at https://github.com/amrisi/amr-guidelines/blob/master/amr.md

Shu Cai and Kevin Knight. 2013. Smatch: an evaluation metric for semantic feature structures. In Proceedings of ACL.

Jeffrey Flanigan, Sam Thomson, Jaime Carbonell, Chris Dyer, and Noah Smith. 2014. A Discriminative Graph-Based Parser for the Abstract Meaning Representation. In Proceedings of ACL 2014.

Dan Flickinger, Emily M. Bender and Stephan Oepen. 2014. Towards an Encyclopedia of Compositional Semantics: Documenting the Interface of the English Resource Grammar. In Proceedings of LREC.

Jan Hajič, Alena Böhmová, Hajičová, Eva, and Hladká, Barbara. (2003). The Prague Dependency Treebank: A Three Level Annotation Scenario. In Abeillé, Anne, editor, Treebanks: Building and Using Annotated Corpora. Kluwer Academic Publishers.

Martha Palmer, Olga Babko-Malaya, Hoa Trang Dang. 2004. Different Sense Granularities for Different Applications. In *Proceedings of Workshop on Scalable Natural Language Understanding.*

Sameer. S. Pradhan, Eduard Hovy, Mitch Marcus, Martha Palmer, Lance Ramshaw, and Ralph Weischedel. 2007. OntoNotes: A Unified Relational Semantic Representation. In Proceedings of the International Conference on Semantic Computing (ICSC '07).

Hisami Suzuki. 2002. A development environment for large-scale multi-lingual parsing systems. In Proceedings of the 2002 workshop on Grammar engineering and evaluation - Volume 15, Pages 1-7.

Lucy Vanderwende. 2015. NLPwin – an introduction. Microsoft Research tech report no. MSR-TR-2015-23, March 2015.

ICE: Rapid Information Extraction Customization for NLP Novices

Yifan He and Ralph Grishman
Computer Science Department
New York University
New York, NY 10003, USA
{yhe,grishman}@cs.nyu.edu

Abstract

We showcase ICE, an Integrated Customization Environment for Information Extraction. ICE is an easy tool for non-NLP experts to rapidly build customized IE systems for a new domain.

1 Introduction

Creating an information extraction (IE) system for a new domain, with new vocabulary and new classes of entities and relations, remains a task requiring substantial time, training, and expense. This has been an obstacle to the wider use of IE technology. The tools which have been developed for this task typically do not take full advantage of linguistic analysis and available learning methods to provide guidance to the user in building the IE system. They also generally require some understanding of system internals and data representations. We have created ICE [the Integrated Customization Environment], which lowers the barriers to IE system development by providing guidance while letting the user retain control, and by allowing the user to interact in terms of the words and phrases of the domain, with a minimum of formal notation.

In this paper, we review related systems and explain the technologies behind ICE. The code, documentation, and a demo video of ICE can be found at `http://nlp.cs.nyu.edu/ice/`

2 Related Work

Several groups have developed integrated systems for IE development:

The extreme extraction system from BBN (Freedman et al., 2011) is similar in several regards: it is based on an extraction system initially developed for ACE[1], allows for the customization of entities and relations, and uses bootstrapping and active learning. However, in contrast to our system, it is aimed at skilled computational linguists.

The Language Computer Corporation has described several tools developed to rapidly extend an IE system to a new task (Lehmann et al., 2010; Surdeanu and Harabagiu, 2002). Here too the emphasis is on tools for use by experienced IE system developers. Events and relations are recognized using finite-state rules, with meta-rules to efficiently capture syntactic variants and a provision for supervised learning of rules from annotated corpora.

A few groups have focused on use by NLP novices:

The WIZIE system from IBM Research (Li et al., 2012) is based on a finite-state rule language. Users prepare some sample annotated texts and are then guided in preparing an extraction plan (sequences of rule applications) and in writing the individual rules. IE development is seen as a rule programming task. This offers less in the way of linguistic support (corpus analysis, syntactic analysis) but can provide greater flexibility for extraction tasks where linguistic models are a poor fit.

The SPIED system (Gupta and Manning, 2014) focuses on extracting lexical patterns for entity recognition in an interactive fashion. Our system, on

[1] `https://www.ldc.upenn.edu/collaborations/past-projects/ace`

Proceedings of NAACL-HLT 2015, pages 31–35,
Denver, Colorado, May 31 – June 5, 2015.

the other hand, aims at extracting both entities and relations. Furthermore, SPIED produces token sequence rules, while our system helps the user to construct lexico-syntactic extraction rules that are based on dependency paths.

The PROPMINER system from T. U. Berlin (Akbik et al., 2013) takes an approach more similar to our own. In particular, it is based on a dependency analysis of the text corpus and emphasizes exploratory development of the IE system, supported by search operations over the dependency structures. However, the responsibility for generalizing initial patterns lies primarily with the user, whereas we support the generalization process through distributional analysis.

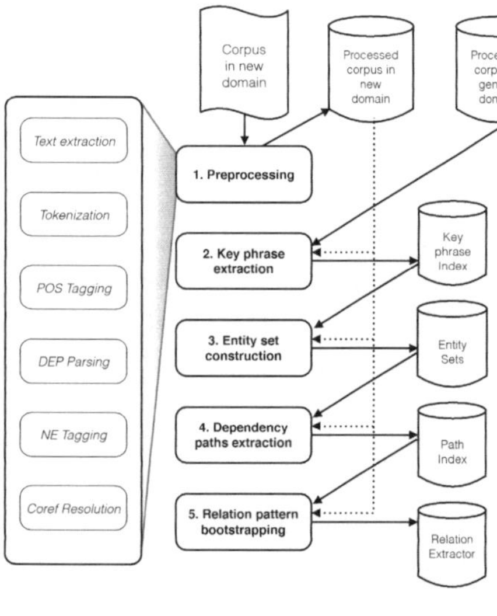

Figure 1: System architecture of ICE

3 System Description

3.1 Overall architecture

The information to be extracted by the IE system consists of user-specified types of entities and user-specified types of relations connecting these entities. Standard types of entities (people, organizations, locations, etc.) are built in; new entity types are defined extensionally as lists of terms. Relation types are captured in the form of sets of lexicalized dependency paths, discussed in more detail below.

For NLP novices, it is much easier to provide examples for what they want and make binary choices, than to come up with linguistic rules or comprehensive lists. ICE therefore guides users through a series of linguistic processing steps, presents them with entities and dependency relations that are potential seeds, and helps them to expand the seeds by answering yes/no questions.

Figure 1 illustrates the five steps of ICE processing: given a new corpus, preprocessing builds a cache of analyzed documents to speed up further processing; key phrase extraction and entity set construction build new entity types; dependency path extraction and relation pattern bootstrapping build new semantic relations.

3.2 Preprocessing

We rely on distributional analysis to collect entity sets and relation patterns on a new domain. Effective distributional analysis requires features from deep linguistic analysis that are too time-consuming to perform more than once. ICE therefore always preprocesses a new corpus with the Jet NLP pipeline[2] when it is first added, and saves POS tags, noun chunks, dependency relations between tokens, types and extents of named-entities, and coreference chains to a cache. After preprocessing, each of the following steps can be completed within minutes on a corpus of thousands of documents, saving the time of the domain expert user.

3.3 Key phrase extraction

In ICE, key phrases of a corpus are either nouns or multi-word terms. We extract multi-word terms from noun chunks: if a noun chunk has N adjectives and nouns preceding the head noun, we obtain $N + 1$ multi-word term candidates consisting of the head noun and its preceding i $(0 \leq i \leq N)$ nouns and adjectives.

We count the absolute frequency of the nouns and multi-word terms and rank them with a ratio score, which is the relative frequency compared to a general corpus. We use the ratio score S_t to measure the representativeness of term t with regard to the given domain, as defined in Eq (1).

$$S_t = \frac{\#pos(t) \cdot \log^{\alpha}(\#pos(t))}{\#neg(t)} \tag{1}$$

where $\#pos(t)$ is the number of occurrences of term t in the in-domain corpus, $\#neg(t)$ is the number of

[2] http://cs.nyu.edu/grishman/jet/jet.html

occurrences of term t in the general corpus, and α is a user-defined parameter to favor either common or rare words, default to 0.

We present the user with a ranked list, where words or multi-word terms that appear more often in the in-domain corpus than in general language will rank higher.

3.4 Entity set construction

ICE constructs entity sets from seeds. Seeds are entities that are representative of a type: if we want to construct a DRUGS type, "methamphetamine" and "oxycodone" can be possible seeds. Seeds are provided by the user (normally from the top scoring terms), but if the user is uncertain, ICE can recommend seeds automatically, using a clustering-based heuristic.

3.4.1 Entity set expansion

Given a seed set, we compute the distributional similarity of all terms in the corpus with the centroid of the seeds, using the dependency analysis as the basis for computing term contexts. We represent each term with a vector that encodes its syntactic context, which is the label of the dependency relation attached to the term in conjunction with the term's governor or dependent in that relation.

Consider the entity set of DRUGS. Drugs often appear in the dependency relations *dobj(sell, drug)* and *dobj(transport, drug)* (where *dobj* is the direct object relation), thus members in the DRUGS set will share the features *dobj_sell* and *dobj_transport*. We use pointwise mutual information (PMI) to weight the feature vectors and use a cosine metric to measure the similarity between two term vectors.

The terms are displayed as a ranked list, and the user can accept or reject individual members of the entity set. At any point the user can recompute the similarities and rerank the list (where the ranking is based the centroids of the accepted and rejected terms, following (Min and Grishman, 2011)). When the user is satisfied, the set of accepted terms will become a new semantic type for tagging further text.

3.5 Dependency path extraction and linearization

ICE captures the semantic relation (if any) between two entity mentions by the lexicalized

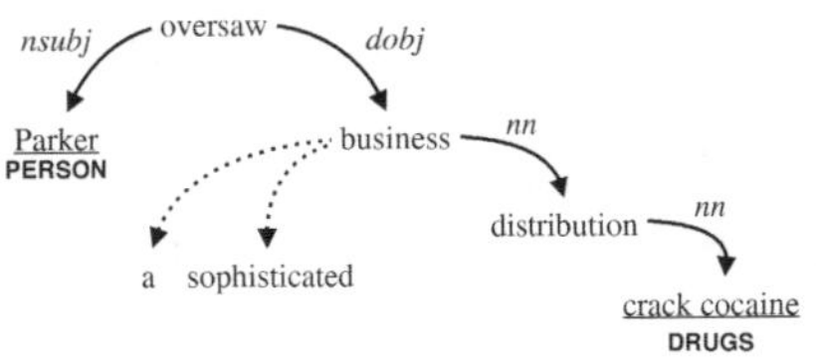

Figure 2: A parse tree; dotted relations ignored by LDP

dependency path (LDP) and the semantic types of the two entities. LDP includes both the labels of the dependency arcs and the lemmatized form of the lexical items along the path. For example, for the sentence "[Parker] oversaw a sophisticated [crack cocaine] distribution business.", consider the parse tree in Figure 2. The path from "Parker" to "crack cocaine" would be $nsubj^{-1}$*:oversee:dobj:business:nn:distribution:nn*, where the $^{-1}$ indicates that the *nsubj* arc is being traversed from dependent to governor. The determiner "a" and the adjective modifier "sophisticated" are dropped in the process, making the LDP more generalized than token sequence patterns.

We linearize LDPs before presenting them to the user to keep the learning curve gentle for NLP novices: given an LDP and the sentence from which it is extracted, we only keep the word in the sentence if it is the head word of the entity or it is on the LDP. The linearized LDP for the path in Figure 2 , "PERSON oversee DRUGS distribution business", is more readable than the LDP itself.

3.6 Bootstrapping relation extractors

3.6.1 Relation extractor

ICE builds two types of dependency-path based relation extractors. Given two entities and an LDP between them, the *exact* extractor extracts a relation between two entities if the types of the two entities match the types required by the relation, and the words on the candidate LDP match the words on an extraction rule. When the two nodes are linked by an arc in the dependency graph (i.e. no word but a type label on the LDP), we require the dependency label to match.

ICE also builds a *fuzzy* extractor that calculates edit distance (normalized by the length of the rule) between the candidate LDP and the rules in the rule set. It extracts a relation if the minimum edit distance between the candidate LDP and the rule set falls below a certain threshold (0.5 in ICE). We tune the edit costs on a development set, and use insertion cost 0.3, deletion cost 1.2, and substitution cost 0.8.

Fuzzy extractors with large rule sets tend to produce false positive relations. ICE therefore bootstraps both positive and negative rules, and requires that the candidate LDP should be closer to (the closest element in) the positive rule set than to the negative rule set, in order to be extracted by the fuzzy LDP matcher.

3.6.2 Bootstrapper

The learner follows the style of Snowball (Agichtein and Gravano, 2000), with two key differences: it bootstraps both positive and negative rules, and performs additional filtering of the top k ($k = 20$ in ICE) candidates to ensure diversity.

Starting with a seed LDP, the learner gathers all the pairs of arguments (endpoints) which appear with this LDP in the corpus. It then collects all other LDPs which connect any of these pairs in the corpus, and presents these LDPs to the user for assessment. If the set of argument pairs connected by any of the seeds is $\mathcal{S}$ and the set of argument pairs of a candidate LDP x is $\mathcal{X}$, the candidate LDPs are ranked by $\mid \mathcal{S} \cap \mathcal{X} \mid / \mid \mathcal{X} \mid$, so that LDPs most distributionally similar to the seed set are ranked highest. The linearized LDPs which are accepted by the user as alternative expressions of the semantic relation are added to the seed set. At any point the user can terminate the bootstrapping and accept the set of LDPs as a model of the relation.

Bidirectional bootstrapping. If the user explicitly rejects a path, but it is similar to a path in the seed set, we still bootstrap from the arg pairs of this path. We save all the paths rejected by the user as the negative rule set.

Diversity-based filtering. When presenting the bootstrapped LDPs, we require paths presented in the first ICE screen (top 20 candidates) to be distant enough from each other.

4 Experiments

We perform end-to-end relation extraction experiments to evaluate the utility of ICE: we start from plain text, extract named entities, and finally extract drug names and relations with models built by ICE. We collect approximately 5,000 web news posts from the U.S. Drug Enforcement Administration [3] (DEA) for our experiments.

	SELL			RESIDENT-OF		
	P	R	F	P	R	F
Fuzzy	0.60	0.22	0.32	0.68	0.51	0.58
-neg	0.59	0.22	0.32	0.55	0.51	0.53
Exact	0.92	0.10	0.18	0.72	0.47	0.57

Table 1: End-to-end relation extraction using small rule sets. *Fuzzy*: fuzzy match relation extractor with negative rule set; -neg: fuzzy match extractor without negative rule set; *Exact*: exact match extractor; P / R / F: Precision / Recall / F-score

	SELL			RESIDENT-OF		
	P	R	F	P	R	F
Fuzzy	0.46	0.36	0.40	0.56	0.53	0.55
-neg	0.31	0.38	0.34	0.30	0.56	0.39
Exact	0.76	0.20	0.32	0.75	0.53	0.62

Table 2: End-to-end relation extraction using large rule sets. Same configurations as Table 1

Entity Set Construction. In our first experiment, we extracted 3,703 terms from this corpus and manually identified 119 DRUGS names and 97 *law enforcement agent* (AGENTS) mentions, which we use as the "gold standard" sets. We then ran our customizer in the following manner: 1) we provided the entity set expansion program with two seeds ("methamphetamine" and "oxycodone" for DRUGS; "special agents" and "law enforcement officers" for AGENTS); 2) the program produced a ranked list of terms; 3) in each iteration, we examined the top 20 terms that had not been examined in previous iterations; 4) if a term is in the gold standard set, we added it to the expander as a positive seed, otherwise, we added it as a negative seed; 5) we continued the expansion with the updated seed set, repeating the process for 10 iterations. This process produced high-recall dictionary-based entity taggers (74% for

[3] http://www.justice.gov/dea/index.shtml

drugs, 82% for agents) in just a few minutes.

Relation Extraction. With the ICE-built DRUGS dictionary, we performed end-to-end extraction of two relations: SELL, in which a PERSON sells DRUGS, using "PERSON sell DRUGS" as seed, and RESIDENT-OF, which indicates that a PERSON resides in a GPE[4], using "PERSON of GPE" as seed. We manually annotated 51 documents from the DEA collection. There are 110 SELL relations and 45 RESIDENT-OF relations in the annotated corpus.

We first extracted small rule sets. For both relations, we asked a user to review the presented LDPs on the first screen (20 LDPs in total) and then ran bootstrapping using the expanded seeds. We did this for 3 iterations, so the user evaluated 60 LDPs, which took less than half an hour. We report the results in Table 1. Note that these are end-to-end scores, reflecting in part errors of entity extraction. After entity tagging and coreference resolution, the recall of entity mentions is 0.76 in our experiments.

We observe that fuzzy LDP match with negative rule sets obtains best results for both relations. If we remove the negative rule set, the precision of RESIDENT-OF is hurt more severely than the SELL relations. On the other hand, if we require exact match, the recall of SELL will decrease very significantly. This discrepancy in performance is due to the nature of the two relations. RESIDENT-OF is a relatively closed binary relation, with fewer lexical variations: the small RESIDENT-OF model covers around 50% of the relation mentions with 7 positive LDPs, so it is easier to rule out false positives than to further boost recall. SELL, in contrast, can be expressed in many different ways, and fuzzy LDP match is essential for reasonable recall.

We report experimental results on larger rule sets in Table 2. The large rule sets were bootstrapped in 3 iterations as well, but the user reviewed 250 LDPs in each iteration. The best score in this setting improves to 0.4 F-score for SELL and 0.62 F-score for RESIDENT-OF, as we have more LDP rules. The exact match extractor performs better than the fuzzy match extractor for RESIDENT-OF, as the latter is hurt by false positives.

[4]Geo-political entity, or GPE, is an entity type defined in Ace, meaning location with a government

5 Conclusion and Future Work

We described ICE, an integrated customization environment for information extraction customization and evaluated its end-to-end performance. We plan to explore more expressive models than LDP that can handle arbitrary number of arguments, which will enable ICE to build event extractors.

Acknowledgements

We thank Lisheng Fu, Angus Grieve-Smith, and Thien Huu Nguyen for discussions.

References

Eugene Agichtein and Luis Gravano. 2000. Snowball: Extracting relations from large plain-text collections. In *Proceedings of the Fifth ACM Conference on Digital Libraries*, pages 85–94.

Alan Akbik, Oresti Konomi, Michail Melnikov, et al. 2013. Propminer: A workflow for interactive information extraction and exploration using dependency trees. In *Proceedings of the 51st Annual Meeting of the Association for Computational Linguistics: Systems Demonstrations*, pages 157–162.

Marjorie Freedman, Lance Ramshaw, Elizabeth Boschee, Ryan Gabbard, Gary Kratkiewicz, Nicolas Ward, and Ralph Weischedel. 2011. Extreme extraction: machine reading in a week. In *Proceedings of the Conference on Empirical Methods in Natural Language Processing*, pages 1437–1446.

Sonal Gupta and Christopher Manning. 2014. SPIED: Stanford pattern based information extraction and diagnostics. In *Proceedings of the Workshop on Interactive Language Learning, Visualization, and Interfaces*, pages 38–44.

John Lehmann, Sean Monahan, Luke Nezda, Arnold Jung, and Ying Shi. 2010. LCC approaches to knowledge base population at tac 2010. In *Proc. TAC 2010 Workshop*.

Yunyao Li, Laura Chiticariu, Huahai Yang, Frederick R Reiss, and Arnaldo Carreno-Fuentes. 2012. WizIE: a best practices guided development environment for information extraction. In *Proceedings of the ACL 2012 System Demonstrations*, pages 109–114.

Bonan Min and Ralph Grishman. 2011. Fine-grained entity refinement with user feedback. In *Proceedings of RANLP 2011 Workshop on Information Extraction and Knowledge Acquisition*.

Mihai Surdeanu and Sanda M. Harabagiu. 2002. Infrastructure for open-domain information extraction. In *Proceedings of the second international conference on Human Language Technology Research*, pages 325–330.

AMRICA: an AMR Inspector for Cross-language Alignments

Naomi Saphra
Center for Language and Speech Processing
Johns Hopkins University
Baltimore, MD 21211, USA
nsaphra@jhu.edu

Adam Lopez
School of Informatics
University of Edinburgh
Edinburgh, United Kingdom
alopez@inf.ed.ac.uk

Abstract

Abstract Meaning Representation (AMR), an annotation scheme for natural language semantics, has drawn attention for its simplicity and representational power. Because AMR annotations are not designed for human readability, we present AMRICA, a visual aid for exploration of AMR annotations. AMRICA can visualize an AMR or the difference between two AMRs to help users diagnose interannotator disagreement or errors from an AMR parser. AMRICA can also automatically align and visualize the AMRs of a sentence and its translation in a parallel text. We believe AMRICA will simplify and streamline exploratory research on cross-lingual AMR corpora.

1 Introduction

Research in statistical machine translation has begun to turn to semantics. Effective semantics-based translation systems pose a crucial need for a practical cross-lingual semantic representation. One such schema, Abstract Meaning Representation (AMR; Banarescu et al., 2013), has attracted attention for its simplicity and expressive power. AMR represents the meaning of a sentence as a directed graph over *concepts* representing entities, events, and properties like names or quantities. Concepts are represented by nodes and are connected by edges representing *relations*—roles or attributes. Figure 1 shows an example of the AMR annotation format, which is optimized for text entry rather than human comprehension.

For human analysis, we believe it is easier to visualize the AMR graph. We present AMRICA, a system for visualizing AMRs in three conditions. First, AMRICA can display AMRs as in Figure 2. Second, AMRICA can visualize differences between aligned AMRs of a sentence, enabling users to diagnose differences in multiple annotations or between an annotation and an automatic AMR parse (Section 2). Finally, to aid researchers studying cross-lingual semantics, AMRICA can visualize differences between the AMR of a sentence and that of its translation (Section 3) using a novel cross-lingual extension to Smatch (Cai and Knight, 2013). The AMRICA code and a tutorial are publicly available.[1]

```
(b / be-located-at-91 :li 4
  :ARG1 (i / i)
  :ARG2 (c / country
    :name (n / name
      :op1 "New" :op2 "Zealand"))
  :time (w / week :quant 2
    :time (p / past)))
```

Figure 1: AMR for "I've been in New Zealand the past two weeks." (Linguistic Data Consortium, 2013)

2 Interannotator Agreement

AMR annotators and researchers are still exploring how to achieve high interannotator agreement (Cai and Knight, 2013). So it is useful to visualize a pair of AMRs in a way that highlights their disagreement, as in Figure 3. AMRICA shows in black those nodes and edges which are shared between the annotations. Elements that differ are red if they appear in one AMR and blue if they appear in the other. This feature can also be used to explore output from an

[1] *http://github.com/nsaphra/AMRICA*

Proceedings of NAACL-HLT 2015, pages 36–40,
Denver, Colorado, May 31 – June 5, 2015.

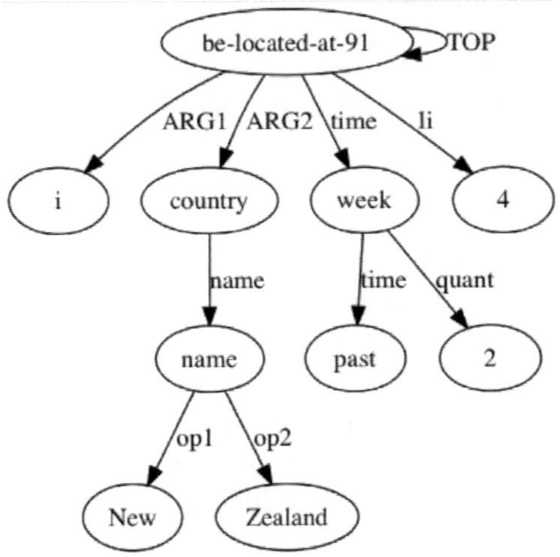

Figure 2: AMRICA visualization of AMR in Figure 1.

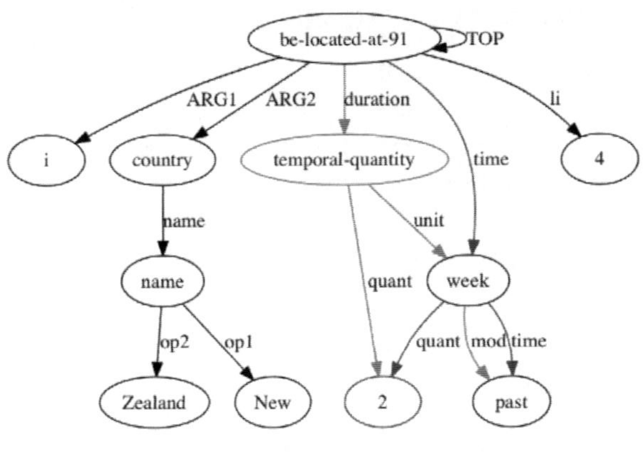

Figure 3: AMRICA visualization of the disagreement between two independent annotations of the sentence in Figure 1.

automatic AMR parser in order to diagnose errors.

To align AMRs, we use the public implementation of Smatch (Cai and Knight, 2013).[2] Since it also forms the basis for our cross-lingual visualization, we briefly review it here.

AMR distinguishes between *variable* and *constant* nodes. Variable nodes, like `i` in Figure 1, represent entities and events, and may have multiple incoming and outgoing edges. Constant nodes, like `2` in Figure 1, participate in exactly one relation, making them leaves of a single parent variable. Smatch compares a pair of AMRs that have each been decomposed into three kinds of relationships:

1. The set V of instance-of relations describe the conceptual class of each variable. In Figure 1, `(c / country)` specifies that `c` is an instance of a `country`. If node v is an instance of concept c, then $(v, c) \in V$.
2. The set E of variable-to-variable relations like `ARG2(b, c)` describe relationships between entities and/or events. If r is a relation from variable v_1 to variable v_2, then $(r, v_1, v_2) \in E$.
3. The set C of variable-to-constant relations like `quant(w, 2)` describe properties of entities or events. If r is a relation from variable v to constant x, then $(r, v, x) \in C$.

Smatch seeks the bijective alignment $\hat{b} : V \to V'$ between an AMR $G = (V, E, C)$ and a larger AMR $G' = (V', E', C')$ satisfying Equation 1, where $\mathbb{I}$ is an indicator function returning 1 if its argument is true, 0 otherwise.

$$\hat{b} = \arg\max_{b} \sum_{(v,c)\in V} \mathbb{I}((b(v), c) \in V') + \sum_{(r,v_1,v_2)\in E} \mathbb{I}((r, b(v_1), b(v_2)) \in E') + \sum_{(r,v,c)\in C} \mathbb{I}((r, b(v), c) \in C') \quad (1)$$

Cai and Knight (2013) conjecture that this optimization can be shown to be NP-complete by reduction to the subgraph isomorphism problem. Smatch approximates the solution with a hill-climbing algorithm. It first creates an alignment b_0 in which each node of G is aligned to a node in G' with the same concept if such a node exists, or else to a random node. It then iteratively produces an alignment b_i by greedily choosing the best alignment that can be obtained from b_{i-1} by swapping two alignments or aligning a node in G to an unaligned node, stopping when the objective no longer improves and returning the final alignment. It uses random restarts since the greedy algorithm may only find a local optimum.

3 Aligning Cross-Language AMRs

AMRICA offers the novel ability to align AMR annotations of bitext. This is useful for analyzing

[2] *http://amr.isi.edu/download/smatch-v2.0.tar.gz*

AMR annotation differences across languages, and for analyzing translation systems that use AMR as an intermediate representation. The alignment is more difficult than in the monolingual case, since nodes in AMRs are labeled in the language of the sentence they annotate. AMRICA extends the Smatch alignment algorithm to account for this difficulty.

AMRICA does not distinguish between constants and variables, since their labels tend to be grounded in the words of the sentence, which it uses for alignment. Instead, it treats all nodes as variables and computes the similarities of their node labels. Since node labels are in their language of origin, exact string match no longer works as a criterion for assigning credit to a pair of aligned nodes. Therefore AMRICA uses a function $L : V \times V \rightarrow \mathbb{R}$ indicating the likelihood that the nodes align. These changes yield the new objective shown in Equation 2 for AMRs $G = (V, E)$ and $G' = (V', E')$, where V and V' are now sets of nodes, and E and E' are defined as before.

$$\hat{b} = \arg\max_{b} \sum_{v \in V} L(v, b(v)) + \sum_{(r,v_1,v_2) \in E} \mathbb{I}((r, b(v_1), b(v_2)) \in E') \qquad (2)$$

If the labels of nodes v and v' match, then $L(v, v') = 1$. If they do not match, then L decomposes over source-node-to-word alignment a_s, source-word-to-target-word alignment a, and target-word-to-node a_t, as illustrated in Figure 5. More precisely, if the source and target sentences contain n and n' words, respectively, then L is defined by Equation 3. AMRICA takes a parameter α to control how it weights these estimated likelihoods relative to exact matches of relation and concept labels.

$$L(v, v') = \alpha \sum_{i=1}^{n} \Pr(a_s(v) = i) \times \sum_{j=1}^{n'} \Pr(a_i = j) \cdot \Pr(a_t(v') = j) \qquad (3)$$

Node-to-word probabilities $\Pr(a_s(v) = i)$ and $\Pr(a_s(v') = j)$ are computed as described in Section 3.1. Word-to-word probabilities $\Pr(a_i = j)$ are computed as described in Section 3.2. AMRICA uses the Smatch hill-climbing algorithm to yield alignments like that in Figure 4.

3.1 Node-to-word and word-to-node alignment

AMRICA can accept node-to-word alignments as output by the heuristic aligner of Flanigan et al. (2014).[3] In this case, the tokens in the aligned span receive uniform probabilities over all nodes in their aligned subgraph, while all other token-node alignments receive probability 0. If no such alignments are provided, AMRICA aligns concept nodes to tokens matching the node's label, if they exist. A token can align to multiple nodes, and a node to multiple tokens. Otherwise, alignment probability is uniformly distributed across unaligned nodes or tokens.

3.2 Word-to-word Alignment

AMRICA computes the posterior probability of the alignment between the ith word of the source and jth word of the target as an equal mixture between the posterior probabilities of source-to-target and target-to-source alignments from GIZA++ (Och and Ney, 2003).[4] To obtain an approximation of the posterior probability in each direction, it uses the m-best alignments $a^{(1)} \ldots a^{(m)}$, where $a_i^{(k)} = j$ indicates that the ith source word aligns to the jth target word in the kth best alignment, and $\Pr(a^{(k)})$ is the probability of the kth best alignment according to GIZA++. We then approximate the posterior probability as follows.

$$\Pr(a_i = j) = \frac{\sum_{k=1}^{m} \Pr(a^{(k)}) \mathbb{I}[a_i^{(k)} = j]}{\sum_{k=1}^{m} \Pr(a^{(k)})}$$

4 Demonstration Script

AMRICA makes AMRs accessible for data exploration. We will demonstrate all three capabilities outlined above, allowing participants to visually explore AMRs using graphics much like those in Figures 2, 3, and 4, which were produced by AMRICA. We will then demonstrate how AMRICA can be used to generate a preliminary alignment for bitext

[3] Another option for aligning AMR graphs to sentences is the statistical aligner of Pourdamghani et al. (2014)

[4] In experiments, this method was more reliable than using either alignment alone.

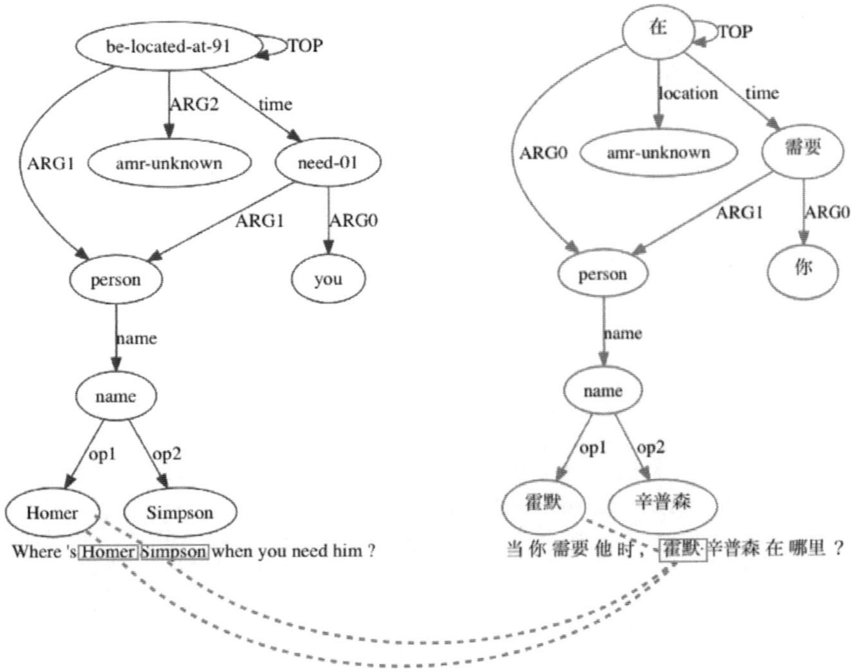

Figure 5: Cross-lingual AMR example from Nianwen Xue et al. (2014). The node-to-node alignment of the highlighted nodes is computed using the node-to-word, word-to-word, and node-to-word alignments indicated by green dashed lines.

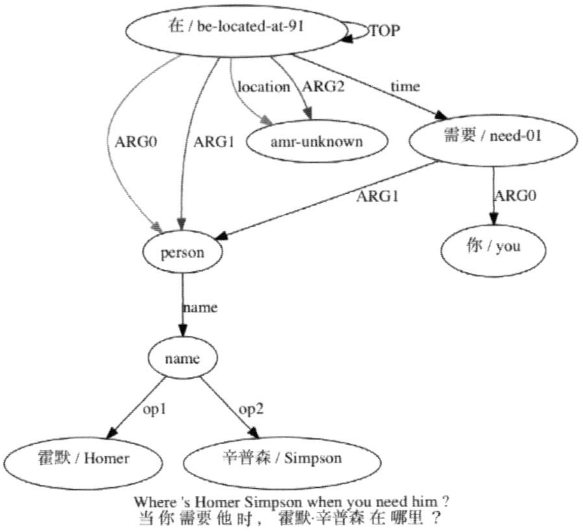

Figure 4: AMRICA visualization of the example in Figure 5. Chinese concept labels are first in shared nodes.

AMRs, which can be corrected by hand to provide training data or a gold standard alignment.

Information to get started with AMRICA is available in the README for our publicly available code.

Acknowledgments

This research was supported in part by the National Science Foundation (USA) under awards 1349902 and 0530118. We thank the organizers of the 2014 Frederick Jelinek Memorial Workshop and the members of the workshop team on Cross-Lingual Abstract Meaning Representations (CLAMR), who tested AMRICA and provided vital feedback.

References

L. Banarescu, C. Bonial, S. Cai, M. Georgescu, K. Griffitt, U. Hermjakob, K. Knight, P. Koehn, M. Palmer, and N. Schneider. 2013. Abstract meaning representation for sembanking. In *Proc. of the 7th Linguistic*

Annotation Workshop and Interoperability with Discourse.

S. Cai and K. Knight. 2013. Smatch: an evaluation metric for semantic feature structures. In *Proc. of ACL.*

J. Flanigan, S. Thomson, C. Dyer, J. Carbonell, and N. A. Smith. 2014. A discriminative graph-based parser for the abstract meaning representation. In *Proc. of ACL.*

Nianwen Xue, Ondrej Bojar, Jan Hajic, Martha Palmer, Zdenka Uresova, and Xiuhong Zhang. 2014. Not an interlingua, but close: Comparison of English AMRs to Chinese and Czech. In *Proc. of LREC.*

F. J. Och and H. Ney. 2003. A systematic comparison of various statistical alignment models. *Computational Linguistics*, 29(1):19–51, Mar.

N. Pourdamghani, Y. Gao, U. Hermjakob, and K. Knight. 2014. Aligning english strings with abstract meaning representation graphs.

Linguistic Data Consortium. 2013. DEFT phase 1 AMR annotation R3 LDC2013E117.

Ckylark: A More Robust PCFG-LA Parser

Yusuke Oda **Graham Neubig** **Sakriani Sakti** **Tomoki Toda** **Satoshi Nakamura**
Graduate School of Information Science
Nara Institute of Science and Technology
8916-5 Takayama, Ikoma, Nara 630-0192, Japan
{oda.yusuke.on9, neubig, ssakti, tomoki, s-nakamura}@is.naist.jp

Abstract

This paper describes Ckylark, a PCFG-LA style phrase structure parser that is more robust than other parsers in the genre. PCFG-LA parsers are known to achieve highly competitive performance, but sometimes the parsing process fails completely, and no parses can be generated. Ckylark introduces three new techniques that prevent possible causes for parsing failure: outputting intermediate results when coarse-to-fine analysis fails, smoothing lexicon probabilities, and scaling probabilities to avoid underflow. An experiment shows that this allows millions of sentences can be parsed without any failures, in contrast to other publicly available PCFG-LA parsers. Ckylark is implemented in C++, and is available open-source under the LGPL license.[1]

1 Introduction

Parsing accuracy is important. Parsing accuracy has been shown to have a significant effect on downstream applications such as textual entailment (Yuret et al., 2010) and machine translation (Neubig and Duh, 2014), and most work on parsing evaluates accuracy to some extent. However, one element that is equally, or perhaps even more, important from the view of downstream applications is parser *robustness*, or the ability to return at least some parse regardless of the input. Every failed parse is a sentence for which downstream applications have no chance of even performing processing in the normal way, and application developers must perform special checks that detect these sentences and either give up entirely, or fall back to some alternative processing scheme.

Among the various methods for phrase-structure parsing, the probabilistic context free grammar with latent annotations (PCFG-LA, (Matsuzaki et al., 2005; Petrov et al., 2006)) framework is among the most popular for several reasons. The first is that it boasts competitive accuracy, both in intrisinic measures such as F1-score on the Penn Treebank (Marcus et al., 1993), and extrinsic measures (it achieved the highest textual entailment and machine translation accuracy in the papers cited above). The second is the availablity of easy-to-use tools, most notably the Berkeley Parser,[2] but also including Egret,[3] and BUBS Parser.[4]

However, from the point of view of robustness, existing tools for PCFG-LA parsing leave something to be desired; to our knowledge, all existing tools produce a certain number of failed parses when run on large data sets. In this paper, we introduce Ckylark, a new PCFG-LA parser specifically designed for robustness. Specifically, Ckylark makes the following contributions:

- Based on our analysis of three reasons why conventional PCFG-LA parsing models fail (Section 2), Ckylark implements three improvements over the conventional PCFG-LA parsing method to remedy these problems (Section 3).

[1] http://github.com/odashi/ckylark

[2] https://code.google.com/p/berkeleyparser/

[3] https://code.google.com/p/egret-parser/

[4] https://code.google.com/p/bubs-parser/

Proceedings of NAACL-HLT 2015, pages 41–45,
Denver, Colorado, May 31 – June 5, 2015.

- An experimental evaluation (Section 4) shows that Ckylark achieves competitive accuracy with other PCFG-LA parsers, and can robustly parse large datasets where other parsers fail.
- Ckylark is implemented in C++, and released under the LGPL license, allowing for free research or commercial use. It is also available in library format, which means that it can be incorporated directly into other programs.

2 Failure of PCFG-LA Parsing

The basic idea behind PCFG-LA parsing is that traditional tags in the Penn Treebank are too coarse, and more accurate grammars can be achieved by automatically splitting tags into finer latent classes. For example, the English words "a" and "the" are classified as determiners (DT), but these words are used in different contexts, so can be assigned different latent classes. The most widely used method to discover these classes uses the EM algorithm to estimate latent classes in stages (Petrov et al., 2006). This method generates hierarchical grammars including relationships between each latent class in a tree structure, and the number of latent classes increases exponentially for each level of the grammar. The standard search method for PCFG grammars is based on the CKY algorithm. However, simply applying CKY directly to the "finest" grammar is not realistic, as the complexity of CKY is propotional to the polynomial of the number of latent classes. To avoid this problem, Petrov et al. (2006) start the analysis with the "coarse" grammar and apply pruning to reduce the amount of computation. This method is called coarse-to-fine analysis. However, this method is not guaranteed to successfully return a parse tree. We describe three reasons why PCFG-LA parsing fails below.

Failure of pruning in coarse-to-fine analysis Coarse-to-fine analysis prunes away candidate paths in the parse graph when their probability is less than a specific threshold ϵ. This pruning can cause problems in the case that all possible paths are pruned and the parser cannot generate any parse tree at the next step.

Inconsistency between model and target If we parse sentences with syntax that diverges from the training data, the parser may fail because the parser needs rules which are not included in the grammar. For example, symbols "(" and ")" become a part of phrase "PRN" only if both of them and some phrase "X" exist with the order "(X)." One approach for this problem is to use smoothed grammars (Petrov et al., 2006), but this increases the size of the probability table needed to save such a grammar.

Underflow of probabilities Parsers calculate joint probabilities of each parse tree, and this value decreases exponentially according to the length of the input sequence. As a result, numerical underflow sometimes occurs if the parser tries to parse longer sentences. Using calculations in logarithmic space is one approach to avoid underflow. However, this approach requires log and exponent operations, which are more computationally expensive than sums or products.

The failure of pruning is a unique problem for PCFG-LA, and the others are general problems of parsing methods based on PCFG. In the next section, we describe three improvements over the basic PCFG-LA method that Ckylark uses to avoid these problems.

3 Improvements of the Parsing Method

3.1 Early Stopping in Coarse-to-fine Analysis

While coarse-to-fine analysis generally uses the parsing result of the finest grammar as output, intermediate grammars also can generate parse trees. Thus, we can use these intermediate results instead of the finest result when parsing fails at later stages. Algorithm 1 shows this "stopping" approach. This approach can avoid all errors due to coarse-to-fine pruning, except in the case of failure during the parsing with the first grammar due to problems of the model itself.

3.2 Lexicon Smoothing

Next, we introduce lexicon smoothing using the probabilities of unknown words at parsing time. This approach not only reduces the size of the grammar, but also allows for treatment of any word as

Algorithm 1 Stopping coarse-to-fine analysis

Require: $\boldsymbol{w}$: input sentence
Require: $G_0, \cdots, G_L$: coarse-to-fine grammars
  $T_{-1} \leftarrow \text{nil}$
  $P_0 \leftarrow \{\}$ ▷ pruned pathes
  for $l \leftarrow 0 .. L$ **do**
    $T_l, P_{l+1} \leftarrow \text{parse\_and\_prune}(\boldsymbol{w}; G_l, P_l)$
    if $T_l = \text{nil}$ **then** ▷ parsing failed
      return T_{l-1} ▷ return intermediate result
    end if
  end for
  return T_L ▷ parsing succeeded

"unknown" if the word appears in an unknown syntactic content. Equation (1) shows the smoothed lexicon probability:

$$P'(X \to w) \equiv (1-\lambda)P(X \to w) + \lambda P(X \to w_{unk}), \quad (1)$$

where X is any pre-terminal (part-of-speech) symbol in the grammar, w is any word, and w_{unk} is the unknown word. λ is an interpolation factor between w and w_{unk}, and should be small enough to cause no effect when the parser can generate the result without interpolation. Our implementation uses $\lambda = 10^{-10}$.

3.3 Probability Scaling

To solve the problem of underflow, we modify model probabilities as Equations (2) to (4) to avoid underflow without other expensive operations:

$$Q(X \to w) \equiv P'(X \to w)/s_l(w), \quad (2)$$
$$Q(X \to Y) \equiv P(X \to Y), \quad (3)$$
$$Q(X \to YZ) \equiv P(X \to YZ)/s_g, \quad (4)$$

where X, Y, Z are any non-terminal symbols (including pre-terminals) in the grammar, and w is any word. The result of parsing using Q is guaranteed to be the same as using original probabilities P and P', because Q maintains the same ordering of P and P' despite the fact that Q is not a probability. Values of Q are closer to 1 than the original values, reducing the risk of underflow. $s_l(w)$ is a scaling factor of a word w defined as the geometric mean of lexicon probabilities that generate w, $P'(X \to w)$, as in Equation (5):

$$s_l(w) \equiv \exp \sum_X P(X) \log P'(X \to w), \quad (5)$$

and s_g is the scaling factor of binary rules defined as the geometric mean of all binary rules in the grammar $P(X \to YZ)$ as in Equation (6):

$$s_g \equiv \exp \sum_X P(X) H(X), \quad (6)$$

$$H(X) \equiv \sum_{Y,Z} P(X \to YZ) \log P(X \to YZ). \quad (7)$$

Calculating $P(X)$ is not trivial, but we can retrieve these values using the graph propagation algorithm proposed by Petrov and Klein (2007).

4 Experiments

We evaluated parsing accuracies of our parser Ckylark and conventional PCFG-LA parsers: Berkeley Parser and Egret. Berkeley Parser is a conventional PCFG-LA parser written in Java with some additional optimization techniques. Egret is also a conventional PCFG-LA parser in C++ which can generate a parsing forest that can be used in downstream application such forest based machine translation (Mi et al., 2008).

4.1 Dataset and Tools

Table 1: Dataset Summaries.

Type	#sent	#word
WSJ-train/dev	41.5 k	990 k
WSJ-test	2.42 k	56.7 k
NTCIR	3.08 M	99.0 M

Table 1 shows summaries of each dataset.

We used GrammarTrainer in the Berkeley Parser to train a PCFG-LA grammar with the Penn Treebank WSJ dataset section 2 to 22 (WSJ-train/dev). Egret and Ckylark can use the same model as the Berkeley Parser so we can evaluate only the performance of the parsers using the same grammar. Each parser is run on a Debian 7.1 machine with an Intel Core i7 CPU (3.40GHz, 4 cores, 8MB caches) and 4GB RAM.

We chose 2 datasets to evaluate the performances of each parser. First, WSJ-test, the Penn Treebank WSJ dataset section 23, is a standard dataset

Table 2: Bracketing F1 scores of each parser.

Parser	**F1** (all)	**F1** ($\|w\| \leq 40$)
Berkeley Parser	89.98	90.54
Egret	89.05	89.70
Ckylark (10^{-5})	89.44	90.07
Ckylark (10^{-7})	89.85	90.39

Table 3: Tagging accuracies of each parser.

Parser	**Acc** (all)	**Acc** ($\|w\| \leq 40$)
Berkeley Parser	97.39	97.37
Egret	97.33	97.28
Ckylark (10^{-5})	97.37	97.35
Ckylark (10^{-7})	97.39	97.38

to evaluate parsing accuracy including about 2000 sentences. Second, we use NTCIR, a large English corpus including more than 3 million sentences, extracted from the NTCIR-8 patent translation task (Yamamoto and Shimohata, 2010).

Input sentences of each parser must be tokenized in advance, so we used a tokenization algorithm equivalent to the Stanford Tokenizer[5] for tokenizing the NTCIR dataset.

4.2 Results

Table 2 shows the bracketing F1 scores[6] of parse trees for each parser on the WSJ-test dataset and Table 3 also shows the part-of-speech tagging accuracies. We show 2 results for Ckylark with pruning threshold ϵ as 10^{-5} and 10^{-7}. These tables show that the result of Ckylark with $\epsilon = 10^{-7}$ achieves nearly the same parsing accuracy as the Berkeley Parser.

Table 4 shows calculation times of each parser on the WSJ-test dataset. When the pruning threshold ϵ is smaller, parsing takes longer, but in all cases Ckylark is faster than Egret while achieving higher accuracy. Berkeley Parser is the fastest of all parsers, a result of optimizations not included in the standard PCFG-LA parsing algorithm. Incorporating these techniques into Ckylark is future work.

Table 5 shows the number of parsing failures of each parser. All parsers generate no failure in the WSJ-test dataset, however, in the NTCIR dataset,

[5]http://nlp.stanford.edu/software/tokenizer.shtml

[6]http://nlp.cs.nyu.edu/evalb/

Table 4: Calculation times of each parser.

Parser	Time [s]
Berkeley Parser	278
Egret	3378
Ckylark (10^{-5})	923
Ckylark (10^{-7})	2157

Table 5: Frequencies of parsing failure of each parser.

Parser	Failure			
	WSJ-test		NTCIR	
	(#)	(%)	(#)	(%)
Berkeley Parser	0	0	419	0.0136
Egret	0	0	17287	0.561
Ckylark (10^{-5})	0	0	0	0

Table 6: Number of failures of each coarse-to-fine level.

Smooth	Failure level						
	0	1	2	3	4	5	6
$\lambda = 0$	1741	135	24	11	5	57	1405
$\lambda = 10^{-10}$	0	130	19	8	4	51	1389

0.01% and 0.5% of sentences could not be parsed with the Berkeley Parser and Egret respectively. In contrast, our parser does not fail a single time.

Table 6 shows the number of failures of Ckylark with $\epsilon = 10^{-5}$ and without the stopping approach; if the parser failed at the level l analysis then it returns the result of the $l - 1$ level. Thus, the stopping approach will never generate any failure, unless failure occurs at the initial level. The reason for failure at the initial level is only due to model mismatch, as no pruning has been performed. These errors can be prevented by lexicon smoothing at parsing time as shown in the case of level 0 with $\lambda = 10^{-10}$ in the table.

5 Conclusion

In this paper, we introduce Ckylark, a parser that makes three improvements over standard PCFG-LA style parsing to prevent parsing failure. Experiments show that Ckylark can parse robustly where other PCFG-LA style parsers (Berkeley Parser and Egret) fail. In the future, we plan to further speed up Ckylark, support forest output, and create interfaces to other programming languages.

Acknowledgement

Part of this work was supported by JSPS's Research Fellowship for Young Scientists.

References

Mitchell P Marcus, Mary Ann Marcinkiewicz, and Beatrice Santorini. 1993. Building a large annotated corpus of english: The Penn Treebank. *Computational linguistics*, 19(2).

Takuya Matsuzaki, Yusuke Miyao, and Jun'ichi Tsujii. 2005. Probabilistic CFG with latent annotations. In *Proc. ACL*.

Haitao Mi, Liang Huang, and Qun Liu. 2008. Forest-based translation. In *Proc. ACL-HLT*.

Graham Neubig and Kevin Duh. 2014. On the elements of an accurate tree-to-string machine translation system. In *Proc. ACL*.

Slav Petrov and Dan Klein. 2007. Improved inference for unlexicalized parsing. In *Proc. NAACL-HLT*.

Slav Petrov, Leon Barrett, Romain Thibaux, and Dan Klein. 2006. Learning accurate, compact, and interpretable tree annotation. In *Proc. COLING-ACL*.

Atsushi Fujii Masao Utiyama Mikio Yamamoto and Sayori Shimohata. 2010. Overview of the patent translation task at the NTCIR-8 workshop. In *Proc. NTCIR-8*.

Deniz Yuret, Aydin Han, and Zehra Turgut. 2010. Semeval-2010 task 12: Parser evaluation using textual entailments. In *Proc. SemEval*.

ELCO3: Entity Linking with Corpus Coherence Combining Open Source Annotators

Pablo Ruiz, **Thierry Poibeau** and **Frédérique Mélanie**
Laboratoire LATTICE
CNRS, École Normale Supérieure, U Paris 3 Sorbonne Nouvelle
1, rue Maurice Arnoux, 92120 Montrouge, France
{pablo.ruiz.fabo,thierry.poibeau,frederique.melanie}@ens.fr

Abstract

Entity Linking (EL) systems' performance is uneven across corpora or depending on entity types. To help overcome this issue, we propose an EL workflow that combines the outputs of several open source EL systems, and selects annotations via weighted voting. The results are displayed on a UI that allows the users to navigate the corpus and to evaluate annotation quality based on several metrics.

1 Introduction

The Entity Linking (EL) literature has shown that the performance of EL systems varies widely depending on the corpora they are applied to and of the types of entities considered (Cornolti et al., 2013). For instance, a system linking to a wide set of entity types can be less accurate at basic types like *Organization*, *Person*, *Location* than systems specializing in those basic types. These issues make it difficult for users to choose an optimal EL system for their corpora.

To help overcome these difficulties, we have created a workflow whereby entities can be linked to Wikipedia via a combination of the results of several existing open source EL systems. The outputs of the different systems are weighted according to how well they performed on corpora similar to the user's corpus.

Our target users are social science researchers, who need to apply EL in order to, for instance, create entity co-occurrence network visualizations. These researchers need to make informed choices about which entities to include in their analyses, and our tool provides metrics to facilitate these choices.

The paper is structured as follows: Section 2 describes related work. Section 3 presents the different steps in the workflow, and Section 4 focuses on the steps presented in the demo.

2 Related work

Cornolti et al. (2013) provide a general survey on EL. Work on combining EL systems and on helping users select a set of linked entities to navigate a corpus is specifically relevant to our workflow. Systems that combine entity linkers exist, e.g. NERD (Rizzo et al., 2012). However, there are two important differences in our workflow. First, the set of entity linkers we combine is entirely open source and public. Second, we use a simple voting scheme to optionally offer automatically chosen annotations when linkers provide conflicting outputs. This type of weighted vote had not previously been attempted for EL outputs to our knowledge, and is inspired on the ROVER method (Fiscus, 1997, De la Clergerie et al., 2008).

Regarding systems that help users navigate a corpus by choosing a representative set of linked entities, our reference is the ANTA tool (Venturini and Guido, 2012).[1] This tool helps users choose entities via an assessment of their corpus frequency and document frequency. Our tool provides such information, besides a measure of each entity's coherence with the rest of entities in the corpus.

[1] https://github.com/medialab/ANTA

Proceedings of NAACL-HLT 2015, pages 46–50,
Denver, Colorado, May 31 – June 5, 2015.

3 Workflow description

The user's corpus is first annotated by making requests to three EL systems' web services: Tagme 2[2] (Ferragina and Scaiella, 2010), DBpedia Spotlight[3] (Mendes et al. 2011) and Wikipedia Miner[4] (Milne and Witten, 2008). Annotations are filtered out if their confidence score is below the optimal thresholds for those services, reported in Cornolti et al. (2013) and verified using the BAT-Framework.[5]

3.1 Annotation voting

The purpose of combining several linkers' results is obtaining combined annotations that are more accurate than each of the linkers' individual results. To select among the different linkers' outputs, a vote is performed on the annotations that remain after the initial filtering described above.

Our voting scheme is based on De la Clergerie et al.'s (2008) version of the ROVER method. An implementation was evaluated in (Ruiz and Poibeau, 2015). Two factors that our voting scheme considers are annotation confidence, and the number of linkers having produced an annotation. An important factor is also the performance of the annotator having produced each annotation on a corpus similar to the user's corpus: At the outset of the workflow, the user's corpus is compared to a set of reference corpora along dimensions that affect EL results, e.g. text-length or lexical cohesion[6] in the corpus' documents. Annotators that perform better on the reference corpus that is most similar along those dimensions to the user's corpus are given more weight in the vote.

In sum, the vote helps to select among conflicting annotation candidates, besides helping identify unreliable annotations.

3.2 Entity types

Entity types are assigned by exploiting information provided in the linkers' responses, e.g. DBpedia ontology types or Wikipedia category labels. The entity types currently assigned are *Organization*, *Person*, *Location*, *Concept*.

3.3 Entity coherence measures

Once entity selection is completed, a score that quantifies an entity's coherence with the rest of entities in the corpus is computed. This notion of coherence consists of two components. The first one is an entity's relatedness to other entities in terms of Milne and Witten's (2008) Wikipedia Link-based Measure (WLM, details below). The second component is the distance between entities' categories in a Wikipedia category graph.

WLM scores were obtained with Wikipedia Miner's *compare* method for Wikipedia entity IDs.[7] WLM evaluates the relatedness of two Wikipedia pages as a function of the number of Wikipedia pages linking to both, and the number of pages linking to each separately. In the literature, WLM has been exploited to disambiguate among competing entity senses within a document, taking into account each sense's relatedness to each of the possible senses for the remaining entity-mentions in the document. We adopt this idea to assess entity relatedness at corpus level rather than at document level. To do so, we obtain each entity's averaged WLM relatedness to the most representative entities in the corpus. The most representative entities in the corpus were defined as a top percentage of the entities, sorted by decreasing annotation confidence, whose annotation frequency and confidence are above given thresholds.

The second component of our entity coherence measure is based on distance between nodes in a Wikipedia category graph (see Strube and Ponzetto, 2006 for a review of similar methods). Based on the category graph, the averaged shortest path[8] between an entity and the most representative entities (see criteria above) of the same type was computed. Some categories like "People from {City}" were ignored, since they created spurious connections.

3.4 Annotation attributes

The final annotations contain information like position (document, character and sentence), confi-

[2] http://tagme.di.unipi.it/tagme_help.html
[3] https://github.com/dbpedia-spotlight/dbpedia-spotlight/wiki
[4] http://wikipedia-miner.cms.waikato.ac.nz/
[5] https://github.com/marcocor/bat-framework
[6] Our notion of lexical cohesion relies on token overlap across consecutive token sequences, inspired on the block comparison method from Hearst (1997).

[7] http://wikipedia-miner.cms.waikato.ac.nz/services/?compare
[8] Using igraph.GraphBase.get_all_shortest_paths from the Python interface to igraph: http://igraph.org/python/

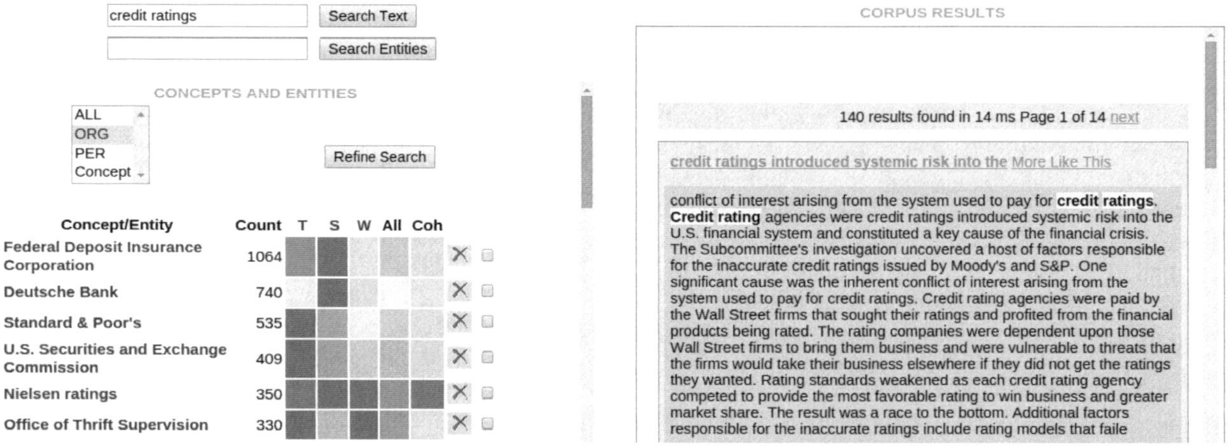

Figure 1: Results for query *credit ratings*. The right panel shows documents matching the query; the left panel shows the entities that have been annotated in those documents.

dence, and entity-type. This can be exploited for further textual analyses, e.g. co-occurrence networks.

4 Demonstrator

The goal of the workflow is to help users choose a representative set of entities to model a corpus, with the help of descriptive statistics and other measures like annotation confidence, or the coherence scores described above. A practical way to access this information is a UI, where users can assess the validity of an entity by simultaneously looking at its metrics, and at the documents where that entity was annotated. We present an early stage prototype of such a UI, which shows some of the features of the workflow above, using preprocessed content—the possibility to tag a new corpus is not online.

The demo interface[9] allows navigating a corpus through search and entity facets. In Figure 1, a *Search Text* query displays, on the right panel, the documents matching the query,[10] while the entities annotated in those documents are shown in the left panel. A *Search Entities* query displays the entities matching the query on the left panel, and, on the right, the documents where those entities were annotated. *Refine Search* restricts the results on the right panel to documents containing certain entities or entity types, if the corresponding checkboxes at the end of each entity row, or items on the entity-types list have been selected. The colors provide a visual indication of the entity's confidence for each linker (columns, *T*, *S*, *W*, *All*), scaled[11] to a range between 0 (red) and 1 (green). Hovering over the table reveals the scores in each cell.

For the prototype, the corpus was indexed in Solr[12] and the annotations were stored in a MySQL DB. The EL workflow was implemented in Python and the UI is in PHP.

Examples of the utility of the information on the UI and of the workflow's outputs follow.

Usage example 1: Spotting incorrect annotations related to a search term. The demo corpus is about the 2008 financial crisis. Suppose the user is interested in organizations appearing in texts that mention *credit ratings* (Figure 1). Several relevant organizations are returned for documents matching the query, but also an incorrect one: *Nielsen ratings*. This entity is related to *ratings* in the sense of audience ratings, not credit ratings. The coherence score (column *Coh*) for the incorrect entity is much lower (red, dark) than the scores for the relevant entities (green, light). The score helps to visually identify the incorrect annotation, based on its lack of coherence with representative entities in the corpus.

Figure 1 also gives an indication how the different linkers complement each other: Some annotations have been missed by one linker (grey cells), but the other two provide the annotation.

[9] http://129.199.228.10/nav/gui/

[10] The application's Solr search server requires access to traffic on port 8983. A *connection refused* (or similar) error message in the search results panel is likely due to traffic blocked on that port at the user's network.

[11] scikit-learn: sklearn.preprocessing.MinMaxScaler.html

[12] http://lucene.apache.org/solr/

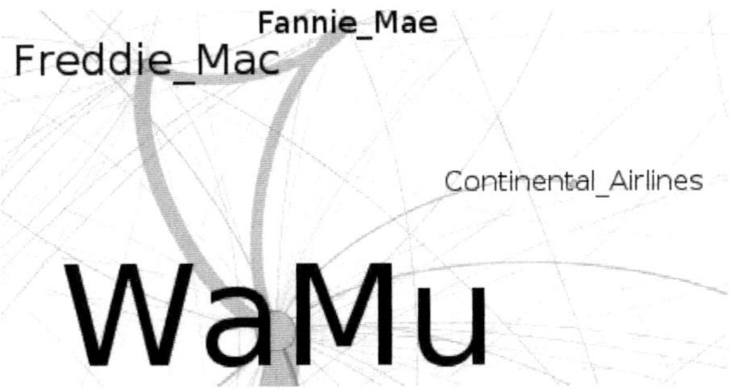

Figure 2: Region of an entity network created outside of our workflow, based on the individual output of one of the EL systems we combine. Node *Continental Airlines* in the network is an error made by that EL system.

Figure 3: Result of a search in our GUI for entity labels containing *Continental*. The lower coherence score (*Coh*) for *Continental Airlines* (orange, dark) vs. *Continental Illinois* (green, light) suggests that the latter is correct and that the airline annotation is an error.

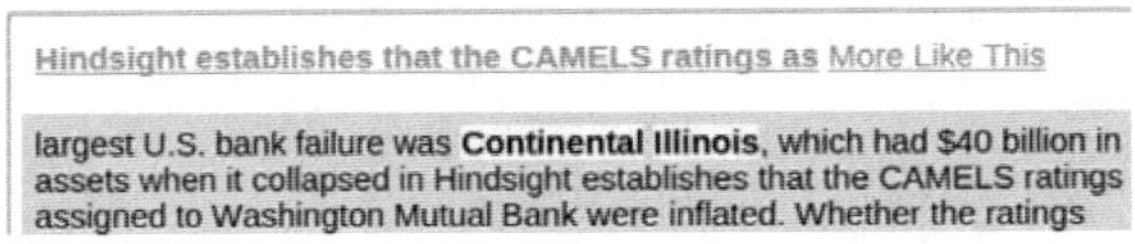
Hindsight establishes that the CAMELS ratings as More Like This

largest U.S. bank failure was **Continental Illinois**, which had $40 billion in assets when it collapsed in Hindsight establishes that the CAMELS ratings assigned to Washington Mutual Bank were inflated. Whether the ratings

Figure 4: Example document showing that *Continental Illinois* is the correct entity in the corpus

Usage example 2: Verifying correctness of entities in networks. A common application of EL is creating co-occurrence networks, e.g. based on an automatic selection of entities above a certain frequency. This can result in errors. Figure 2 shows a small area from an entity co-occurrence network for our corpus. Our corpus comes from the 2014 PoliInformatics challenge (Smith et al., 2014), and the corpus topic is the 2008 financial crisis. The network was created independently of the workflow described in this paper, using Gephi,[13] based on entities annotated by Wikipedia Miner, which is one of the EL systems whose outputs our workflow combines. Node *Continental Airlines* in the network seems odd for the corpus, in the sense that the corpus is about the financial crisis, and Continental Airlines was not a major actor in the crisis. A *Search Entities* query for *Continental* on our GUI returns two annotations (Figure 3): the airline, and *Continental Illinois* (a defunct bank). The coherence (*Coh*) score for the bank is higher than for the airline. If we run a *Search Text* query for *Continental* on our GUI, the documents returned for the query confirm that the correct entity for the corpus is the bank (Figure 4 shows one of the documents returned).

The example just discussed also shows that the coherence scores can provide information that is not redundant with respect to annotation frequency or annotation confidence. It is the bank's coherence score that suggests its correctness: The incorrect annotation (for the airline) is more frequent, and the confidence scores for both annotations are equivalent.

In short, this second example is another indication how our workflow helps spot errors made by annotation systems and decide among conflicting annotations.

A final remark about entity networks: Our workflow segments documents into sentences, which would allow to create co-occurrence networks at sentence level. Some example networks based on our outputs and created with Gephi are available on the demo site.[14] These networks were not created programmatically from the workflow: The current implementation does not automatically call a visualization tool to create networks, but this is future work that would be useful for our target users.

5 Conclusion

Since entity linking (EL) systems' results vary widely according to the corpora and to the annotation types needed by the user, we present a workflow that combines different EL systems' results, so that the systems complement each other. Conflicting annotations are resolved by a voting scheme which had not previously been attempted for EL. Besides an automatic entity selection, a measure of coherence helps users decide on the validity of an annotation. The workflow's results are presented on a UI that allows navigating a corpus using text-search and entity facets. The UI helps users assess annotations via the measures displayed and via access to the corpus documents.

[13] http://gephi.github.io

[14] Follow link *Charts* on http://129.199.228.10/nav/gui

Acknowledgements

Pablo Ruiz was supported through a PhD scholarship from Région Île-de-France.

References

Cornolti, M., Ferragina, P., & Ciaramita, M. (2013). A framework for benchmarking entity-annotation systems. In *Proc. of WWW*, 249–260.

De La Clergerie, É. V., Hamon, O., Mostefa, D., Ayache, C., Paroubek, P., & Vilnat, A. (2008). Passage: from French parser evaluation to large sized treebank. In *Proc. LREC 2008*, 3570–3576.

Ferragina, P., & Scaiella, U. (2010). Tagme: on-the-fly annotation of short text fragments (by wikipedia entities). In *Proc. of CIKM'10*, 1625–1628.

Fiscus, J. G. (1997). A post-processing system to yield reduced word-error rates: Recognizer output voting error reduction (ROVER). In *Proc. of the IEEE Workshop on Automatic Speech Recognition and Understanding*, 347–354.

Hearst, M. A. (1997). TextTiling: Segmenting text into multi-paragraph subtopic passages. *Computational Linguistics, 23*(1), 33–64.

Mendes, P. N., Jakob, M., García-Silva, A., & Bizer, C. (2011). DBpedia spotlight: shedding light on the web of documents. In *Proc. I-SEMANTICS'11*, 1–8.

Milne, D. & Witten, I. (2008). An effective, low-cost measure of semantic relatedness obtained from Wikipedia links. In *Proc. of AAAI Workshop on Wikipedia and Artificial Intelligence,* 25–30

Rizzo, G., & Troncy, R. (2012). NERD: a framework for unifying named entity recognition and disambiguation extraction tools. In *Proc. of the Demonstrations at EACL'12*, 73–76.

Ruiz, P. and Poibeau, T. (2015). Combining Open Source Annotators for Entity Linking through Weighted Voting. In *Proceedings of *SEM. Fourth Joint Conference on Lexical and Computational Semantics.* Denver, U.S.

Venturini, T. and Daniele Guido. 2012. Once upon a text: an ANT tale in Text Analytics. *Sociologica*, 3:1-17. Il Mulino, Bologna.

Smith, N. A., Cardie, C., Washington, A. L., Wilkerson, J. D. (2014). Overview of the 2014 NLP Unshared Task in PoliInformatics. *Proceedings of the ACL Workshop on Language Technologies and Computational Social Science*, 5–7.

Strube, M. and Ponzetto, S. (2006). WikiRelate! Computing semantic relatedness using Wikipedia. In *AAAI*, vol. 6, 1419–1424.

SETS: Scalable and Efficient Tree Search in Dependency Graphs

Juhani Luotolahti[1], Jenna Kanerva[1,2], Sampo Pyysalo[1] and Filip Ginter[1]
[1]Department of Information Technology
[2]University of Turku Graduate School (UTUGS)
University of Turku, Finland
first.last@utu.fi

Abstract

We present a syntactic analysis query toolkit geared specifically towards massive dependency parsebanks and morphologically rich languages. The query language allows arbitrary tree queries, including negated branches, and is suitable for querying analyses with rich morphological annotation. Treebanks of over a million words can be comfortably queried on a low-end netbook, and a parsebank with over 100M words on a single consumer-grade server. We also introduce a web-based interface for interactive querying. All contributions are available under open licenses.

1 Introduction

Syntactic search is one of the basic tools necessary to work with syntactically annotated corpora, both manually annotated treebanks of modest size and massive automatically analyzed parsebanks, which may go into hundreds of millions of sentences and billions of words. Traditionally, tools such as *TGrep2* (Rohde, 2004) and *TRegex* (Levy and Andrew, 2006) have been used for tree search. However, these tools are focused on constituency trees annotated with simple part-of-speech tags, and have not been designed to deal with dependency graphs and rich morphologies. Existing search systems are traditionally designed for searching from treebanks rarely going beyond million tokens. However, treebank sized corpora may not be sufficient enough for searching rare linguistic phenomena, and therefore ability to cover billion-word parsebanks is essential. Addressing these limitations in existing tools, we present SETS, a toolkit for search in dependency treebanks and parsebanks that specifically emphasizes expressive search of dependency graphs including detailed morphological analyses, simplicity of querying, speed, and scalability.

Operator	Meaning
<	governed by
>	governs
<@L	governed by on the left
<@R	governed by on the right
>@L	has dependent on the left
>@R	has dependent on the right
!	negation
& |	and / or
+	match if both sets not empty
->	universal quantification

Table 1: Query language operators.

2 Demonstration outline

We demonstrate the query system on the set of all available Universal Dependencies[1] treebanks, currently covering 10 languages with the largest treebank (Czech) consisting of nearly 90K trees with 1.5M words. We demonstrate both the command line functionality as well as an openly accessible web-based interface for the graph search and visualization on multiple languages. We also demonstrate how new treebanks in the CoNLL formats are added to the system.

3 Query language

The query language is loosely inspired by TRegex, modified extensively for dependency structures. Each query specifies the words together with any restrictions on their tags or lemmas, and then connects them with operators that specify the dependency structure. Table 1 shows the operators defined in the query language, and Table 2 illustrates a range of queries from the basic to the moderately complex.

[1]universaldependencies.github.io/docs. Note that while the SETS system is completely generic, we here use UD tagsets and dependency relations in examples throughout.

Proceedings of NAACL-HLT 2015, pages 51–55,
Denver, Colorado, May 31 – June 5, 2015. ©2015 Association for Computational Linguistics

Target	Query
The word *dog* as subject	`dog <nsubj _`
A verb with *dog* as the object	`VERB >dobj dog`
A word with two nominal modifiers	`_ >nmod _ >nmod _`
A word with a nominal modifier that has a nominal modifier	`_ >nmod (_ >nmod _)`
An active verb without a subject	`VERB&Voice=Act !>nsubj _`
A word which is a nominal modifier but has no adposition	`_ <nmod _ !>case _`
A word governed by *case* whose POS tag is not an adposition	`!ADP <case _`

Table 2: Example queries.

The query language is explained in detail in the following.

3.1 Words

Word positions in queries can be either unspecified, matching any token, or restricted for one or more properties. Unspecified words are marked with the underscore character. Lexical token restrictions include wordform and lemma. Wordforms can appear either as-is (`word`) or in quotation marks (`"word"`). Quotation marks are required to disambiguate queries where the wordform matches a feature name, such as a query for the literal word *NOUN* instead of tokens with the `NOUN` POS tag. Words can be searched by lemma using the `L=` prefix: for example, the query `L=be` matches all tokens with the lemma *(to) be*.

Words can also be restricted based on any tags, including POS and detailed morphological features. These tags can be included in the query as-is: for example, the query for searching all pronouns is simply `PRON`. All word restrictions can also be negated, combined arbitrarily using the *and* and *or* logic operators, and grouped using parentheses. For example, `(L=climb|L=scale)&VERB&!Tense=Past` searches for tokens with either *climb* or *scale* as lemma whose POS is verb and that are not in the past tense.

3.2 Dependency relations

Dependency relations between words are queried with the dependency operators (`<` and `>`), optionally combined with the dependency relation name. For example, the query to find tokens governed by an *nsubj* relation is `_ <nsubj _`, and tokens governing an *nsubj* relation can be searched with `_ >nsubj _`. The left-most word in the search expression is always the target, and is identified in the results. While the two preceding *nsubj* queries match the same graphs, they thus differ in the target token. To constrain the linear direction of the dependency relation, the operators `@R` and `@L` can be used, where e.g. `_ >nsubj@R _` means that the token must have a *nsubj* dependent to the right.

Negations and logical operators can be applied to the dependency relations in the same manner as to words. There are two different ways to negate relations; the whole relation can be negated, as in `_ !>nsubj _`, which means that the tokens may not have an *nsubj* dependent (not having any dependent is allowed), or only the type can be negated, as in `_ >!nsubj _`, where the token must have a dependent but it cannot be *nsubj*. Tokens which have either a nominal or clausal subject dependent can be queried for with the logical *or* operator: `_ >nsubj|>csubj _`.

Subtrees can be identified in the search expression by delimiting them with parentheses. For example, in `_ >nmod (_ >nmod _)`, the target token must have a nominal modifier which also has a nominal modifier (i.e a chain of two modifiers), whereas in `_ >nmod _ >nmod _` the token must have two (different) nominal modifiers. Note that queries such as `_ >nmod _ >nmod _` are interpreted so that all sibling nodes in the query must be unique in the match to guarantee that the restriction is not satisfied twice by the same token in the target tree.

There is no restriction on the complexity of subtrees, which may also include any number of negations and logical operators. It is also possible to negate entire subtrees by placing the negation operator `!` before the opening parenthesis.

3.3 Sentence

The more general properties of the sentence instead of just the properties of certain token, can be queried using the operators +, match a sentence if both sets are not empty and ->, universal quantification – operators. For example, if we wanted to find a sentence where all subject dependents are in the third person, we could query (_ <nsubj _) -> (Person=3 <nsubj _). And to find sentences where we have a token with two nmod dependents and a word dog somewhere in the sentence we could query (_ >nmod _ >nmod _) + "dog".

4 Design and implementation

The scalability and speed of the system stem from several key design features, the most important of which is the that every query is used to generate an algorithmic implementation that is then compiled into native binary code, a process which takes typically less than a second. Search involves the following steps:

1) The user query is translated into a sequence of set operations (intersection, complement, etc.) over tokens. For example, a query for tokens that are in the partitive case and dependents of a subject relation is translated into an intersection of the set of partitive case tokens and the set of subject dependents. Similarly, negation can in most cases be implemented as the set complement. The code implementing these operations is generated separately for each query, making it possible to only include the exact operations needed to execute each specific query.

2) The code implementing this sequence of operations is translated into C by the Cython compiler. The set operations are implemented as bit operations on integers (bitwise and, or, etc.) and can thus be executed extremely fast.

3) An SQL statement is generated and used to fetch from a database the token sets that are needed to evaluate the query. The query retrieves the token sets only for those trees containing at least one token meeting each of the restrictions (dependency relations, morphological tags, etc.).

4) The sequence of set operations implementing the query is used to check whether their configuration matches the query. For each match, the whole tree is retrieved from the database, reformatted and output in the CoNLL-U format.

The data is stored in an embedded database as precomputed token sets, with separate sets for all different lemmas, wordforms, and morphological features. These sets are stored as native integers with each bit corresponding to a single token position in a sentence. Since the vast majority of sentences are shorter than 64 words, these sets typically fit into a single integer. However, the system imposes no upper limit on the sentence length, using several integers when necessary.

The system uses SQLite as its database backend and the software is written as a combination of Python, Cython and C++. Cython enables easy integration of Python code with fast C-extensions, vital to assure the efficiency of the system. As it uses the embedded SQLite database, the system is fully self-contained and requires no server applications.

In addition to the primary search system, we created a simple browser-based frontend to the query system that provides a dynamic visualization of the retrieved trees and the matched sections (Figure 1). This interface was implemented using the Python Flask[2] framework and the BRAT annotation tool (Stenetorp et al., 2012).

5 Benchmarks

Our graph-search tool is tested and timed on three different machines and two datasets. Evaluation platforms include a server-grade machine with good resources, a standard laptop computer and a small netbook with limited performance. To compare the efficiency of our system to the state-of-the-art treebank searching solutions, we employ ICARUS (Gärtner et al., 2013) search and visualization tool which also focuses on querying dependency trees. ICARUS system loads the data into the computer's main memory, while our system uses a database, which is optimized by caching. The comparison of our graph-search tool and the ICARUS baseline is run on server machine with a dataset of roughly 90K trees.

Three test queries are chosen so that both systems support the functionality needed in or-

[2] http://flask.pocoo.org/

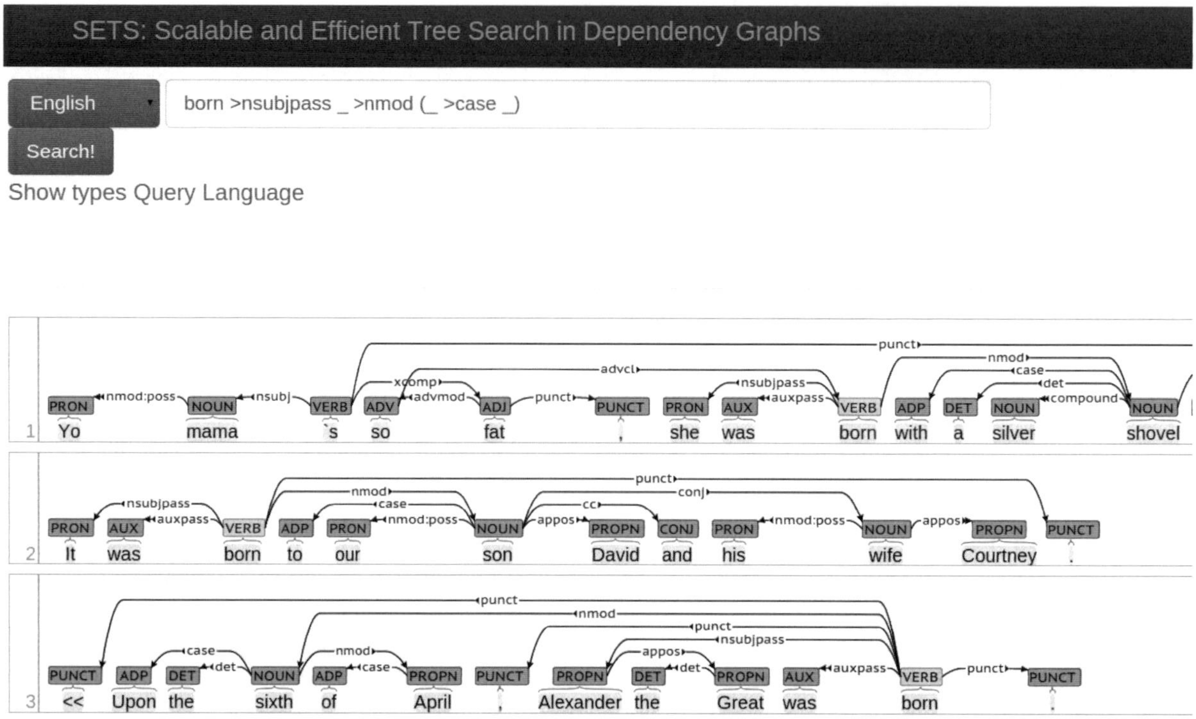

Figure 1: Web interface showing trees in Finnish.

der to run the tests. The first query is a straightforward search for all subject dependents (`_ <nsubj _`) and the second query adds a lexical restraint to it and requires the lemma to be I (`L=I <nsubj _`). The third query is much more complex and is inspired by an actual linguistic use case to find examples of an exceptionally rare transitive verb usage in Finnish. The query includes chaining of dependencies and a negation (`_ >nsubj (Case=Gen > _) >dobj ... _ !<xcomp _`).

	Query 1	Query 2	Query 3
ICARUS	2m30s	2m30s	2m30s
SETS	1.61s	1.2s	2.18s

Table 3: The speed of our system compared to the baseline on the three different test queries when a treebank of about 90K sentences is used.

As can be seen from Table 3, when our system and the baseline system are tested on the server machine using the three example queries our system clearly outperforms the baseline. The speed of the baseline seems to be relatively unaffected by the complexity of the query, suggesting a bottle-neck somewhere else than tree-verification. It should be noted that these measurements are only to illustrate the relative speed and performance differences, and are subject to change depending on system cache. Due to their architecture, neither system has a major advantage in the use of memory and the results are broadly comparable.

Our system is also tested on a standard laptop, and a netbook using the same three queries and the same input corpus. The first test query was finished by a netbook in 37 seconds, the third query, most complex of them, was finished in 13.5 seconds. The laptop finished the first query in 16 seconds, the second in 7 seconds and the third in 16 seconds.

As our system is meant for searching from very large corpora, we test it with a parsebank of 10 million trees and over 120 million tokens. A variant of the test query number 3, the most complex of the queries, was executed in time between 1m52s and 48s (depending the system cache). The test query 1 took from 5m10s to 4m30s and the lexicalized version (query 2) from 12s to 9s. The test queries were performed on the same server-machine as the runs shown in Table 3.

Since our system uses pre-indexed databases the disk space needed for holding the data slightly increases. Indexing the 90K sentence treebank used in our tests requires about 550M of free disk space, whereas indexing the 10 million sentence parsebank uses 35G of space.

6 Conclusion

We have presented a syntax query system especially geared towards very large treebanks and parsebanks. In the future, we will implement support for graph queries, e.g. coindexing of the tokens, since many treebanks have multiple layers of dependency structures. Related to this goal, we aim to include support for properties of the tokens and dependencies, for example the annotation layer of the dependency, word sense labels, etc.

The full source code of the system is available under an open license at `https://github.com/fginter/dep_search`. Additionally, we maintain a server for public online search in all available Universal Dependencies treebanks (Nivre et al., 2015) at `http://bionlp-www.utu.fi/dep_search`.

Acknowledgments

This work was supported by the Kone Foundation and the Emil Aaltonen Foundation. Computational resources were provided by CSC – IT Center for Science.

References

[Gärtner et al.2013] Markus Gärtner, Gregor Thiele, Wolfgang Seeker, Anders Björkelund, and Jonas Kuhn. 2013. Icarus – an extensible graphical search tool for dependency treebanks. In *Proceedings of Demonstrations at ACL'13*, pages 55–60.

[Levy and Andrew2006] Roger Levy and Galen Andrew. 2006. Tregex and Tsurgeon: tools for querying and manipulating tree data structures. In *Proceedings of LREC'06)*.

[Nivre et al.2015] Joakim Nivre, Cristina Bosco, Jinho Choi, Marie-Catherine de Marneffe, Timothy Dozat, Richárd Farkas, Jennifer Foster, Filip Ginter, Yoav Goldberg, Jan Hajič, Jenna Kanerva, Veronika Laippala, Alessandro Lenci, Teresa Lynn, Christopher Manning, Ryan McDonald, Anna Missilä, Simonetta Montemagni, Slav Petrov, Sampo Pyysalo, Natalia Silveira, Maria Simi, Aaron Smith, Reut Tsarfaty, Veronika Vincze, and Daniel Zeman. 2015. Universal dependencies 1.0.

[Rohde2004] Douglas L. T. Rohde, 2004. *TGrep2 User Manual*. Available at http://tedlab.mit.edu/~dr/Tgrep2.

[Stenetorp et al.2012] Pontus Stenetorp, Sampo Pyysalo, Goran Topić, Tomoko Ohta, Sophia Ananiadou, and Jun'ichi Tsujii. 2012. Brat: a web-based tool for nlp-assisted text annotation. In *Proceedings of Demonstrations at EACL'12*, pages 102–107.

Visualizing Deep-Syntactic Parser Output

Juan Soler-Company[1] **Miguel Ballesteros**[1] **Bernd Bohnet**[2]
Simon Mille[1] **Leo Wanner**[1,3]
[1]Natural Language Processing Group, Pompeu Fabra University, Barcelona, Spain
[2]Google Inc.
[3]Catalan Institute for Research and Advanced Studies (ICREA)
[1,3]{name.lastname}@upf.edu [2]bohnetbd@google.com

Abstract

"Deep-syntactic" dependency structures bridge the gap between the surface-syntactic structures as produced by state-of-the-art dependency parsers and semantic logical forms in that they abstract away from surface-syntactic idiosyncrasies, but still keep the linguistic structure of a sentence. They have thus a great potential for such downstream applications as machine translation and summarization. In this demo paper, we propose an online version of a deep-syntactic parser that outputs deep-syntactic structures from plain sentences and visualizes them using the Brat tool. Along with the deep-syntactic structures, the user can also inspect the visual presentation of the surface-syntactic structures that serve as input to the deep-syntactic parser and that are produced by the joint tagger and syntactic transition-based parser ran in the pipeline before deep-syntactic parsing takes place.

1 Introduction

"Deep-syntactic" dependency structures bridge the gap between surface-syntactic structures as produced by state-of-the-art dependency parsers and semantic logical forms in that they abstract away from surface-syntactic idiosyncrasies, but still keep the linguistic structure of a sentence. More precisely, a deep-syntactic structure (DSyntS) is a dependency tree that captures the argumentative, attributive and coordinative relations between full (i.e., meaningful) words of a sentence. For illustration, Figure 1 shows a surface-syntactic structure (above) and deep-syntactic structure (below) for the sentence: *almost 1.2 million jobs have been created by the state in that time.*

DSyntSs have a great potential for such downstream applications as deep machine translation, summarization or information extraction. In deep machine translation as discussed, e.g., by Jones et al. (2012), DSyntSs simplify the alignment between the source and target language structures considerably. In extractive summarization, sentence fusion (Filippova and Strube, 2008) becomes much more straightforward at the level of DSyntSs. A stochastic sentence realizer that takes as input DSyntSs can then be used to generate surface sentences (Ballesteros et al., 2015). In information extraction (Attardi and Simi, 2014) the procedures for the distillation of the information to fill the slots of the corresponding patterns are also simpler at the DSyntS level.

However, it is only recently that deep-syntactic parsing has been introduced as a new parsing paradigm; see, e.g., (Ballesteros et al., 2014).[1] No visualization interfaces are available as yet to control the output of deep-syntactic parsers. In this paper, we propose such a visualization interface. The interface can be used for both a pipeline consisting of a syntactic parser and a deep parser and a joint syntactic+deep parser. In the first configuration, it facilitates the visualization of the output of the syntactic parser and of the output of the deep parser. In the second configuration, it visualizes directly the output of the joint parser.

In what follows, we present its use for the first configuration applied to English. As surface-syntactic parser, we use Bohnet and Nivre (2012)'s joint tagger+lemmatizer+parser. As deep parser, we use Ballesteros et al. (2014)'s implementation. Both have been trained on the dependency Penn Treebank (Johansson and Nugues, 2007), which has been extended by the DSyntS-annotation. The interface can be inspected online; cf. `http://dparse.`

[1]The source code of Ballesteros et al.'s deep parser and a short manual on how to use it can be downloaded from `https://github.com/talnsoftware/deepsyntacticparsing/wiki`.

Proceedings of NAACL-HLT 2015, pages 56–60,
Denver, Colorado, May 31 – June 5, 2015.

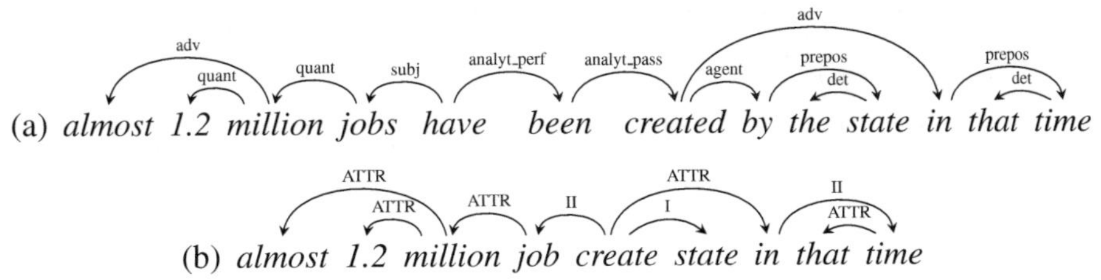

Figure 1: Sample equivalent (a) SSynt- and (b) DSynt-structures. A SSyntS contains all tokens of the sentence, while in the corresponding DSyntS the grammatical tokens that are void of lexical meaning are omitted.

`multisensor.taln.upf.edu/main`. It accepts as input an English sentence and delivers as output the surface- and deep-syntactic structures of this sentence.

Section 2 shows how the online model of the deep parser is trained and displays its performance for the English model. Section 3 describes the visualization interface and its use online. In Section 4, a number of other existing visualizers of the output of dependency parsers are briefly listed. Section 5, finally, concludes and makes some suggestions for future work.

2 Deep-Syntactic Parser

As already mentioned above, we use the joint PoS-tagger+lemmatizer+parser of Bohnet and Nivre (2012)[2] as surface parser, setting up a pipeline with the deep-syntactic parser of Ballesteros et al. (2014).[3] The output of the first serves as input to the latter.

The online versions of the joint PoS-tagger+lemmatizer+parser and the deep-syntactic parser have been trained on the dependency Penn Treebank (Johansson and Nugues, 2007) in CoNLL09 format. To have an English training dataset for the deep-syntactic parser, we derived DSyntSs from the syntactic structures of the dependency Penn Treebank, extending thus the Penn Treebank by a new layer of annotation, as described in Section 2.1. The performance figures obtained using this dataset are shown in Section 2.2.

[2]The joint PoS-tagger+Lemmatizer+parser is available for downloading at https://code.google.com/p/mate-tools/.

[3]The deep-syntactic parser is availabe for download at https://code.google.com/p/deepsyntacticparsing/.

2.1 Training Dataset for the Deep-Syntactic Parser

The English deep-syntactic dataset has been obtained using a rule-based graph transducer that converts the syntactic annotation of the dependency Penn Treebank into a DSyntS annotation in the CoNLL09 format. The conversion removes definite and indefinite determiners, auxiliaries, THAT complementizers, TO infinitive markers, and all functional (or *lexically-bound*) prepositions which we were able to recover in PropBank and NomBank. In these two resources, 11,781 disambiguated predicates are described and their semantic roles are listed. We use two fields of their XML files to gather prepositions: the last word of the field "descr" in "roles", and the first word of the field of the corresponding role in "example". In this way, we retrieve, for instance, for the lexical unit *beg.01* the preposition *from* for the second semantic role (as in *beg from someone*), and the preposition *for* for the third role (as in *beg someone for something*). The correspondence between prepositions and semantic roles is also used for the mapping of dependency relations (Mille and Wanner, 2015).

For each surface dependency relation, a default mapping that is conditioned by the encountered syntactic structure and dictionary entries is defined. Thus, a subject is by default mapped to a first argument *I* unless it is the subject of a passive verb. In this case, the subject is mapped to the second argument *II*. Along similar lines, a dictionary entry may specify in the subcategorization pattern of a headword the association of a given preposition to a different argument slot than indicated by the default mapping. For instance, in the sentence *Sony announced its plans to hire Mr. Guber*, *to* is a depen-

	POS	LEMMA	LAS	UAS
English	98.50	99.46	89.70	92.21

Table 1: Performance of Bohnet and Nivre's joint PoS-tagger+dependency parser trained on the PTB Treebank for English.

Hypernode Detection (English)	
Measure	SSyntS–DSyntS Transducer
p_h	98.42 (41967/42461)
r_h	98.82 (41967/42467)
$F1_h$	98.62
Attachment and labeling (English)	
Measure	SSynS–DSyntS Transducer
LAP	81.80 (34882/42461)
UAP	85.82 (36598/42461)
LA-P	89.11 (37998/42641)
LAR	82.14 (34882/42467)
UAR	86.18 (36598/42467)
LA-R	89.48 (37998/42467)

Table 2: Performance of the Ballesteros et al. deep-syntactic parser trained on the adapted version of the PTB Treebank for English.

dent of *plan* with the surface dependency *NMOD*. *NMOD* is by default mapped to the deep relation *ATTR*, but in the dictionary entry of *plan* it is stated that a dependent introduced by *to* is mapped to *II*, such that in the case of *plan*, the default will be overwritten in that *NMOD* will be mapped to *II*.

2.2 Parser Results

Our models offer state-of-the-art performance for part-of-speech tagging, lemmatization, syntactic dependency parsing and deep-syntactic parsing.[4] Tables 1[5] and 2[6] show the results of both parsers.

[4]This is the first attempt to build English deep-syntactic structures; Ballesteros et al. (2014) report results for Spanish only.

[5]'POS' stands for part-of-speech accuracy, 'LEMMA' for lemma accuracy, 'LAS' for labeled attachment score, and 'UAS' for unlabeled attachment score

[6]'p_h' stands for hypernode detection precision, 'r_h' for hypernode detection recall, '$F1_h$' for hypernode detection F1 measure, 'LAP' for labeled attachment precision, 'UAP' for unlabeled attachment precision, 'LA-P' for label accuracy precision, 'LAR' for labeled attachment recall, 'UAR' for unlabeled attachment recall, and 'LA-R' for label accuracy recall.

3 Tree Visualization

Our visualization interface is built with a Java HTTPServer, which is bound to an IP address and port number that listens to incoming connections from users. The HTTPServer Java class connects with both the joint tagger+lemmatizer+parser and the deep-syntactic parser and provides the output of plain text input sentences in real time. To ensure real time performance, a model of both parsers is already loaded, and the interface waits for new input given by the users.

The main page (see `http://dparse.multisensor.taln.upf.edu/main`) lets the user introduce a text and select what kind of parsing she wants to see in the output, the surface-syntactic, deep-syntactic or both at the same time. Depending on the choice of the user, after parsing the CoNLL outputs (surface- and/or deep-syntactic) are shown. If desired, they can be also downloaded. A click on the corresponding link takes the user to the graphic representation of the parse tree.

The visualization of the output is performed by the annotation tool Brat (Stenetorp et al., 2012). Brat takes an annotation file, which is produced by transforming the CoNLL files that the parsers output into Brat's native format, and generates the graphical interface for the dependency trees.

Figure 2 shows three sample surface syntactic structures in Brat. In Figure 3, their equivalent deep-syntactic structures are displayed. As already Figure 1, the figures illustrate the difference of both types of structures with respect to the abstraction of linguistic phenomena. The DSyntSs are clearly much closer to semantics. As a matter of fact, they are equivalent to PropBank structures (Palmer et al., 2005). However, this does not mean that they must *per se* be "simpler" than their corresponding surface-syntactic structures—compare, for instance, the structures (3a) and (3b) in Figures 2 and 3, where both SSyntS and DSyntS contain the same number of nodes, i.e., are isomorphic.

The structures (2a) and (2b) illustrate the capacity of the deep parser to correctly identify the arguments of a lexical item without that explicit hints are available in the surface structure.

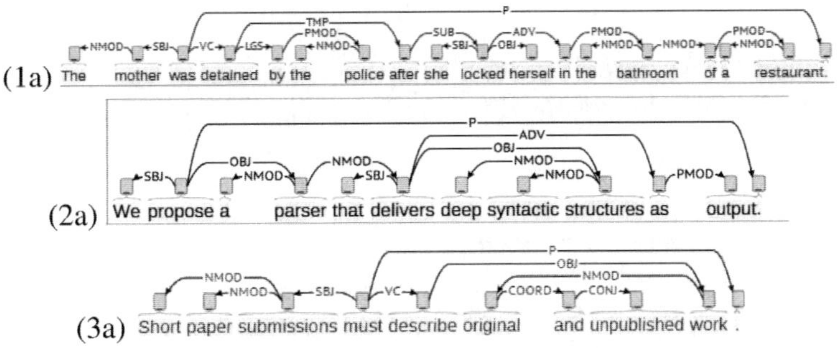

Figure 2: Visualization of surface syntactic structures with Brat

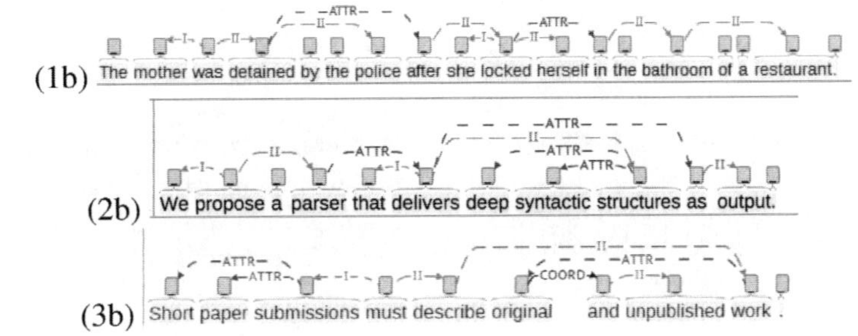

Figure 3: Visualization of deep-syntactic structures with Brat

4 Related Work

Visualization interfaces normally offer a universal and simple way to access the output of NLP tools, among them parsers. This leads to better comprehension of their outputs and a better usability for downstream applications. Therefore, it is not surprising that visualization interfaces have been a relevant topic during the last years in the NLP community; see, e.g., (Collins et al., 2008; Collins et al., 2009; Feng and Lapata, 2010). In the parsing area, tools such as MaltEval (Nilsson and Nivre, 2008), the Mate Tools (Bohnet and Wanner, 2010), XLDD (Culy et al., 2011), TreeExplorer (Thiele et al., 2013), ViZPar (Ortiz et al., 2014), MaltDiver (Ballesteros and Carlini, 2013), or XLike Services (Carreras et al., 2014) have been proposed for the visualization of parse trees and their subsequent evaluation. The interface described in this paper serves a similar purpose. To the best of our knowledge, it is the first interface that uses the flexible off-the-shelf tool Brat and that serves for the visualization of deep-syntactic structures.

5 Conclusions and Future Work

We have presented an operational interface for the visualization of the output of a deep-syntactic parser and of surface-syntactic structures that serve it as input. The interface is flexible in that it allows for the display of any additional structural information provided by an extended parsing pipeline. For instance, if the obtained deep-syntactic structure is projected onto a frame-like structure (Chen et al., 2010) with semantic roles as arc labels, this frame structure can be displayed as well. We are currently working on such an extension. Furthermore, we aim to expand our visualization interface to facilitate active exploration of linguistic structures with Brat and thus add to the static display of structures the dimension of *Visual Analytics* (Keim et al., 2008).

Acknowledgments

This work has been partially funded by the European Union's Seventh Framework and Horizon 2020 Research and Innovation Programmes under the Grant Agreement numbers FP7-ICT-610411, FP7-SME-606163, and H2020-RIA-645012.

References

G. Attardi and M. Simi. 2014. Dependency parsing techniques for information extraction. In *Proceedings of Evalita 2014*.

M. Ballesteros and R. Carlini. 2013. Maltdiver: A transition-based parser visualizer. In *Demonstrations of the Sixth International Joint Conference on Natural Language Processing*, page 25. IJCNLP.

M. Ballesteros, B. Bohnet, S. Mille, and L. Wanner. 2014. Deep-syntactic parsing. In *Proceedings of the 25th International Conference on Computational Linguistics (COLING)*.

M. Ballesteros, B. Bohnet, S. Mille, and L. Wanner. 2015. Data-driven sentence generation with non-isomorphic trees. In *Proceedings of the 2015 Conference of the North American Chapter of the Association for Computational Linguistics – Human Language Technologies (NAACL HLT 2015)*.

B. Bohnet and J. Nivre. 2012. A transition-based system for joint part-of-speech tagging and labeled non-projective dependency parsing. In *EMNLP-CoNLL*.

B. Bohnet and L. Wanner. 2010. Open Source Graph Transducer Interpreter and Grammar Development Environment. In *Proceedings of the International Conference on Linguistic Resources and Evaluation (LREC)*.

X. Carreras, L. Padró, L. Zhang, Z. Rettinger, A.and Li, E. Garcıa-Cuesta, Z. Agic, B. Bekavec, B. Fortuna, and T. Štajner. 2014. Xlike project language analysis services. *Proceedings of the Demonstrations Session at EACL*, pages 9–12.

D. Chen, N. Schneider, D. Das, and N.A. Smith. 2010. Semafor: Frame argument resolution with log-linear models. In *Proceedings of the 5th international workshop on semantic evaluation*, pages 264–267. Association for Computational Linguistics.

C. Collins, G. Penn, and S. Carpendale. 2008. Interactive visualization for computational linguistics. In *Proceedings of the 46th Annual Meeting of the Association for Computational Linguistics on Human Language Technologies*, Stroudsburg, PA, USA. Association for Computational Linguistics.

C. Collins, S. Carpendale, and G. Penn. 2009. DocuBurst: Visualizing Document Content Using Language Structure. In *Proceedings of the Eurographics/IEEE-VGTC Symposium on Visualization (EuroVis '09)*, pages 1039–1046. Eurographics Association.

C. Culy, V. Lyding, and H. Dittmann. 2011. xLDD: Extended Linguistic Dependency Diagrams. In *Proceedings of the 2011 15th International Conference on Information Visualisation*, IV '11, pages 164–169, Washington, DC, USA. IEEE Computer Society.

Y. Feng and M. Lapata. 2010. Visual Information in Semantic Representation. In *Proceedings of the 2010 Conference of the North American Chapter of the Association for Computational Linguistics – Human Language Technologies (NAACL HLT 2010)*, pages 91–99, Stroudsburg, PA, USA. Association for Computational Linguistics.

K. Filippova and M. Strube. 2008. Sentence fusion via dependency graph compression. In *Proceedings of the International Conference on Empirical Methods in Natural Language Processing (EMNLP)*.

R. Johansson and P. Nugues. 2007. Extended constituent-to-dependency conversion for English. In *Proceedings of the 16th Nordic Conference of Computational Linguistics (NODALIDA)*, pages 105–112, Tartu, Estonia, May 25-26.

B. Jones, J. Andreas, D. Bauer, K.-M. Hermann, and K. Knight. 2012. Semantics-based machine translation with hyperedge replacement grammars. In *Proceedings of the International Conference on Computational Linguistics (COLING)*.

D.A. Keim, F. Mansmann, J. Schneidewind, J. Thomas, and H. Ziegler. 2008. Visual Analytics: Scope and Challenges. In S. Simoff, editor, *Visual Data Mining, LNCS 4404*, pages 76–90. Springer Verlag, Berlin.

S. Mille and L. Wanner. 2015. Towards large-coverage detailed lexical resources for data-to-text generation. In *Proceedings of the First International Workshop on Data-to-Text Generation*, Edinburgh, Scotland.

Jens Nilsson and Joakim Nivre. 2008. Malteval: an evaluation and visualization tool for dependency parsing. In *Proceedings of the Sixth International Conference on Language Resources and Evaluation (LREC'08)*, Marrakech, Morocco, may. European Language Resources Association (ELRA).

I. Ortiz, M. Ballesteros, and Y. Zhang. 2014. ViZPar: A GUI for ZPar with Manual Feature Selection. *Procesamiento del lenguaje natural*, 53.

Martha Palmer, Paul Kingsbury, and Daniel Gildea. 2005. The Proposition Bank: An annotated corpus of semantic roles. *Computational Linguistics*, 31.

P. Stenetorp, S. Pyysalo, G. Topić, T. Ohta, S. Ananiadou, and J. Tsujii. 2012. BRAT: A Web-based Tool for NLP-Assisted Text Annotation. In *13th Conference of the European Chapter of the Association for Computational Linguistics*, pages 102–107. Association for Computational Linguistics.

G. Thiele, M. Gärtner, W. Seeker, A. Björkelund, and J. Kuhn. 2013. Treeexplorer – An extensible Graphical Search Tool for Dependency Treebanks. In *Proceedings of the Demonstrations of the 51st Annual Meeting of the Association for Computational Linguistics (ACL 2013)*.

WOLFE: An NLP-friendly Declarative Machine Learning Stack

Sameer Singh[†] **Tim Rocktäschel**[*] **Luke Hewitt**[*] **Jason Naradowsky**[*] **Sebastian Riedel**[*]
[†]University of Washington
Seattle WA
sameer@cs.washington.edu
[*]University College London
London UK
{t.rocktaschel,luke.hewitt.10,j.narad,s.riedel}@cs.ucl.ac.uk

Abstract

Developing machine learning algorithms for natural language processing (NLP) applications is inherently an iterative process, involving a continuous refinement of the choice of model, engineering of features, selection of inference algorithms, search for the right hyper-parameters, and error analysis. Existing probabilistic program languages (PPLs) only provide partial solutions; most of them do not support commonly used models such as matrix factorization or neural networks, and do not facilitate interactive and iterative programming that is crucial for rapid development of these models.

In this demo we introduce WOLFE, a stack designed to facilitate the development of NLP applications: (1) the WOLFE *language* allows the user to concisely define complex models, enabling easy modification and extension, (2) the WOLFE *interpreter* transforms declarative machine learning code into automatically differentiable terms or, where applicable, into factor graphs that allow for complex models to be applied to real-world applications, and (3) the WOLFE *IDE* provides a number of different visual and interactive elements, allowing intuitive exploration and editing of the data representations, the underlying graphical models, and the execution of the inference algorithms.

1 Introduction

Machine learning has become a critical component of practical NLP systems, however designing and training an appropriate, accurate model is an iterative and time-consuming process for a number of reasons. First, initial intuitions that inform model design (such as which features to use) are often inaccurate, requiring incremental model tweaking based on performance. Even if the model is accurate, the final performance depends quite critically on the choice of the algorithms and their hyper-parameters. Further, bugs that are introduced by the user may not even be reflected directly in the performance (such as a feature computation bug may not degrade performance). All these concerns are further compounded due to the variety of approaches commonly used in NLP, such as conditional random fields (Sutton and McCallum, 2007), Markov random networks (Poon and Domingos, 2007), Bayesian networks (Haghighi and Klein, 2010), matrix factorization (Riedel et al., 2013), and Deep learning (Socher et al., 2013).

Probabilistic programming languages (PPLs), by closing the gap between traditional programming and probabilistic modeling, go a long way in aiding quick design and modification of expressive models[1]. However, creating accurate machine learning models using these languages remains challenging. Of the probabilistic programming languages that exist today, no language can easily express the variety of models used in NLP, focusing instead on a restricted set of modeling paradigms, for example, Markov logic networks can be models by Alchemy (Richardson and Domingos, 2006), Bayesian generative networks by Church (Goodman et al., 2008), undirected graphical models by Factorie (McCallum et al., 2009), and so on. Further, these toolkits are only restricted to model design and inference execution, and do not provide the appropriate debugging and interactive

[1]For a comprehensive list of PPLs, see `http://probabilistic-programming.org/`.

Proceedings of NAACL-HLT 2015, pages 61–65,
Denver, Colorado, May 31 – June 5, 2015.

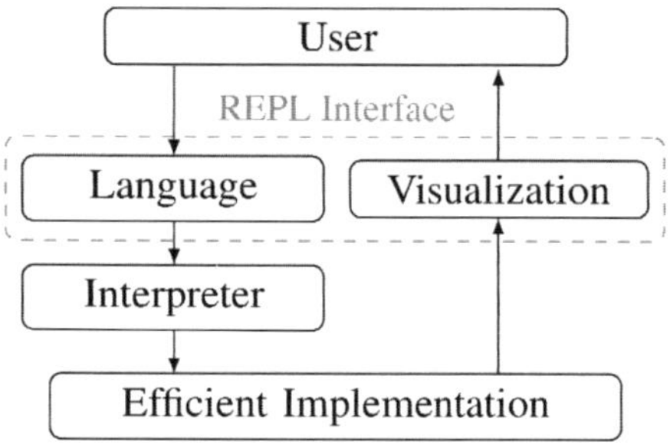

Figure 1: Overview of the WOLFE Stack.

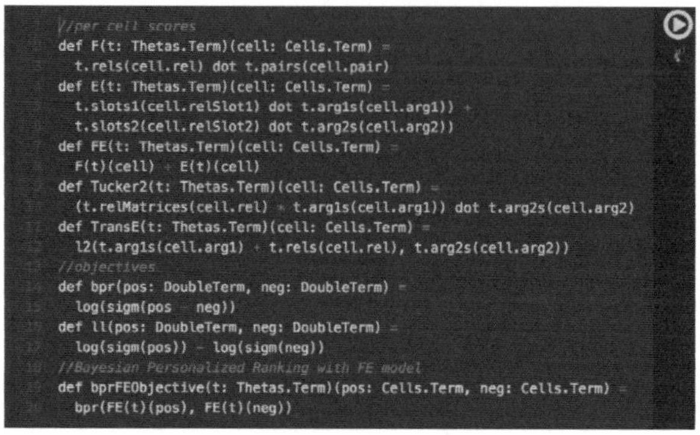

Figure 2: Implementation of various matrix and tensor factorization models in WOLFE.

visualization tools required for developing such models in practice. Due to these concerns, probabilistic programming has not found significant adoption in natural language processing, and application of machine learning to NLP still consists either of arduously designing, debugging, and iterating over a variety of models, or more commonly, giving up and using the first model that is "good enough".

In this demo, we introduce our probabilistic programming toolkit WOLFE (Riedel et al., 2014) that aids in the iterative design of machine learning models for NLP applications. The underlying probabilistic programming language can be used to concisely express a wide range of models, including undirected graphical models, matrix factorization, Bayesian networks, neural networks, and further, its modular nature allows combinations of these modeling paradigms. We additionally present an easy-to-use IDE for the interactive designing of NLP models, consisting of an interactive and visual presentation of structured data, graphical models, and inference execution. Using the WOLFE language and IDE can thus enable the users to quickly create, debug, and iterate on complex models and inference.

2 Overview of the WOLFE Stack

The overall goal of the demo will be to guide users in creating complex graphical models using an easy-to-use mathematical language for defining models, and in performing learning and inference for the created model using an IDE. Figure 1 summarizes the overview of the WOLFE stack, consisting of the language and the visualization that form the user-facing interface, with the interpreter and efficient learning and inference engine as the back-end.

2.1 Declarative Modeling Language

Existing PPLs primarily focus on a single representation for the probabilistic models, and either do not support, or provide only inefficient implementations for other kinds of machine learning models. Thus a practitioner either has to write her own customized implementation of the models she is trying to explore, or decide apriori on the family of models she will be restricted to; both undesirable options. Instead, we introduce a probabilistic programming language that is universal in its expression of models, yet allows for efficient implementations of these models.

The design of the WOLFE language is inspired by the observation that most machine learning algorithms can be formulated in terms of scalar functions (such as distributions and objectives/losses), search spaces (such as the universe of possible labels) and a small set of mathematical operations such as maximization, summation and expectations that operate on these functions and spaces. Using this insight, a program in WOLFE consists of a declarative description of the machine learning algorithm in terms of implementations of these scalar functions, definitions of the search spaces, and the use of appropriate operators on these. For example, named-entity recognition tagging using conditional random fields consists of a scalar function that defines the model *score* using a dot product between the parameters and the *sum* of node and edge features, while inference using this model involves finding the label sequence that has the *maximum* model score over all label sequences.

The focus on scalar functions as building blocks allows for rapid prototyping of a large range of machine learning models. For instance, there exist a variety of matrix and tensor factorization methods for knowledge base population that have a succinct, unified mathematical formulation (Nickel et al., 2015). In WOLFE these models can be easily implemented with a few lines of code. See Figure 2 for examples of a Tucker2 decomposition, TransE (Bordes et al., 2013), and Riedel et al. (2013)'s feature model (F), entity model (E), and combination of the two (FE), either based on a log likelihood or Bayesian Personalized Ranking (Rendle et al., 2009) objective.

2.2 Interpreter, and Efficient Implementations

In WOLFE users write models using a domain-specific-language that supports a wide range of mathematical expressions. The WOLFE *interpreter* then evaluates these expressions. This is non-trivial as expressions usually contain operators such as the *argmax* functions which are, in general, intractable to compute. For efficient evaluation of WOLFE programs our interpreter *compiles* WOLFE expressions into representations that enable efficient computation in many cases. For example, for terms that involve maximization over continuous search spaces WOLFE generates a computation tree that supports efficient forward and back-propagation for automatic differentiation. Likewise, when maximizing over discrete search spaces, WOLFE constructs *factor graphs* that support efficient message passing algorithm such as Max-Product or Dual Decomposition. Crucially, due to the compositional nature of WOLFE, discrete and continuous optimization problems can be nested to support a rich class of *structured prediction* objectives. In such cases the interpreter constructs nested computational structures, such as a factor graph within a back-propagation graph.

2.3 Visual and Interactive IDE

In this demonstration, we present an integrated developing, debugging and visualization toolkit for machine learning for NLP. The IDE is based on the read-eval-print loop (REPL) to allow quick iterations of writing and debugging, and consists of the following elements: (1) Editor (read): Users define the model and inference in the declarative, math-like language described in Section 2.1 using a syntax highlighted code editor. (2) Build Automation (eval): The use of the interpreter as described in the previous section to provide efficient code that is executed. (3) Debugging/Visualization (print): Our tool presents the underlying factor graph as an interactive UI element that supports clicking, drag and drop, hover, etc. to explore the structure and the factors of the model. We visualize the results of inference in a graphical manner that adapts to the type of the result (bar charts for simple distributions, shaded maps for matrix-like objects, circles/arrows for NLP data types, etc.). For further fine-grained debugging, we can also surface intermediate results from inference, for example, visualizing the messages in belief propagation for each edge in the factor graph.

3 Demo Outline

The overall objective of the demo is for users to design, debug, and modify a machine learning model for an NLP application, starting from scratch. The demo takes the user through all the steps of loading data, creating an initial model, observing the output errors, modifying the model accordingly, and rerunning to see the errors fixed: the complete set of steps often involved in real-life application of ML for NLP. We provide pre-built functions for the menial tasks, such as data loading and feature computation functions, leaving the more interesting aspects of model design to the user. Further, we include an "open-ended" option for interested users to develop arbitrary models. Based on their interest or area of expertise, the user has an option of investigating any (or all) of the following applications: (1) sequence tagging using CRFs, (2) relational learning using MLNs, (3) matrix factorization for relation extraction, and (4) dependency parsing (for advanced users). Each of these are similar in the overall "script", differing in the data, models, and inference algorithms used; we describe the steps of the demo using the CRF example. All of the demo applications are available online at `http://wolfe.ml/demos/nlp`.

1. The first step of the demo allows the user to read as input a standard dataset of the task, and visualize instances in an easy-to-read manner. In Figure 3a for example, we show two sentences read for the purpose of sequence tagging.

2. The user then defines an initial model for the task, which is visualized as a factor graph for

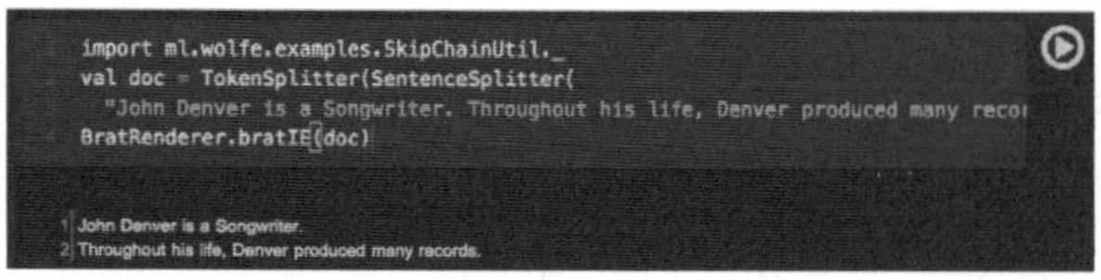

(a) Data Loading

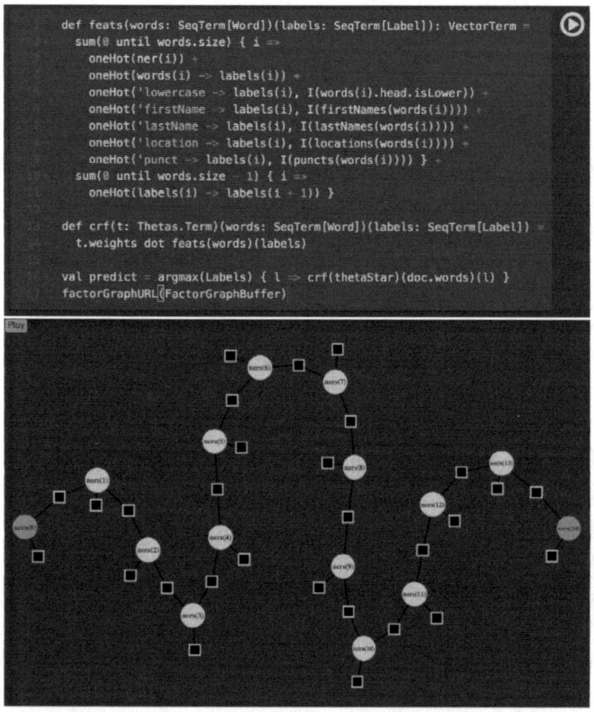

(b) Initial Model

(c) Error in Prediction

Figure 3: **Model Creation and Evaluation:** An example instance of the demo showing the *creation* steps, including the loading and visualization of the sentences, designing and presentation of a linear chain CRF, and Viterbi decoding for the sentences.

the purpose of debugging the model definition. The initial model for sequence tagging is a simple linear chain, defined and visualized for a sentence in Figure 3b.

3. The user writes the declarative definition of inference, and makes predictions of the input data. The predictions are appropriately visualized, allowing the user to detect mistakes (for example, the incorrect NER tag of location to "Denver" in Figure 3c).

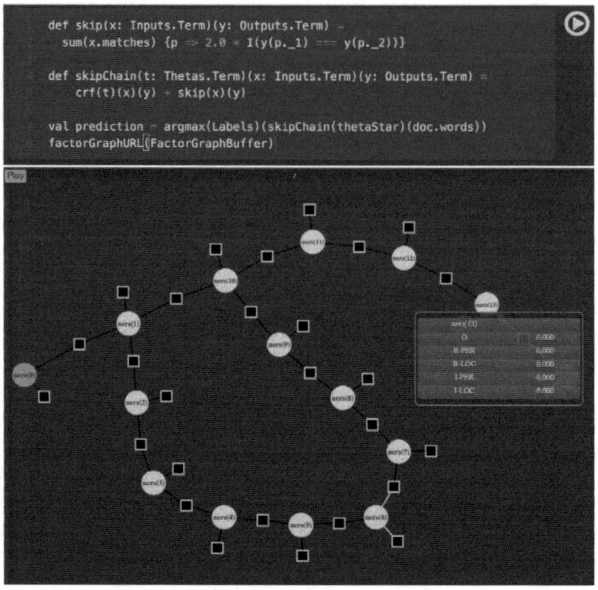

(a) Modify the Model (add skip edge)

(b) Fixed Prediction

Figure 4: **Debugging Loop:** The remaining steps of the iterative development, consisting of modification of the model to fix the error from Figure 3c by adding a skip-factor to the original model, and confirming the inference in the skip-chain model results in the correct prediction.

4. The user then modifies the model (adding a skip-factor in Figure 4a) that will likely correct the mistake. The modified model is then visualized to confirm it is correct. (Optionally, the user can, at any point, visualize the execution of the inference to confirm the modifications as well, for example Figure 4a shows the state of messages in belief propagation.)

5. On the execution of the model, the user confirms that the original error has been fixed, for example the skip factor allows the correct tag of person for "Denver" in Figure 4b.

4 Conclusions

This demo describes WOLFE, a language, interpreter, and an IDE for easy, iterative development of complex machine learning models for NLP applications. The language allows concise definition of the models and inference by using universal, mathematical syntax. The interpreter performs program analysis on the user code to automatically generate efficient low-level code. The easy-to-use IDE allows the user to iteratively write and execute such programs, but most importantly supports intuitive visualizations of structured data, models, and inference to enable users to understand and debug their code. The demo thus allows a user to design, debug, evaluate, and modify complex machine learning models for a variety of NLP applications.

Acknowledgments

We would like to thank Larysa Visengeriyeva, Jan Noessner, and Vivek Srikumar for contributions to early versions of WOLFE. This work was supported in part by Microsoft Research through its PhD Scholarship Programme, an Allen Distinguished Investigator Award, a Marie Curie Career Integration Grant, and in part by the TerraSwarm Research Center, one of six centers supported by the STARnet phase of the Focus Center Research Program (FCRP) a Semiconductor Research Corporation program sponsored by MARCO and DARPA.

References

Antoine Bordes, Nicolas Usunier, Alberto Garcia-Duran, Jason Weston, and Oksana Yakhnenko. 2013. Translating embeddings for modeling multi-relational data. In *Advances in Neural Information Processing Systems*, pages 2787–2795.

Noah D. Goodman, Vikash K. Mansinghka, Daniel Roy, Keith Bonawitz, and Joshua B. Tenenbaum. 2008. Church: a language for generative models. In *Uncertainty in Artificial Intelligence (UAI)*.

Aria Haghighi and Dan Klein. 2010. Coreference resolution in a modular, entity-centered model. In *North American Chapter of the Association for Computational Linguistics - Human Language Technologies (NAACL HLT)*, pages 385–393.

Andrew McCallum, Karl Schultz, and Sameer Singh. 2009. FACTORIE: Probabilistic programming via imperatively defined factor graphs. In *Neural Information Processing Systems (NIPS)*.

Maximilian Nickel, Kevin Murphy, Volker Tresp, and Evgeniy Gabrilovich. 2015. A review of relational machine learning for knowledge graphs: From multi-relational link prediction to automated knowledge graph construction. *arXiv preprint arXiv:1503.00759*.

Hoifung Poon and Pedro Domingos. 2007. Joint inference in information extraction. In *Proceedings of the 22nd AAAI Conference on Artificial Intelligence (AAAI '07)*, pages 913–918.

Steffen Rendle, Christoph Freudenthaler, Zeno Gantner, and Lars Schmidt-Thieme. 2009. BPR: Bayesian personalized ranking from implicit feedback. In *Uncertainty in Artificial Intelligence (UAI)*.

Matthew Richardson and Pedro Domingos. 2006. Markov logic networks. *Machine Learning*, 62(1-2):107–136.

Sebastian Riedel, Limin Yao, Benjamin M. Marlin, and Andrew McCallum. 2013. Relation extraction with matrix factorization and universal schemas. In *Joint Human Language Technology Conference/Annual Meeting of the North American Chapter of the Association for Computational Linguistics (HLT-NAACL '13)*, June.

Sebastian Riedel, Sameer Singh, Vivek Srikumar, Tim Rocktaschel, Larysa Visengeriyeva, and Jan Noessner. 2014. Wolfe: Strength reduction and approximate programming for probabilistic programming. In *International Workshop on Statistical Relational AI (StarAI)*.

Richard Socher, Alex Perelygin, Jean Y Wu, Jason Chuang, Christopher D Manning, Andrew Y Ng, and Christopher Potts Potts. 2013. Recursive deep models for semantic compositionality over a sentiment treebank. In *Empirical Methods in Natural Language Processing (EMNLP)*.

Charles Sutton and Andrew McCallum. 2007. An introduction to conditional random fields for relational learning. In *Introduction to Statistical Relational Learning*.

Lean Question Answering over Freebase from Scratch

Xuchen Yao
kitt.ai *
2157 N Northlake Way
Seattle, WA 98103, USA

Abstract

For the task of question answering (QA) over Freebase on the WebQuestions dataset (Berant et al., 2013), we found that 85% of all questions (in the training set) can be directly answered via a single binary relation. Thus we turned this task into slot-filling for <*question topic, relation, answer*> tuples: predicting *relations* to get *answers* given a *question's topic*. We design efficient data structures to identify question topics organically from 46 million Freebase topic names, without employing *any* NLP processing tools. Then we present a lean QA system that runs in real time (in offline batch testing it answered two thousand questions in 51 seconds on a laptop). The system also achieved 7.8% better F_1 score (harmonic mean of average precision and recall) than the previous state of the art.

1 Introduction

Large-scale open-domain question answering from structured Knowledge Base (KB) provides a good balance of precision and recall in everyday QA tasks, executed by search engines and personal assistant applications. The release of WebQuestions dataset (Berant et al., 2013) has drawn a lot of interest from both academia and industry. One tendency to notice is that the general trend of research is becoming more complex, utilizing various techniques such as semantic parsing and deep neural networks.

We took a radically different approach by heading for the other direction: simplifying the task as much as possible with no compromise on speed and accuracy. We treat the task of QA from Freebase as a two-step problem: identifying the correct topic (*search* problem) and predicting the correct answer (*prediction* problem). The common approach to the first problem is applying basic linguistic processing, such as part-of-speech (POS) tagging and chunking to identify noun phrases, and named entity recognition (NER) for interesting topics. The common approach to the second problem is detailed question analysis, which usually involves parsing. In any case, various components from the natural language processing (NLP) pipeline are usually applied.

With an emphasis on real-time prediction (usually making a prediction within 100 milliseconds after seeing the question), we chose not to use *any* NLP preprocessing – not even POS tagging. Instead we design efficient data structures to help identify named entities to tackle the search problem.

For the prediction problem, we found that given a question and its topic, simply predicting the KB relation between the topic and the answer is sufficient. In other words, we turned QA from Freebase into a slot-filling problem in the form of <*topic, relation, answer*> tuples: given a *question*, the task is to find the *answer*, while the search problem is to find the *topic* and the prediction problem is to find the *relation*. For instance, given the question what's sweden's currency?, the task can be turned into a tuple of <Sweden, */location/country/currency_used*, Swedish krona>. In Section 3 we address how to identify the topic (Sweden) and in Section 4 how to predict the relation (*/location/country/currency_used*). There are obvious limitations in this task format, which are discussed in Section 6.

Going beyond reporting evaluation scores, we describe in details our design principle and also report performance in speed. This paper makes the follow-

* Incubated by the Allen Institute for Artificial Intelligence.

Proceedings of NAACL-HLT 2015, pages 66–70,
Denver, Colorado, May 31 – June 5, 2015.

ing technical contributions to QA from KB:

- We design and compare several data structures to help identify question topics using the KB resource itself. The key to success is to search through 46 million Freebase topics efficiently while still being robust against noise (such as typographical or speech recognition errors).

- Our algorithm is high-performance, real-time, and simple enough to replicate. It achieved state-of-the-art result on the WEBQUESTIONS dataset. Training time in total is less than 5 minutes and testing on 2032 questions takes less than 1 minute. There are no external NLP library dependencies: the only preprocessing is lowercasing.

2 Related Work

The task of question answering from Freebase was first proposed by Berant et al. (2013), who crawled Google Suggest and annotated 5810 questions that had answers from Freebase with Amazon Mechanical Turk, thus the WEBQUESTIONS dataset. Researchers have approached this problem from different angles. Semantic parsing (Berant et al., 2013; Berant and Liang, 2014) aims to predict the logic forms of the question given the distant supervision of direct answers. Their logic forms were derived from dependency parses and then converted into database queries. Reddy et al. (2014) conceptualized semantic parsing as a graph matching problem by building graphs with Combinatory Categorial Grammar parses. Edges and nodes in parsing graphs were grounded with respect to Freebase relations and entities. Other research explored the graph nature of Freebase. For instance, Bordes et al. (2014) learned low-dimensional word embeddings for both the question and related topic subgraph. A scoring function was defined over these embeddings so that correct answers yielded a higher score. Yao and Van Durme (2014) treated this task as a direct information extraction problem: each entity node from a topic graph was ranked against others by searching a massively generated feature space.

All of the above work resorted to using the Freebase annotation of ClueWeb (Gabrilovich et al., 2013) to gain extra advantage of paraphrasing QA pairs or dealing with data sparsity problem. However, ClueWeb is proprietary data and costs hundreds of dollars to purchase. Moreover, even though the implementation systems from (Berant et al., 2013; Yao and Van Durme, 2014; Reddy et al., 2014) are open-source, they all take considerable disk space (in tens of gigabytes) and training time (in days). In this paper we present a system that can be easily implemented in 300 lines of Python code with no compromise in accuracy and speed.

3 Search

Given a question, we need to find out all named entities (or *topics* in Freebase terms). For instance, for the question what character did natalie portman play in star wars?, we are mainly interested in the topics of natalie portman and star wars. Note that all sentences in WEBQUESTIONS are lowercased.

Normal approaches require a combination of basic NLP processing. For instance, an NER tagger might recognize natalie portman as a PERSON, but would not recognize star wars as a movie, unless there is a pre-defined gazetteer. Then one needs to resort to basic chunking to at least identify star wars as a noun phrase. Moreover, these NLP tools need to be trained to better adapt lowercased sentences. Even though, one is still limited to a small number of recognizable types: noun phrases, person, location, organization, time, date, etc.

Freebase contains 46 million topics, each of which is annotated with one or more types. Thus a natural idea is to use these 46 million topics as a gazetteer and recognizes named entities from the question (with ambiguities), with two steps:

1. enumerate all adjacent words (of various length) of the question, an $O(N^2)$ operation where N is the length of question in words;
2. check whether each adjacent word block exists in the gazetteer.

We use two common data structures to search efficiently, with three design principles:

1. compact and in-memory, to avoid expensive hard disk or solid state drive I/O;
2. fuzzy matching, to be robust against noise;
3. easily extensible, to accommodate new topics.

3.1 Fuzzy Matching and Generation

To check whether one string is a Freebase topic, the easiest way is to use a hash set. However, this is not robust against noise unless a fuzzy matching hashing function (e.g., locality sensitive hashing) is designed. Moreover, 46 million keys in a giant hash set might cause serious problems of key collision or set resizing in some programming languages. Instead, we propose to use two common data structures for the purpose of fuzzy matching or generation.

Fuzzy Matching with Sorted List [1]: a sorted list can provide basic fuzzy matching while avoiding the key collision problem with slightly extra computing time. The search is done via 3 steps:

1. build a sorted list of 46 million topics;
2. to identify whether a string appears in the list, do a binary search. Since 46 million is between 2^{25} and 2^{26}, a search would require in the worst case 26 steps down the binary random access ladder, which is a trivial computation on modern CPUs;
3. For each string comparison during the binary search, also compute the edit distance. This checks whether there is a similar string within an edit distance of d in the list given another string.

Note that a sorted list does not compute *all* similar strings within an edit distance of d efficiently. Adjacent strings in the list also wastes space since they are highly similar. Thus we also propose to use a prefix tree:

Fuzzy Generation with Prefix Tree (Trie): a prefix tree builds a compact representation of all strings where common prefixes are shared towards the root of the tree. By careful back tracing, a prefix tree can also output all similar strings within a fixed edit distance to a given string. This efficiently solves the wasted space and generation problems.

3.2 Implementation and Speed Comparison

We maximally re-used existing software for robustness and quick implementation:

	d = 0	d = 1	d = 2
Fuzzy Matching (Sorted List, PyPy)	<0.01ms	7.9ms	7.5ms
Fuzzy Generation (Trie, Elasticsearch)	29ms	210ms	1969ms

Table 1: Fuzzy query time per question. d is the edit distance while $d = 0$ means strict matching. HTTP roundtrip overhead from Elasticsearch was also counted.

Sorted List was implemented with vanilla Python list, compiled with the PyPy just-in-time compiler.

Prefix Tree was implemented with Elasticsearch, written in Java.

Both implementations held 46 million topic names (each topic name is 20 characters long on average) in memory. Specifically, sorted list took 2.06GB RAM while prefix tree took 1.62GB RAM.

Then we tested how fast it was to find out all topics from a question. To do this, we used the DEV set of WEBQUESTIONS. Enumerating all adjacent words of various length is an $O(N^2)$ operation where N is a sentence length. In practice we counted 27 adjacent words on average for one question, thus 27 queries per question. Elasticsearch follows the client-server model where client sends HTTP queries to the backend database server. To reduce HTTP roundtrip overhead, we queried the server in burst mode: client only sends one "mega" query to the server per question where each "mega" query contains 27 small queries on average. Experiments were conducted with an Intel Core i5-4278U CPU @ 2.60GHz.

Table 1 shows the query time per question. Note that this is an evaluation of real-world computing situation, not how efficiently either search structure was implemented (or in what programming language). Thus the purpose of comparison is to help choose the best implementation solution.

3.3 Ranking

After identifying all possible topic names in a question, we send them to the official Freebase Search API to rank them. For instance, for the question what character did natalie portman play in star wars?, possible named entities include character, natalie, natalie portman, play, star, and star wars.

[1]We mix the notion of array vs. list as long as the actual implementation satisfies two conditions: O(1) random access time and O(1) appending(resizing) time.

But in general natalie portman and star wars should be ranked higher. Due to the crowd-sourced nature, many topics have duplicate entries in Freebase. For instance, we counted 20 different natalie portman's (each one has a unique machine ID), but only one is extensively edited. One can either locally rank them by the number of times each topic is cross-referenced with others, or use the Freebase Search API in an online fashion. In our experiments the latter yielded significantly better results. The Freebase Search API returns a ranked list of topic candidates. Our next job is to predict answers from this list.

4 Prediction

Given a question and its topic, we directly predict the relation that connects the topic with the answer. Our features and model are extremely simple: we took unigram and bigram words from the question as our features and used logistic regression to learn a model that associates lexical words with relations.

The training set of WEBQUESTIONS contains 3778 question and answer pairs. Each question is also annotated with the Freebase topic used to identify the answers. Then for each of the topic-answer pairs, we extracted a direct relation from the topic to the answer, for instance (TOPIC: Sweden, RELATION: */location/country/currency_used*, ANSWER: Swedish krona). If there were more than one relations between the topic and the answer (mostly due to dummy "compound" nodes in between), we chose the nearest one to the answer node as the direct relation. To be more specific: we first selected the the shortest path between the topic and answer node, then chose the relation from the answer node to its parent node, regardless of whether the parent node was the topic node. In this way we found direct relations for 3634 of these questions, which count as 96.2% of the whole training set.

Note that we "reverse-engineered" the slot-filling relations that would predict the correct answers based on annotated gold answers. It does not mean that these relations will predict the answers with 100% accuracy. For instance, for the question what was the first book dr. seuss wrote?, the direct relation was */book/author/book_editions_published*. However, this relation would predict *all* books Dr. Seuss wrote, instead of just the first one. Thus in the training set, we further counted the number of relations that point to the *exact* gold answers. In all, 62% of questions out of the whole training set can be exactly answered by a single relation.

The remaining 38% presented a complicated case. We sampled 100 questions and did a manual analysis. There were mainly two reasons that contributed to the 38%:

1. **Noisy Annotation**: questions with incomplete answers. For instance,

   (a) for the question what does bob dylan sing?, the annotated answer was only "like a rolling stone", while the direct relation */music/artist/-track* gave a full list;

   (b) for the question what kind of currency does cuba use?, the annotated answer was Cuban Peso, while the direct relation */location/country/currency_used* led to two answers: Cuban Peso and Cuban Convertible Peso.

2. **Complex Questions**: questions with constraints that cannot be answered by binary relations. For instance:

   (a) who does david james play for 2011?

   (b) which province in canada is the most populated?

   (c) who does jodelle ferland play in eclipse?

For category 1, the answers provided by direct binary relations will only hurt evaluation scores, but not user experience. For category 2, we counted about 40% of them from the samples. Thus in total, complex questions constructed $38\% \times 40\% = 15\%$ of the whole training set. In other words, 85% of questions can be answered by predicting a single binary relation. This provides statistical evidence that the task of QA on WEBQUESTIONS can be effectively simplified to a tuple slot-filling task.

5 Results

We applied Liblinear (Fan et al., 2008) via its Scikit-learn Python interface (Pedregosa et al., 2011) to train the logistic regression model with L2 regularization. Testing on 2032 questions took 51 seconds.[2]

[2]This excluded the time used to call the Freebase Search API, which is highly dependent on the network and server node.

	F_1 (Berant)	F_1 (Yao)
Yao and Van Durme (2014)	33.0	42.0
Berant and Liang (2014)	39.9	43.0
Reddy et al. (2014)	41.3	-
Bordes et al. (2014)	41.8	45.7
this work	**44.3**	**53.5**

Table 2: Results on the WEBQUESTIONS test set.

We found no difference in quality but only slightly in speed in the search results between using sorted list and prefix tree. Moreover, in specifically the WEBQUESTIONS dataset, there was no difference in strict matching and fuzzy matching – the dataset is somehow void of typographical errors. [3]

We evaluated both the average F_1 over all questions (Berant) and the F_1 of average precision and recall values (Yao) following Bordes et al. (2014), shown in Table 2. Our method outperformed all previous systems in both F_1 measures, with possibly two reasons: 1, the simplicity of this method minimizes error propagation down the processing pipeline; 2, we used direct supervision while most previous work used distant supervision.

6 Limitation and Discussion

The limitation of our method comes from the assumption: most questions can be answered by predicting a direct binary relation. Thus it cannot handle complex questions that require to resolve a chain of relations. These complex questions appear about 15% of the time.

Note that WEBQUESTIONS is a realistic dataset: it was mined off Google Suggest, which reflects people's everyday searches. Our manual analysis showed that these complex questions usually only contain one type of constraint that comes from either a ranking/superlative describer (first, most, etc) or a preposition phrase (in 1998, in some movie, etc). To adapt to these questions, we can take a further step of learning to filter a returned list of results. For instance, first (first husband, first novel, etc) requires learning a time ordering; a prepositional constraint usually picks out a single result from a list of results. To go beyond to "crossword-like" questions with multiple constraints, more powerful mechanisms are certainly needed.

In summary, we have presented a system with a focus on efficiency and simplicity. Computation time is minimized to allow more time for network traffic, while still being able to respond in real time. The system is based on a simpler assumption: most questions can be answered by directly predicting a binary relation from the question topic to the answer. The assumption is supported by both statistics and observation. From this simple but verified assumption we gained performance advantages of not only speed, but also accuracy: the system achieved the best result so far on this task.

[3] This is likely due to the fact that the dataset was crawled with the Google Suggest API, which aggregates common queries and common queries are mostly free of typos. For real-world everyday queries, fuzzy matching should still be applied.

References

Jonathan Berant and Percy Liang. 2014. Semantic parsing via paraphrasing. In *Proceedings of ACL*.

Jonathan Berant, Andrew Chou, Roy Frostig, and Percy Liang. 2013. Semantic Parsing on Freebase from Question-Answer Pairs. In *Proceedings of EMNLP*.

Antoine Bordes, Sumit Chopra, and Jason Weston. 2014. Question answering with subgraph embeddings. In *Proceedings of EMNLP 2014*, pages 615–620.

Rong-En Fan, Kai-Wei Chang, Cho-Jui Hsieh, Xiang-Rui Wang, and Chih-Jen Lin. 2008. LIBLINEAR: A library for large linear classification. *The Journal of Machine Learning Research*, 9:1871–1874.

Evgeniy Gabrilovich, Michael Ringgaard, , and Amarnag Subramanya. 2013. FACC1: Freebase annotation of ClueWeb corpora. http://lemurproject.org/clueweb09/FACC1/.

Fabian Pedregosa, Gaël Varoquaux, Alexandre Gramfort, Vincent Michel, Bertrand Thirion, Olivier Grisel, Mathieu Blondel, Peter Prettenhofer, Ron Weiss, Vincent Dubourg, et al. 2011. Scikit-learn: Machine learning in Python. *The Journal of Machine Learning Research*, 12:2825–2830.

Siva Reddy, Mirella Lapata, and Mark Steedman. 2014. Large-scale semantic parsing without question-answer pairs. *Transactions of the Association for Computational Linguistics*, 2:377–392.

Xuchen Yao and Benjamin Van Durme. 2014. Information extraction over structured data: Question answering with freebase. In *Proceedings of ACL*.

A Web Application for Automated Dialect Analysis

Sravana Reddy
Neukom Institute
Dartmouth College
Hanover, NH.
sravana@cs.dartmouth.edu

James N. Stanford
Linguistics and Cognitive Science
Dartmouth College
Hanover, NH.
james.n.stanford@dartmouth.edu

Abstract

Sociolinguists are regularly faced with the task of measuring phonetic features from speech, which involves manually transcribing audio recordings – a major bottleneck to analyzing large collections of data. We harness automatic speech recognition to build an online end-to-end web application where users upload untranscribed speech collections and receive formant measurements of the vowels in their data. We demonstrate this tool by using it to automatically analyze President Barack Obama's vowel pronunciations.

1 Introduction

There has been recent interest in technologies for the automated analysis of web-scale corpora in sociolinguistics, the study of language usage and variation in society. The subfield of sociophonetics is concerned with how certain speech sounds are manifested, giving rise to distinctive speech accents. While there have been computational tools developed for sociophoeticians in the last few years, they require that the speech is manually transcribed at the word level, which is painstaking for large corpora.

Our insight is that, for many types of recordings, transcriptions produced by current automatic speech recognition (ASR) systems are not significantly worse than manual transcriptions for the purpose of measuring certain key phonetic characteristics of speakers, such as their vowel formants – which are essential to dialect research.

We have created an open-access website, DARLA (short for Dartmouth Linguistic Automation)[1], where linguists and other researchers working on speech dialects can upload their data, and receive automatic transcriptions of the recordings as well as measurements of the speakers' vowels. We envision this tool being used by linguists for a first-pass qualitative study of dialect features in speech data without the effort of manual transcription.

We choose to implement the system online rather than as a downloadable toolkit to eliminate the overhead of program installation for users. Furthermore, since this is an ongoing project, it is seamless to incorporate new features in a web application rather than pushing updates to a desktop program. DARLA currently supports English speech.

Details about our methods as well as studies using sociolinguistic data appear in Reddy and Stanford (2015). In this paper, we focus on describing the interface and an overview of the system components.

2 Background

2.1 Vowel Formants

Every vowel sound is associated with a set of resonance frequencies, or formants, characteristic to the vowel as well as the speaker. Sociophoneticians typically study how the first two formants of stressed vowels, denoted by F_1 and F_2, systematically differ across speakers of the language. For example, as shown in Fig. 1, a speaker saying the vowel `EY`[2] (the first vowel in *paper*) with a Southern accent would

[1] http://darla.dartmouth.edu

[2] We use the standard CMU Arpabet phoneme set (http://www.speech.cs.cmu.edu/cgi-bin/cmudict)

Proceedings of NAACL-HLT 2015, pages 71–75,
Denver, Colorado, May 31 – June 5, 2015.

have a higher F_1 and lower F_2 than a Northern US speaker for the same vowel.

Figure 1: Words and phonemes aligned to speech (represented by its waveform and frequency spectrogram, visualized in Praat). The vowel formants are the dark 'bands', or local frequency peaks.

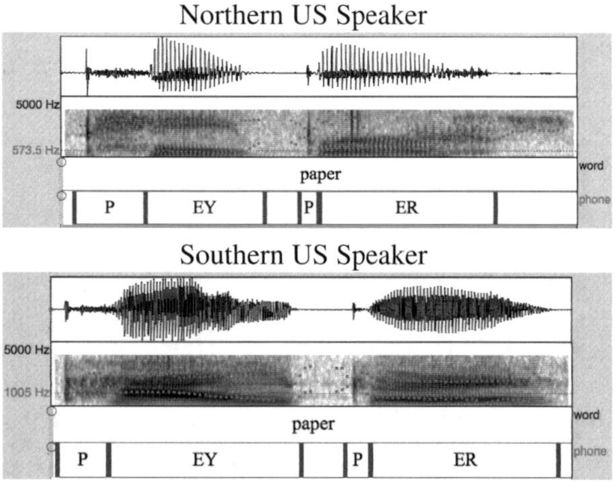

2.2 Motivation

We observe that the stressed vowel error rate of our automatic speech recognition system is about a third of the word error rate for several different test corpora. Unlike typical applications of ASR like dictation or command-and-control systems where accurate word recognition is the primary objective, perfect transcription accuracy is not always necessary. For many sociophonetic purposes, it is sufficient to get the vowel correct. Errors like *depend* in place of *spend* that retain the identity of the stressed vowel account for many of the word errors. Furthermore, with the opportunity to easily analyze speech containing several examples of each vowel type, a few errors will make little difference to the overall dialect analysis.

3 Existing Work

DARLA is inspired by two online tools used by the phonetics and sociolinguistics communities:

1. FAVE (Rosenfelder et al., 2011), short for Forced Alignment Vowel Extraction, takes as input a speech file along with word-level manual transcriptions. It performs Viterbi alignment of the phonemes in the transcription to the speech using HMM-based acoustic models. The locations of vowels are identified from the alignment, and the vowel formants measured at the appropriate locations using Linear Predictive Coding, which in turn is computed by the Praat toolkit for phonetics (Boersma and Weenink, 2014).

Other programs for phoneme alignment include the ProsodyLab Aligner (Gorman et al., 2011) and WebMAUS (Kisler et al., 2012). Recently, Winkelmann and Raess (2014) developed a web tool for spectral analysis and visualization of speech.

The key difference between our system and prior work is that we do not require any transcriptions for the input speech.

2. The NORM suite for vowel normalization and plotting (Thomas and Kendall, 2007) lets users upload formant measurements, and generates scatterplots of the first two formants.

4 System Description

4.1 Input

Fig. 2 is a screenshot of the interface, which is implemented in HTML and Javascript, and connected to the server through CGI and Ajax. Users upload their speech data and can optionally select parameters for the ASR decoder. The options consist of a dialect-specific acoustic model, and the type of speech: free speech or dictation, for which we use a high language model scaling factor, or lists of words – commonly used in sociophonetic research – for which a lower scaling factor is appropriate. Once the upload is complete, users are prompted to enter a speaker ID and sex for each file (Fig. 3), used as parameters for formant extraction. The inputs are validated and sanitized on the client and server sides.

4.2 Back-End Computation

The system currently contains an HMM-based speech recognizer built using the CMU Sphinx toolkit[3], with acoustic and language models that we trained on a variety of American English speech corpora (broadcast news and telephone conversations). We currently have one dialect-specific acoustic model for Southern speech, trained on portions of the Switchboard corpus (Godfrey and Holliman,

[3]http://cmusphinx.sourceforge.net

Figure 2: Input interface for the completely automated vowel extraction system.

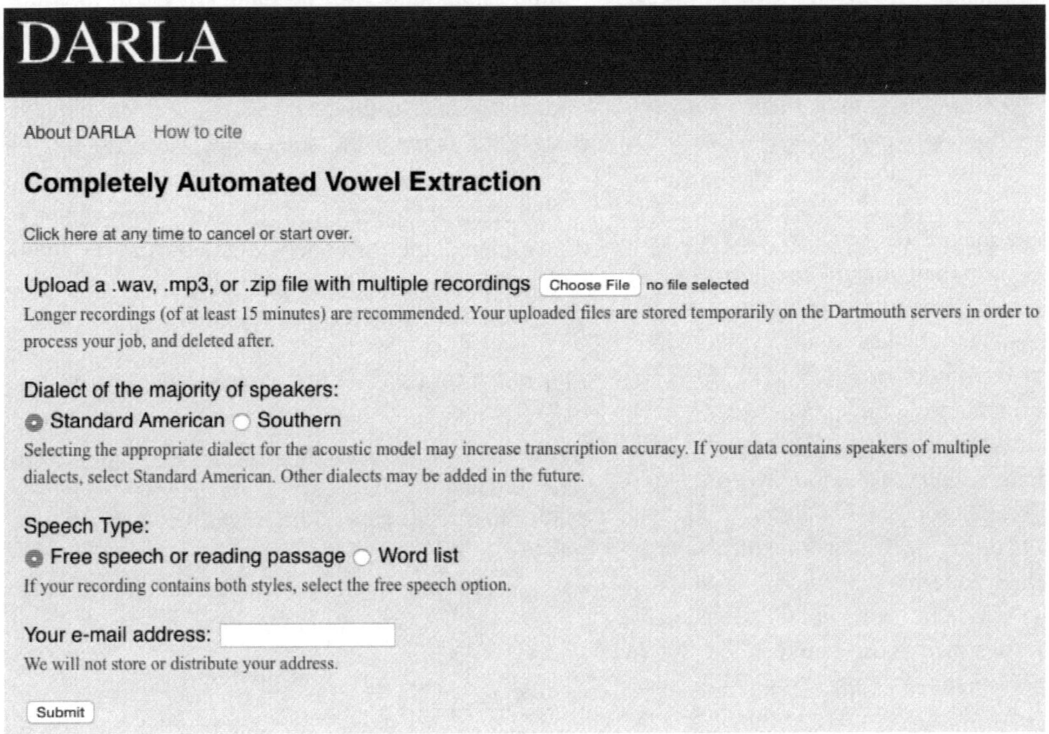

Figure 3: Speaker information prompt.

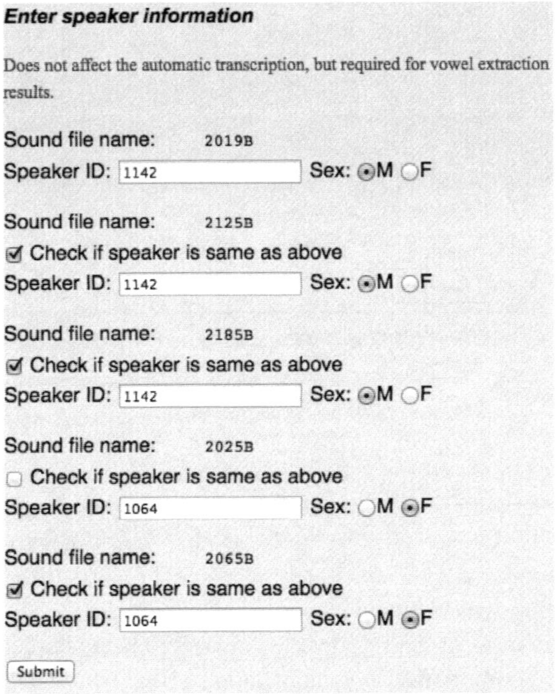

1993). The feature representation uses 13 MFCCs, deltas, and delta-deltas sampled every 10ms.

Long audio files are split into smaller segments, and down-sampled to 16 kHz (or 8 kHz if the original sampling rate is below 16 kHz). We use PocketSphinx for decoding, and HTK to force-align the output transcriptions to produce phoneme-to-audio alignments. The system then converts the alignments to TextGrid format[4], and uses the formant extraction portion of the FAVE code[5] to measure the formant values for all the vowel tokens in the transcriptions. The processing is distributed over eight CPUs so simultaneous jobs can be supported.

Since the transcriptions are likely to contain errors, we filter out low-confidence vowel tokens based on the acoustic likelihood of the word containing that token under the acoustic model. Previous work on identifying potential errors in the transcription suggests using models of duration in addition to acoustic features (Das et al., 2010), which we plan

[4]Conversion was facilitated by the Python TextGrid library available at http://github.com/kylebgorman/textgrid.py

[5]https://github.com/JoFrhwld/FAVE

to incorporate. We also filter out function words, unstressed vowel tokens, and tokens with high formant bandwidths (indicating that the formant values may not be reliable). Finally, we generate scatter plots of the mean values of the first two formants for each vowel type using the R vowels package[6].

4.3 Output

The results are e-mailed to the user once the task is completed. The e-mail includes scatter plots of the first two vowel formants for each speaker, and the complete raw formant data in a CSV file which is adapted from the output of FAVE. This file contains the raw formant measurements of every vowel, including the unfiltered tokens, the formant bandwidths, the phonetic contexts, adjacent words, and other relevant information.

Phonetic contexts are particularly important since many vowel shift patterns are context-dependent. We separate the phonetic contexts into place, manner, and voicing features – for example, the sound `P` would be represented as {place: bilabial, manner: stop, and voicing: unvoiced}. Probabilities are computed under the acoustic model for each of these features. This allows researchers to discard low-probability contexts, or incorporate the probabilities as a gradient measure of the phonetic environment.

The e-mail also includes the filtered formant measurements formatted in a tab-separated file for input to the NORM plotting suite in case the user wants more plotting options, and the aligned ASR transcriptions as TextGrid files, which can be opened by Praat and visualized as in Fig. 1. The user can then check the transcriptions and alignments, make corrections as needed, and re-run the formant extraction step using FAVE for more accurate vowel measurements if desired.

5 Case Study: Obama's State of the Union

We ran the audio of US President Barack Obama's 2015 State of the Union address[7] through our system. The audio of the address is reasonably clean, but the speech is sometimes interrupted by clapping sounds and background noise. The recording is a just over an hour long, and contains 6793 words according to the manual transcript. The decoding, alignment, and formant extraction pipeline takes about 90 minutes to complete.

The ASR transcriptions show a 42% word error rate, and a total stressed vowel error rate of 13%. Of the filtered tokens, the stressed vowel error rate is even better at 9%.

The mean formants from the ASR transcriptions are similar to the formants extracted from the manual text (Fig. 4). The largest discrepancies are in vowels like `OY` which occur less frequently.

Figure 4: Plot of formants averaged over filtered tokens of stressed vowels. This plot shows Obama's vowels as exhibited in the 2015 State of the Union, analyzed using ASR as well as manual transcriptions for comparison. This is the scatterplot that the user receives in the e-mailed output (except that the manual transcription results will not be included).

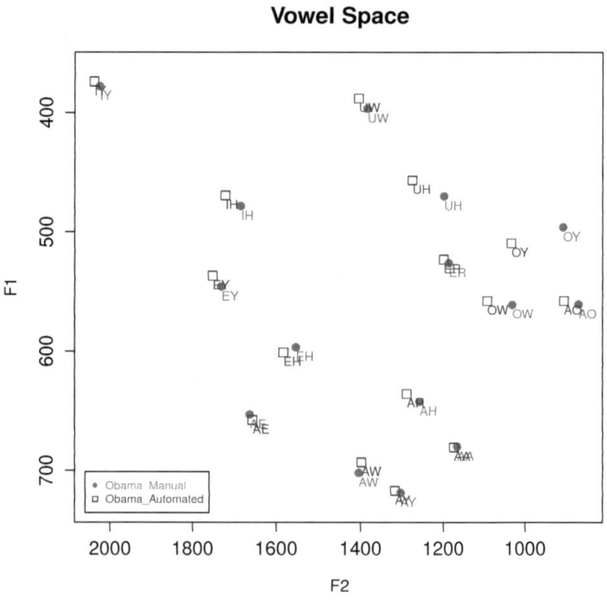

Obama's regional background is often described as a mix of Hawai'i where he spent most of his childhood, Kansas (his mother's home), and Chicago where he worked for much of his professional life. Sociolinguists have shown that children usually acquire most of their dialect features from peers in the local community, not their parents (Labov, 1991). We therefore expect to find influences from Hawai'i

[6] http://cran.r-project.org/web/packages/vowels

[7] The speech and transcripts are taken from http://www.americanrhetoric.com/barackobamaspeeches.htm

and Chicago, and perhaps also a politician's tendency to appeal to a wider audience: in this case, a general northern US audience.

The results in Fig. 4 indicate that Obama has a mix of conservative Northern US vowels with some Midland and Southern influences, based on sociolinguistic dialect descriptions (Labov et al., 2006; Labov, 2007; Eckert, 2008).

(1) In this data, Obama does not show an advanced stage of the Northern Cities Vowel Chain Shift (NCS) prevalent in Chicago. The F_1 of Obama's `AE` vowel is lower than average, which is a prevalent pattern in Chicago, but also in other regions of the US.

(2) He shows clear evidence of "fronting" (high F_2) of the vowels `UW` (*boot*) and `UH` (*hood*). This pattern is common in the West and other regions, and is spreading to the North.

(3) His `AO` and `AA` vowels are distinct, which is common for Chicago and the Inland North and the South, but interestingly, not the West and Hawai'i.

(4) Finally, his `AW` (*bout*) is somewhat fronted – a feature of the Midland and South.

We also analyzed Obama's previous State of the Union addresses and found that his vowels have remained remarkably stable since 2011.

6 Future Work

Since our system is an ongoing project, we will be rolling out several new features in the upcoming months. We are developing an interface to allow users to make corrections to the speech recognition transcriptions (with low-confidence regions highlighted), and receive updated formant measurements. In the longer term, we hope to expand beyond vowel formants by developing phonetic feature classifiers for other dialect variables such as rhoticity, nasality, and prosody. Finally, since the speech recognizer is the most vital component of the system, we are working on improving the ASR error rate by incorporating state-of-the-art technologies that use deep neural nets.

Acknowledgments

We would like to thank Irene Feng for programming assistance, and the developers of FAVE and NORM for permission to use their formant measurement and plotting code. We are grateful for the feedback received from the sociolinguistics community at the NWAV conference and during pilot testing of the application. The first author was supported by a Neukom Fellowship, and further development of the tool is being supported by a Neukom CompX grant.

References

Paul Boersma and David Weenink. 2014. Praat: doing phonetics by computer [computer program]. Available at http://www.praat.org/.

Rajarshi Das, Jonathan Izak, Jiahong Yuan, and Mark Liberman. 2010. Forced alignment under adverse conditions. Unpublished manuscript.

Penelope Eckert. 2008. Where do ethnolects stop? *International Journal of Bilingualism*, 12:25–42.

John Godfrey and Edward Holliman. 1993. *Switchboard-1 Release 2 LDC97S62*. Linguistic Data Consortium, Philadelphia.

Kyle Gorman, Jonathan Howell, and Michael Wagner. 2011. Prosodylab-aligner: A tool for forced alignment of laboratory speech. *Canadian Acoustics*, 39(3):192–93.

Thomas Kisler, Florian Schiel, and Han Sloetjes. 2012. Signal processing via web services: the use case WebMAUS. In *Proceedings of Digital Humanities*.

William Labov, Sharon Ash, and Charles Boberg. 2006. *The Atlas of North American English (ANAE)*. Mouton, Berlin.

William Labov. 1991. *Sociolinguistic patterns*. University of Pennsylvania Press, Philadelphia.

William Labov. 2007. Transmission and diffusion. *Language*, 83(2):344–387.

Sravana Reddy and James N. Stanford. 2015. Toward completely automated vowel extraction: Introducing DARLA. Manuscript. Under review at *Linguistics Vanguard*.

Ingrid Rosenfelder, Josef Fruehwald, Keelan Evanini, Scott Seyfarth, Kyle Gorman, Hilary Prichard, and Jiahong Yuan. 2011. FAVE (Forced Alignment and Vowel Extraction) Program Suite v1.2 doi:10.5281/zenodo.12325. Available at http://fave.ling.upenn.edu.

Erik Thomas and Tyler Kendall. 2007. NORM: The vowel normalization and plotting suite [online resource]. Available at http://ncslaap.lib.ncsu.edu/tools/norm/.

Raphael Winkelmann and Georg Raess. 2014. Introducing a web application for labeling, visualizing speech and correcting derived speech signals. In *Proceedings of LREC*.

An Open-source Framework for Multi-level Semantic Similarity Measurement

Mohammad Taher Pilehvar and **Roberto Navigli**
Department of Computer Science
Sapienza University of Rome
{pilehvar,navigli}@di.uniroma1.it

Abstract

We present an open source, freely available Java implementation of *Align, Disambiguate, and Walk* (ADW), a state-of-the-art approach for measuring semantic similarity based on the Personalized PageRank algorithm. A pair of linguistic items, such as phrases or sentences, are first disambiguated using an alignment-based disambiguation technique and then modeled using random walks on the WordNet graph. ADW provides three main advantages: (1) it is applicable to all types of linguistic items, from word senses to texts; (2) it is all-in-one, i.e., it does not need any additional resource, training or tuning; and (3) it has proven to be highly reliable at different lexical levels and multiple evaluation benchmarks. We are releasing the source code at https://github.com/pilehvar/adw/. We also provide at http://lcl.uniroma1.it/adw/ a Web interface and a Java API that can be seamlessly integrated into other NLP systems requiring semantic similarity measurement.

1 Introduction

Semantic similarity quantifies the extent of shared semantics between two linguistics items, e.g., between *deer* and *moose* or *cat* and *a feline mammal*. Lying at the core of many Natural Language Processing systems, semantic similarity measurement plays an important role in their overall performance and effectiveness. Example applications of semantic similarity include Information Retrieval (Hliaoutakis et al., 2006), Word Sense Disambiguation (Patwardhan et al., 2003), paraphrase recognition (Glickman and Dagan, 2003), lexical substitution (McCarthy and Navigli, 2009) or simplification (Biran et al., 2011), machine translation evaluation (Lavie and Denkowski, 2009), tweet search (Sriram et al., 2010), question answering (Mohler et al., 2011), and lexical resource alignment (Pilehvar and Navigli, 2014).

Owing to its crucial importance a large body of research has been dedicated to semantic similarity. This has resulted in a diversity of similarity measures, ranging from corpus-based methods that leverage the statistics obtained from massive corpora, to knowledge-based techniques that exploit the knowledge encoded in various semantic networks. Align, Disambiguate, and Walk (ADW) is a knowledge-based semantic similarity approach which was originally proposed by Pilehvar et al. (2013). The measure is based on the Personalized PageRank (PPR) algorithm (Haveliwala et al., 2002) applied on the WordNet graph (Miller et al., 1990), and can be used to compute the similarity between arbitrary linguistic items, all the way from word senses to texts. Pilehvar et al. (2013) reported state-of-the-art performance on multiple evaluation benchmarks belonging to different lexical levels: senses, words, and sentences.

In this demonstration we present an open-source implementation of our system together with a Java API and a Web interface for online measurement of semantic similarity. We also introduce a method for offline calculation of the PPR stationary distribution for multiple starting nodes. Moreover, we release the compressed semantic signatures for all the 118K synsets and 155K words of WordNet 3.0.

Proceedings of NAACL-HLT 2015, pages 76–80,
Denver, Colorado, May 31 – June 5, 2015.

2 Align, Disambiguate, and Walk (ADW)

ADW uses a two-phase procedure to model a given pair of linguistic items:

1. The pair is first disambiguated using an alignment-based disambiguation technique. Let a and b be two linguistic items to be compared, and S_w be the set of senses of a word w in the item a which is to be disambiguated. The alignment-based disambiguation measures the semantic similarity of each sense in S_w to all the senses of all the words in the compared item, i.e., b. The sense of w that produces the maximal similarity is taken as its intended sense. The procedure is repeated for all the other words in a and also in the opposite direction for all the words in b.

2. By using the PPR algorithm on the WordNet network, the two disambiguated items are modeled as high-dimensional vectors, called semantic signatures. To this end, ADW initializes the PPR algorithm from all the nodes in the semantic network that correspond to the disambiguated senses of the linguistic item being modeled. The resulting stationary distribution, which has WordNet synsets as its individual dimensions, is taken as the semantic signature of that item.

Finally, the similarity of the two linguistic items is computed as the similarity of their corresponding semantic signatures. We describe in Section 2.2 the four different signature comparison techniques that are implemented and offered in the package. Note that the two phases of ADW are inter-connected, as the alignment-based disambiguation in the first phase requires the generation of the semantic signatures for individual senses of each word in an item, i.e., the second phase.

2.1 Pre-computed semantic signatures

For each measurement of the semantic similarity between two linguistic items, ADW requires the semantic signatures for the two items to be calculated. Moreover, the alignment-based disambiguation of a pair of textual items requires the computation of all the semantic signatures of all their content words. Therefore, a comparison of two items which contain an average of n words involves around $n \times p$ times the calculation of the PPR, where p is the average polysemy of the n words. This can be time-consuming and computationally expensive, particularly for larger textual items such as paragraphs. In order to speed up ADW we pre-computed the semantic signatures for individual WordNet synsets and words. We also provide a procedure for offline computation of semantic signatures for textual items comprising of multiple words, i.e., corresponding to multiple WordNet synsets, boosting the speed of signature generation for these items.

The WordNet graph is constructed by including all types of WordNet relations, and further enriched by means of relations obtained from Princeton Annotated Gloss Corpus[1]. The graph consists of 117,522 nodes (WordNet synsets) which are connected by means of more than half a million non-directed edges.

Individual synsets. We used the UKB package[2] to generate the semantic signatures for all the 118K synsets in WordNet 3.0. Each signature is truncated to the top 5000 most significant dimensions and compressed for better space utilization.

Words. We also generated semantic signatures for around 155K WordNet 3.0 words. To this end, for each word we initialized the PPR algorithm from all the synsets that contained its different senses. The word signatures can be used for faster computation of similarity, if it is not intended to perform alignment-based disambiguation on the items.

Other textual items. ADW computes the semantic signature of a textual item by initializing the PPR algorithm from all the nodes associated with its disambiguated content words. Given that it is simply unfeasible to pre-compute semantic signatures for all possible linguistic items, we put forward an approach which, given the pre-computed signatures for all WordNet synsets, can generate the semantic signature for an arbitrary linguistic item without the need to resort to the PPR algorithm. Let S be the set of synsets s corresponding to all the disambiguated

[1]http://wordnet.princeton.edu/glosstag.shtml

[2]http://ixa2.si.ehu.es/ukb/

```
//the two linguistic items to be compared
String t1 = "fire#v#4";
ItemType t1Type = ItemType.WORD_SENSE;

String t2 = "terminating the employment of a worker";
ItemType t2Type = ItemType.SURFACE;

//method for comparing semantic signatures
SignatureComparison compMethod = new WeightedOverlap();

double similarity = ADW.getInstance().getPairSimilarity(t1, t2,
        DisambiguationMethod.ALIGNMENT_BASED, compMethod, t1Type, t2Type);

System.out.println(similarity);
```

Figure 1: Sample ADW API usage for similarity measurement between a word sense and a phrase.

content words of a given linguistic item T. Considering each normalized semantic signature as a multinomial distribution, the semantic signature of the item T can be alternatively computed as the mean multinomial distribution of the signatures for individual synsets $s \in S$. It can be shown mathematically that the resulting mean distribution is equal to the same stationary distribution obtained by initializing the PPR algorithm from all the nodes corresponding to synsets $s \in S$.

2.2 Signature comparison

Four different methods are included in the package for comparing pairs of semantic signatures: Jensen-Shannon and Kullback-Leibler divergence, cosine, and Weighted Overlap (Pilehvar et al., 2013). Weighted Overlap is a rank similarity measure that computes the similarity of a pair of ranked lists in a harmonic manner, attributing more importance to the top elements than to the bottom ones. Pilehvar et al. (2013) reported improvements over the conventional cosine measure when using Weighted Overlap in multiple tasks and frameworks.

3 Availability

The Java source code can be obtained from ADW's github repository at https://github.com/pilehvar/adw/. We also provide a Java API, an online demo and the set of pre-computed semantic signatures for all the synsets and words in WordNet 3.0 at http://lcl.uniroma1.it/adw/.

4 Using ADW

Figure 1 shows a sample usage of the ADW API. The `getPairSimilarity` method in the `ADW` class receives six parameters: the two linguistic items, the disambiguation method (`ALIGNMENT_BASED` or `NONE`), the signature comparison method, and the types of the two inputs. ADW supports five different types of input:[3]

- **SURFACE**: Raw text (e.g., *A baby plays with a dog*).
- **SURFACE_TAGGED**: Lemmas with part of speech tags (e.g., *baby#n play#v dog#n*). We support only the four open-class parts of speech: nouns (*n*), verbs (*v*), adjectives (*a*), and adverbs (*r*).
- **SENSE_KEYS**: WordNet 3.0 sense keys (e.g., *baby%1:18:00:: play%2:33:00:: dog%1:05:00::*).
- **SENSE_OFFSETS**: WordNet 3.0 synset offsets (e.g., *09827683-n 01072949-v 02084071-n*).
- **WORD_SENSE**: Word senses in the form of lemma[#.]tag[#.]sense_number (e.g., *baby#n#1 play#v#1 dog#n#1* or *baby.n.1 play.v.1 dog.n.1*).

Figure 2 provides a snapshot of ADW's online demo. Two items from two different linguistic levels are being compared: the fourth sense of the verb *fire*[4] and the phrase "terminating the employment of a worker." The user can either choose the input type for each item from the drop-down menu or leave it to be automatically detected by the interface (the "detect automatically" option). The online demo also

[3]All word senses, sense keys and offsets are defined according to WordNet 3.0.

[4]Defined as "terminate the employment of; discharge from an office or position."

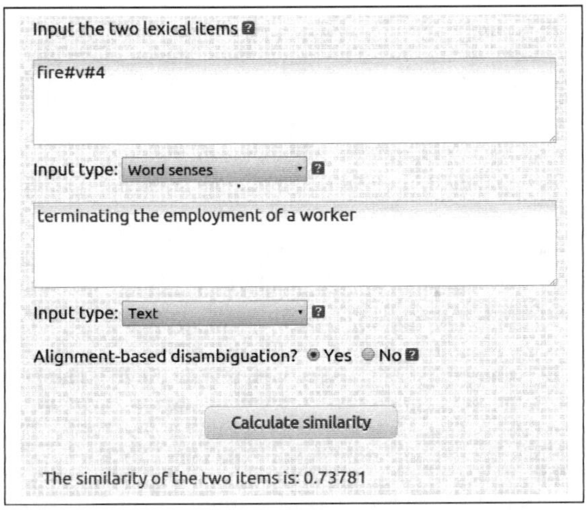

Figure 2: A screenshot of ADW Web interface.

provides users with the possibility to test similarity measurement with no involvement of the disambiguation step.

5 Evaluation

We assessed the implementation of ADW on two evaluation benchmarks: similarity judgement correlation on the RG-65 dataset (Rubenstein and Goodenough, 1965) and synonym recognition on the TOEFL dataset (Landauer and Dumais, 1997). Given a set of word pairs, the task in judgement correlation is to automatically compute the similarity between each pair and judgements are ideally expected to be as close as possible to those assigned by humans. The closeness is usually measured in terms of correlation statistics. In the synonym recognition task, a target word is paired with a set of candidate words from which the most semantically similar word (to the target word) is to be selected.

Table 1 shows the results according to the Spearman ρ and Pearson r correlations on RG-65 and accuracy, i.e., the number of correctly identified synonyms, on TOEFL. We show results for two sets of vectors: full vectors of size 118K and truncated vectors of size 5000 which are provided as a part of the package. As can be seen, despite reducing the space requirement by more than 15 times, our compressed vectors obtain high performance on both the datasets, matching those of the full vectors on the TOEFL dataset and also the cosine measure.

Dataset		Full vector		Truncated (top 5000)	
		Cosine	WO	Cosine	WO
RG-65	r	0.65	0.81	0.65	0.80
	ρ	0.82	0.86	0.82	0.85
TOEFL	%	96.3	95.0	96.3	95.0

Table 1: Performance of ADW on two different word similarity datasets, i.e., RG-65 (according to Spearman ρ and Pearson r correlations) and TOEFL (accuracy percentage), for two different vector comparison methods, i.e., cosine and Weighted Overlap (WO). We show results for two sets of vectors: full vectors with 118K dimensions and truncated vectors of size 5000 which are provided as a part of the package.

6 Related Work

As the de facto standard lexical database, WordNet has been used widely in measuring semantic similarity. Budanitsky and Hirst (2006) provide an overview of WordNet-based similarity measures. WordNet::Similarity, a software developed by Pedersen et al. (2004), provides a Perl implementation of a number of these WordNet-based measures. UMLS::Similarity is an adaptation of WordNet::Similarity to the Unified Medical Language System (UMLS) which can be used for measuring the similarity and relatedness of terms in the biomedical domain (McInnes et al., 2009). Most of these WordNet-based measures suffer from two major drawbacks: (1) they usually exploit only the subsumption relations in WordNet; and (2) they are limited to measuring the semantic similarity of pairs of synsets with the same part of speech. ADW improves both issues by obtaining rich and unified representations for individual synsets, enabling effective comparison of arbitrary word senses or concepts, irrespective of their part of speech.

Distributional semantic similarity measures have also attracted a considerable amount of research attention. The S-Space Package (Jurgens and Stevens, 2010) is an evaluation benchmark and a development framework for word space algorithms, such as Latent Semantic Analysis (Landauer and Dumais, 1997). The package is integrated in DKProSimilarity (Bär et al., 2013), a more recently developed package geared towards semantic similarity of textual items. DKProSimilarity provides an open-source implementation of several semantic similarity techniques, from simple string-based measures such as character n-gram overlap, to more sophisticated vector-based measures such as Explicit Semantic Analysis (Gabrilovich and Markovitch, 2007). ADW was shown to improve the performance of DKProSimilarity (Pilehvar et al., 2013) on the task of semantic textual similarity (Agirre et al., 2012).

Acknowledgments

The authors gratefully acknowledge the support of the ERC Starting Grant MultiJEDI No. 259234.

References

Eneko Agirre, Daniel Cer, Mona Diab, and Aitor Gonzalez-Agirre. 2012. SemEval-2012 task 6: A pilot on semantic textual similarity. In *Proceedings of SemEval-2012*, pages 385–393, Montreal, Canada.

Daniel Bär, Torsten Zesch, and Iryna Gurevych. 2013. DKPro Similarity: An open source framework for text similarity. In *Proceedings of ACL: System Demonstrations*, pages 121–126, Sofia, Bulgaria.

Or Biran, Samuel Brody, and Noémie Elhadad. 2011. Putting it simply: a context-aware approach to lexical simplification. In *Proceedings of ACL*, pages 496–501, Portland, Oregon.

Alexander Budanitsky and Graeme Hirst. 2006. Evaluating WordNet-based measures of Lexical Semantic Relatedness. *Computational Linguistics*, 32(1):13–47.

Evgeniy Gabrilovich and Shaul Markovitch. 2007. Computing semantic relatedness using Wikipedia-based explicit semantic analysis. In *Proceedings of IJCAI*, pages 1606–1611, Hyderabad, India.

Oren Glickman and Ido Dagan. 2003. Acquiring lexical paraphrases from a single corpus. In *Proceedings of RANLP*, pages 81–90, Borovets, Bulgaria.

Taher Haveliwala, A. Gionis Dan Klein, and P. Indyk. 2002. Evaluating strategies for similarity search on the web. In *Proceedings of WWW*, pages 432–442, Honolulu, Hawaii.

Angelos Hliaoutakis, Giannis Varelas, Epimenidis Voutsakis, Euripides GM Petrakis, and Evangelos Milios. 2006. Information retrieval by semantic similarity. *International Journal on Semantic Web and Information Systems*, 2(3):55–73.

David Jurgens and Keith Stevens. 2010. The S-Space package: An open source package for word space models. In *Proceedings of the ACL: System Demonstrations*, pages 30–35, Uppsala, Sweden.

Thomas K. Landauer and Susan T. Dumais. 1997. A solution to Plato's problem: The latent semantic analysis theory of acquisition, induction, and representation of knowledge. *Psychological Review*, 104(2):211.

Alon Lavie and Michael J. Denkowski. 2009. The Meteor metric for automatic evaluation of Machine Translation. *Machine Translation*, 23(2-3):105–115.

Diana McCarthy and Roberto Navigli. 2009. The English lexical substitution task. *Language Resources and Evaluation*, 43(2):139–159.

Bridget T. McInnes, Pedersen Ted, and Serguei V.S. Pakhomov. 2009. UMLS-interface and UMLS-similarity: open source software for measuring paths and semantic similarity. In *Proceedings of AMIA*, pages 431–435, San Fransico, CA.

George A. Miller, R.T. Beckwith, Christiane D. Fellbaum, D. Gross, and K. Miller. 1990. WordNet: an online lexical database. *International Journal of Lexicography*, 3(4):235–244.

Michael Mohler, Razvan Bunescu, and Rada Mihalcea. 2011. Learning to grade short answer questions using semantic similarity measures and dependency graph alignments. In *Proceedings of ACL*, pages 752–762, Portland, Oregon.

Siddharth Patwardhan, Satanjeev Banerjee, and Ted Pedersen. 2003. Using measures of semantic relatedness for Word Sense Disambiguation. In *Proceedings of CICLing*, pages 241–257.

Ted Pedersen, Siddharth Patwardhan, and Jason Michelizzi. 2004. WordNet::Similarity: Measuring the relatedness of concepts. In *Proceedings of HLT-NAACL 2004: Demonstration Papers*, pages 38–41, Boston, Massachusetts.

Mohammad Taher Pilehvar and Roberto Navigli. 2014. A robust approach to aligning heterogeneous lexical resources. In *Proceedings of ACL*, pages 468–478, Baltimore, USA.

Mohammad Taher Pilehvar, David Jurgens, and Roberto Navigli. 2013. Align, Disambiguate and Walk: a Unified Approach for Measuring Semantic Similarity. In *Proceedings of ACL*, pages 1341–1351, Sofia, Bulgaria.

Herbert Rubenstein and John B. Goodenough. 1965. Contextual correlates of synonymy. *Communications of the ACM*, 8(10):627–633.

Bharath Sriram, Dave Fuhry, Engin Demir, Hakan Ferhatosmanoglu, and Murat Demirbas. 2010. Short text classification in Twitter to improve information filtering. In *Proceedings of ACM SIGIR*, pages 841–842, Geneva, Switzerland.

Brahmi-Net: A transliteration and script conversion system for languages of the Indian subcontinent

Anoop Kunchukuttan *
IIT Bombay
anoopk@cse.iitb.ac.in

Ratish Puduppully *†
IIIT Hyderabad
ratish.surendran@research.iiit.ac.in

Pushpak Bhattacharyya
IIT Bombay
pb@cse.iitb.ac.in

Abstract

We present *Brahmi-Net* - an online system for transliteration and script conversion for all major Indian language pairs (306 pairs). The system covers 13 Indo-Aryan languages, 4 Dravidian languages and English. For training the transliteration systems, we mined parallel transliteration corpora from parallel translation corpora using an unsupervised method and trained statistical transliteration systems using the mined corpora. Languages which do not have parallel corpora are supported by transliteration through a bridge language. Our script conversion system supports conversion between all Brahmi-derived scripts as well as ITRANS romanization scheme. For this, we leverage co-ordinated Unicode ranges between Indic scripts and use an extended ITRANS encoding for transliterating between English and Indic scripts. The system also provides top-k transliterations and simultaneous transliteration into multiple output languages. We provide a Python as well as REST API to access these services. The API and the mined transliteration corpus are made available for research use under an open source license.

1 Introduction

The Indian subcontinent is home to some of the most widely spoken languages of the world. It is unique in terms of the large number of scripts used for writing these languages. Most of the these are *abugida* scripts derived from the Brahmi script. *Brahmi* is one of the oldest writing systems of the Indian subcontinent which can be dated to at least the 3rd century B.C.E. In addition, Arabic-derived and Roman scripts are also used for some languages. Given the diversity of languages and scripts, transliteration and script conversion are extremely important to enable effective communication.

The goal of **script conversion** is to represent the source script accurately in the target script, without loss of phonetic information. It is useful for exactly reading manuscripts, signboards, etc. It can serve as a useful tool for linguists, NLP researchers, etc. whose research is multilingual in nature. Script conversion enables reading text written in foreign scripts accurately in a user's native script. On the other hand, **transliteration** aims to conform to the phonology of the target language, while being close to the source language phonetics. Transliteration is needed for phonetic input systems, cross-lingual information retrieval, question-answering, machine translation and other cross-lingual applications.

Brahmi-Net is a general purpose transliteration and script conversion system that aims to provide solutions for South Asian scripts and languages. While transliteration and script conversion are challenging given the scale and diversity, we leverage the commonality in the phonetics and the scriptural systems of these languages. The major features of *Brahmi-Net* are:

1. It supports 18 languages and 306 language pairs for statistical transliteration. The supported languages cover 13 Indo-Aryan language (Assamese, Bengali, Gujarati, Hindi, Konkani, Marathi, Nepali, Odia, Punjabi, Sanskrit, Sindhi, Sinhala, Urdu) , 4 Dravidian lan-

*These authors contributed equally to this project
†Work done while the author was at IIT Bombay

Proceedings of NAACL-HLT 2015, pages 81–85,
Denver, Colorado, May 31 – June 5, 2015. ©2015 Association for Computational Linguistics

guages (Kannada, Malayalam, Tamil, Telugu) and English. To the best of our knowledge, no other system covers as many languages and scripts.

2. It supports script conversion among the following 10 scripts used by major Indo-Aryan and Dravidian languages: Bengali, Gujarati, Kannada, Malayalam, Odia, Punjabi, Devanagari, Sinhala, Tamil and Telugu. Some of these scripts are used for writing multiple languages. Devanagari is used for writing Hindi, Sanskrit, Marathi, Nepali, Konkani and Sindhi. The Bengali script is also used for writing Assamese. Also, Sanskrit has historically been written in many of the above mentioned scripts.

3. The system also supports an extended ITRANS transliteration scheme for romanization of the Indic scripts.

4. The transliteration and script conversion systems are accessible via an online portal. Some additional features include the ability to simultaneously view transliterations to all available languages and the top-k best transliterations.

5. An Application Programming Interface (API) is available as a Python package and a REST interface for easy integration of the transliteration and script conversion systems into other applications requiring transliteration services.

6. As part of the project, parallel transliteration corpora has been mined for transliteration between 110 languages pairs for the following 11 languages: Bengali, Gujarati, Hindi, Konkani, Marathi, Punjabi, Urdu, Malayalam, Tamil, Telugu and English. The parallel transliteration corpora is comprised of 1,694,576 word pairs across all language pairs, which is roughly 15,000 mined pairs per language pair.

2 Script Conversion

Our script conversion engine contains two rule-based systems: one for script conversion amongst scripts of the Brahmi family, and the other for romanization of Brahmi scripts.

2.1 Among scripts of the Brahmi family

Each Brahmi-derived Indian language script has been allocated a distinct codepoint range in the Unicode standard. These scripts have a similar character inventory, but different glyphs. Hence, the first 85 characters in each Unicode block are in the same order and position, on a script by script basis. Our script conversion method simply maps the codepoints between the two scripts.

The Tamil script is different from other scripts since it uses the characters for unvoiced, unaspirated plosives for representing voiced and/or aspirated plosives. When converting into the Tamil script, we substitute all voiced and/or aspirated plosives by the corresponding unvoiced, unaspirated plosive in the Tamil script. For Sinhala, we do an explicit mapping between the characters since the Unicode ranges are not coordinated.

This simple script conversion scheme accounts for a vast majority of the characters. However, there are some characters which do not have equivalents in other scripts, an issue we have not addressed so far. For instance, the Dravidian scripts do not have the *nukta* character.

2.2 Between a Roman transliteration scheme and scripts from the Brahmi family

We chose ITRANS[1] as our transliteration scheme since: (i) it can be entered using Roman keyboard characters, (ii) the Roman character mappings map to Indic script characters in a phonetically intuitive fashion. The official ITRANS specification is limited to the Devanagari script. We have added a few extensions to account for some characters not found in non-Devanagari scripts. Our extended encoding is backward compatible with ITRANS. We convert Devanagari to ITRANS using Alan Little's python module[2]. For romanization of other scripts, we use Devanagari as a pivot script and use the inter-Brahmi script converter mentioned in Section 2.1.

3 Transliteration

Though Indian language scripts are phonetic and largely unambiguous, script conversion is not a sub-

[1] `http://www.aczoom.com/itrans/`

[2] `http://www.alanlittle.org/projects/transliterator/transliterator.html`

stitute for transliteration which needs to account for the target language phonology and orthographic conventions. The main challenges that machine transliteration systems encounter are: script specifications, missing sounds, transliteration variants, language of origin, etc. (Karimi et al., 2011). A summary of the challenges specific to Indian languages is described by Antony, P. J. and Soman, K.P. (2011).

3.1 Transliteration Mining

Statistical transliteration can address these challenges by learning transliteration divergences from a parallel transliteration corpus. For most Indian language pairs, parallel transliteration corpora are not publicly available. Hence, we mine transliteration corpora for 110 language pairs from the ILCI corpus, a parallel translation corpora of 11 Indian languages (Jha, 2012). Transliteration pairs are mined using the unsupervised approach proposed by Sajjad et al. (2012) and implemented in the *Moses* SMT system (Durrani et al., 2014). Their approach models parallel translation corpus generation as a generative process comprising an interpolation of a transliteration and a non-transliteration process. The parameters of the generative process are learnt using the EM procedure, followed by extraction of transliteration pairs from the parallel corpora.

Table 1 shows the statistics of mined pairs. We mined a total of 1.69 million word pairs for 110 language pairs. We observed disparity in the counts of mined transliteration pairs across languages. Language pairs of the Indo-Aryan family from geographically contiguous regions have more number of mined pairs. For instance, the *hin-pan, hin-guj, mar-guj, kok-mar* pairs have high number of mined transliterations averaging more than 30,000 entries. The mined pairs are diverse, containing spelling variations, orthographic variations, sound shifts, cognates and loan words.

3.2 Training transliteration systems

We model the transliteration problem as a phrase based translation problem, a common approach which learns mappings from character sequences in the source language to the target language. The systems were trained on the mined transliteration parallel corpus using *Moses*. The mined pairs are first segmented and a phrase-based machine translation system is trained on them.

We used a hybrid approach for transliteration involving languages for which we could not mine a parallel transliteration corpus. Source languages which cannot be statistically transliterated are first transliterated into a phonetically close language (bridge language) using the above-mentioned rule-based system. The bridge language is then transliterated into the target language using statistical transliteration. Similarly, for target languages which cannot be statistically transliterated, the source is first statistically transliterated into a phonetically close language, followed by rule-based transliteration into the target language.

4 *Brahmi-Net* Interface

Brahmi-Net is accessible via a web interface as well an API. We describe these interfaces in this section.

4.1 Web Interface

The purpose of the Web interface is to allow users quick access to transliteration and script conversion services. They can also choose to see the transliteration/script conversion output in all target languages, making comparison easier. Alternative choices of transliteration can also be studied by requesting the top-5 transliterations for each input. A snapshot of the interface is shown in Figure 1. The web interface is accessible at:

`http://www.cfilt.iitb.ac.in/brahminet/`

4.2 REST API

We provide a REST interface to access the transliteration and script conversion services. Simultaneous transliterations/script conversion into all languages and top-k transliterations are also available. The REST endpoints have an intuitive signature. For instance, to fetch the transliteration for a word from English (en) to Hindi (hi), the REST endpoint is:

```
http://www.cfilt.iitb.ac.in/indicnlpweb/
indicnlpws/transliterate/en/hi/<input>/statistical
```

The API returns a serialized JSON object containing a dictionary of target language to top-k transliterations. The detailed API reference is available on the website.

	hin	urd	pan	ben	guj	mar	kok	tam	tel	mal	eng
hin	-	21185	40456	26880	29554	13694	16608	9410	17607	10519	10518
urd	21184	-	23205	11379	14939	9433	9811	4102	5603	3653	5664
pan	40459	23247	-	25242	29434	21495	21077	7628	15484	8324	8754
ben	26853	11436	25156	-	33125	26947	26694	10418	18303	11293	7543
guj	29550	15019	29434	33166	-	39633	35747	12085	22181	11195	6550
mar	13677	9523	21490	27004	39653	-	31557	10164	18378	9758	4878
kok	16613	9865	21065	26748	35768	31556	-	9849	17599	9287	5560
tam	9421	4132	7668	10471	12107	10148	9838	-	12138	10931	3500
tel	17649	5680	15598	18375	22227	18382	17409	12146	-	12314	4433
mal	10584	3727	8406	11375	11249	9788	9333	10926	12369	-	3070
eng	10513	5609	8751	7567	6537	4857	5521	3549	4371	3039	-

Table 1: Mined Pairs Statistics (ISO-639-2 language codes are shown)

Figure 1: *Brahmi-Net* Web Interface

Lang Pair	**Rule**	**Statistical**	
		top-1	*top-5*
ben-mar	64.6	68.3	87.1
mal-tam	27.9	30.9	66.0
mar-ben	68.0	67.3	85.2
tel-mar	68.2	70.9	87.5

Table 2: Transliteration Accuracy (%)

5 Evaluation

5.1 Transliteration Accuracy

We evaluated the top-1 and top-5 transliteration accuracy for a sample set of language pairs. For this evaluation, we used an internally available, manually created corpus of 1000 transliteration pairs for each language pair. These transliterations were manually curated from synsets in *IndoWordNet*[3] Though this corpus does not reflect the diversity in the mined transliterations, evaluation on this corpus could be a pointer to utility of the transliteration corpus. We compare the accuracy of match for transliteration against the rule based script conversion output for some language pairs. Table 2 shows the accuracy values. *top-1* indicates exact match for the first transliteration output returned by our system, whereas *top-5* indicates match in the top 5 transliterations returned by the system.

5.2 Case Study: Improving SMT output

Our work in developing the transliteration systems was initially motivated by the need for transliterating the untranslated words in SMT output. To evaluate the transliteration systems in the context of machine translation, we post-edited the phrase based system (PB-SMT) outputs of Indian language pairs provided by Kunchukuttan et al. (2014) using our transliteration systems. Each untranslated word was replaced by each of its top-1000 transliterations and the resulting candidate sentences were re-ranked using a language model. We observe a significant improvement in translation quality across language pairs, as measured by the BLEU evaluation metric. Due to space constraints, we present results for only 8 language pairs in Table 3. We observed that though the system's best transliteration is not always correct, the sentence context and the language model select the right transliteration from the top-k transliteration

[3] `http://www.cfilt.iitb.ac.in/indowordnet`

Lang Pair	PB-SMT	PB-SMT +translit
urd-eng	21.0	21.59
tel-eng	12.09	12.34
kok-ben	24.61	27.69
pan-hin	71.26	75.25
mar-pan	34.75	36.92
tel-mal	6.58	7.54
guj-tel	16.57	18.61
tal-urd	15.65	16.22

Table 3: Results of PB-SMT output + transliteration of OOVs (%BLEU)

candidates. The top-k transliterations can thus be disambiguated by SMT or other downstream applications.

6 Conclusion

Brahmi-Net is an effort to provide a comprehensive transliteration and script conversion solution for all languages of the Indian subcontinent. Unsupervised transliteration mining and leveraging the phonetic and scriptural similarities between the languages have been the key ingredients in scaling the system to a large number of languages. Even the simple phrase based SMT model of transliteration has proved useful for transliterating the output of MT systems. A natural extension would be to employ richer transliteration models. There is scope for improvement in the hybrid models of transliteration used in the system. Some of the finer details regarding script conversions have to be ironed out. Finally, a long term goal is to support other major languages from South Asia, which differ phonetically from the Indo-Aryan and Dravidian languages or use non-Brahmi scripts.

Acknowledgments

We would like to thank Arjun Atreya for making available parallel transliterations from *IndoWordNet* for evaluation of our system.

References

Antony, P. J. and Soman, K.P. 2011. Machine Transliteration for Indian Languages: A Literature Survey. *International Journal of Scientific and Engineering Research.*

Nadir Durrani, Hieu Hoang, Philipp Koehn, and Hassan Sajjad. 2014. Integrating an Unsupervised Transliteration Model into Statistical Machine Translation. *EACL 2014.*

Girish Nath Jha. 2012. The TDIL program and the Indian Language Corpora Initiative. In *Language Resources and Evaluation Conference.*

Sarvnaz Karimi, Falk Scholer, and Andrew Turpin. 2011. Machine transliteration survey. *ACM Computing Surveys.*

Anoop Kunchukuttan, Abhijit Mishra, Rajen Chatterjee, Ritesh Shah, and Pushpak Bhattacharyya. 2014. Sata-Anuvadak: Tackling Multiway Translation of Indian Languages. In *Language Resources and Evaluation Conference.*

Hassan Sajjad, Alexander Fraser, and Helmut Schmid. 2012. A statistical model for unsupervised and semi-supervised transliteration mining. In *Proceedings of the 50th Annual Meeting of the Association for Computational Linguistics.*

A Concrete Chinese NLP Pipeline

Nanyun Peng, Francis Ferraro, Mo Yu, Nicholas Andrews,
Jay DeYoung, Max Thomas, Matthew R. Gormley, Travis Wolfe,
Craig Harman, Benjamin Van Durme, Mark Dredze
Human Language Technology Center of Excellence
Johns Hopkins University, Baltimore, Maryland USA

Abstract

Natural language processing research increasingly relies on the output of a variety of syntactic and semantic analytics. Yet integrating output from multiple analytics into a single framework can be time consuming and slow research progress. We present a CONCRETE Chinese NLP Pipeline: an NLP stack built using a series of open source systems integrated based on the CONCRETE data schema. Our pipeline includes data ingest, word segmentation, part of speech tagging, parsing, named entity recognition, relation extraction and cross document coreference resolution. Additionally, we integrate a tool for visualizing these annotations as well as allowing for the manual annotation of new data. We release our pipeline to the research community to facilitate work on Chinese language tasks that require rich linguistic annotations.

1 Introduction

Over the past few years, the natural language processing community has shifted its attention towards the Chinese language, with numerous papers covering a range of NLP tasks for Chinese. Last year's EMNLP and ACL alone featured two dozen papers focused primarily on Chinese data[1], not including many others that considered Chinese language data within a broader context. The large number of Chinese speakers, coupled with the unique challenges of Chinese compared to well studied Romance and Germanic languages, have driven these research efforts. This focus has given rise to new NLP systems that enable the automated processing of Chinese data. While some pipelines cover multiple tasks, such as Stanford CoreNLP (Manning et al., 2014), other tasks such as relation extraction are not included.

Modern NLP research, including research focused on Chinese, often relies on automatically produced analytics, or annotations, from multiple stages of linguistic analysis. Downstream systems, such as sentiment analysis and question answering, assume that data has been pre-processed by a variety of syntactic and semantic analytics. Consider the task of knowledge base population (KBP), in which information is extracted from text corpora for inclusion in a knowledge base. Associated information extraction systems rely on various NLP analytics run on the data of interest, such as relation extractors that require the identification of named entities and syntactically parsed text. Similarly, entity linking typically assumes the presence of within document coreference resolution, named entity identification and relation extraction. These analytics themselves rely on other core NLP systems, such as part of speech tagging and syntactic parsing.

While each of these tasks have received extensive attention and have associated research software for producing annotations, the output of these components must be integrated into a single cohesive framework for use in a downstream task. This integration faces a wide variety of challenges resulting from the simple fact that most research systems are designed to produce good performance on an eval-

[1] Excluding the Chinese Restaurant Process.

Proceedings of NAACL-HLT 2015, pages 86–90,

uation metric, but are not designed for integration in a pipeline. Beyond the production of integrated NLP pipelines, research groups often produce resources of corpora annotated by multiple systems, such as the Annotated Gigaword Corpus (Napoles et al., 2012). Effective sharing of these corpora requires a common standard.

These factors lead to the recent development of CONCRETE, a data schema that represents numerous types of linguistic annotations produced by a variety of NLP systems (Ferraro et al., 2014). CONCRETE enables interoperability between NLP systems, facilitates the development of large scale research systems, and aids sharing of richly annotated corpora.

This paper describes a Chinese NLP pipeline that ingests Chinese text to produce richly annotated data. The pipeline relies on existing Chinese NLP systems that encompass a variety of syntactic and semantic tasks. Our pipeline is built on the CONCRETE data schema to produce output in a structured, coherent and shareable format. To be clear, our goal is *not* the development of new methods or research systems. Rather, our focus is the integration of multiple tools into a single pipeline. The advantages of this newly integrated pipeline lie in the fact that the components of the pipeline communicate through a unified data schema: CONCRETE. By doing so, we can

- easily switch each component of the pipeline to any state-of-the-art model;
- keep several annotations of the same type generated by different tools; and
- easily share the annotated corpora.

Furthermore, we integrate a visualization tool for viewing and editing the annotated corpora. We posit all the above benefits as the contributions of this paper and hope the efforts can facilitate ongoing Chinese focused research and aid in the construction and distribution of annotated corpora. Our code is available at `http://hltcoe.github.io`.

2 The CONCRETE Data Schema

We use CONCRETE, a recently introduced data schema designed to capture and layer many different types of NLP output (Ferraro et al., 2014).[2] A primary purpose of CONCRETE is to ease analytic pipelining. Based on Apache Thrift (Slee et al., 2007), it captures NLP output via a number of inter-working structs, which are translated automatically into in-memory representations for many common programming languages, including Java, C++ and Python. In addition to being, in practice, language-agnostic, CONCRETE and Thrift try to limit programmer error: Thrift generates I/O libraries, making it easy for analytics to read and write CONCRETE files; with this common format and I/O libraries, developers can more easily share NLP output. Unlike XML or JSON, Thrift's automatic validation of strongly typed annotations help ensure legitimate annotations: developers cannot accidentally populate a field with the wrong type of object, nor must they manually cast values.

CONCRETE allows both within-document and cross-document annotations. The former includes standard tagging tasks (e.g., NER or POS), syntactic parses, relation extraction and entity coreference, though Ferraro et al. (2014) show how CONCRETE can capture deeper semantics, such as frame semantic parses and semantic roles. These within-document annotations, such as entity coref, can form the basis of cross-document annotations.

We chose CONCRETE as our data schema to support as many NLP analytics as possible. In the future, we plan to add additional analytics to our pipeline, and we expect other research groups to integrate their own tools. A flexible and well documented data schema is critical for these goals. Furthermore, the release of multiple corpora in CONCRETE (Ferraro et al., 2014) support our goal of facilitating the construction and distribution of new Chinese corpora.

3 Analytic Pipeline

We describe each stage of our pipeline with a brief description of the associated tool and relevant details of its integration into the pipeline.

[2]CONCRETE, language interfaces, and utility libraries are open-source projects (`https://hltcoe.github.io/`).

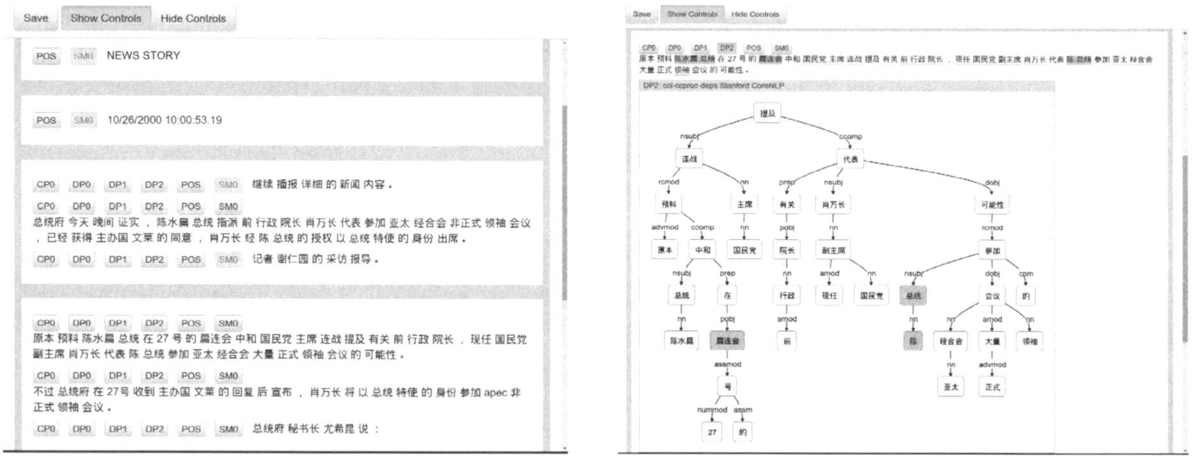

(a) The basic visualization of a `Communication`. Each line is a tokenized sentence, with options to view the part of speech, constituency and dependency parse, and entity relation information.

(b) Multiple types of annotations can be viewed simultaneously. Here, entity information is laid atop a dependency parse. A particular mention-of-interest is shown in yellow, with all other mentions in pink.

Figure 1: CONCRETE `Communication` containing Chinese text displayed in Quicklime (section 3.7).

3.1 Data Ingest

The first stage of our pipeline requires ingesting existing Chinese text into CONCRETE `Communication` objects, the core document representation of CONCRETE. The existing CONCRETE Java and Python utilities support ingesting raw text files. Part of this process requires not only ingesting the raw text, but identifying section (paragraph) and sentence boundaries.

Not all corpora contain raw text, as many corpora come with existing manual (or automatic) linguistic annotations. We provide code to support two data formats of existing Chinese corpora: the Chinese ACE 2005 relation extraction dataset (Walker et al., 2006) and the new Chinese Entities, Relations, and Events (ERE) dataset (Consortium, 2013). Both data sets include annotations for entities and a variety of relations (Aguilar et al., 2014). The labeled entities and relations are represented by CONCRETE `EntityMentions` and stored in a `EntityMentionSetList`. Additional annotations that are typically utilized by relation extraction systems, such as syntactic parses, are provided automatically by the pipeline.

3.2 Word Segmentation

Chinese text processing requires the identification of word boundaries, which are not indicated in written Chinese as they are in most other languages. Our word segmentation is provided by the Stanford CoreNLP[3] (Manning et al., 2014) Chinese word segmentation tool, which is a conditional random field (CRF) model with character based features and lexicon features according to Chang et al. (2008). Word segmentations decisions are represented by CONCRETE `Token` objects and stored in the `TokenList`. We follow the Chinese Penn Treebank segmentation standard (Xue et al., 2005). Our system tracks token offsets so that segmentation is robust to unexpected spaces or line breaks within a Chinese word.

3.3 Syntax

Part of speech tagging and syntactic parsing are also provided by Stanford CoreNLP. The part of speech tagger is based on Toutanova et al. (2003) adapted for Chinese, which is a log-linear model underneath. Integration with CONCRETE was facilitated by the concrete-stanford library [4], though supporting Chinese required significant modifications to the

[3] http://nlp.stanford.edu/software/corenlp.shtml

[4] https://github.com/hltcoe/concrete-stanford

library. Resulting tags are stored in a CONCRETE `TokenTaggingList`.

Syntactic constituency parsing is based on the model of Klein and Manning (2003) adapted for Chinese. We obtained dependency parses from the CoreNLP dependency converter. We store the constituency parses as a CONCRETE `Parse`, and the dependency analyses as CONCRETE `DependencyParses`.

3.4 Named Entity Recognition

We support the two most common named entity annotation standards: the CoNLL standard (four types: person, organization, location and miscellaneous), and the ACE standard, which includes the additional types of geo-political entity, facility, weapon and vehicle. The ACE standard also includes support for nested entities. We used the Stanford CoreNLP NER toolkit which is a CRF model based on the method in Finkel et al. (2005), plus features based on Brown clustering. For the CoNLL standard annotations, we use one CRF model to label all the four types of entities. For the ACE standard annotations, in order to deal with the nested cases, we build one tagger for each entity type. Each entity is stored in a CONCRETE `EntityMention`.

3.5 Relation Extraction

Relations are extracted for every pair of entity mentions. We use a log-linear model with both traditional hand-crafted features and word embedding features. The hand-crafted features include all the baseline features of Zhou et al. (2005) (excluding the Country gazeteer and WordNet features), plus several additional carefully-chosen features that have been highly tuned for ACE-style relation extraction over years of research (Sun et al., 2011). The embedding-based features are from Yu et al. (2014), which represent each word as the outer product between its word embedding and a list of its associated non-lexical features. The non-lexical features indicate the word's relative positions comparing to the target entities (whether the word is the head of any target entity, in-between the two entities, or on the dependency path between entities), which improve the expressive strength of word embeddings. We store the extracted relations in CONCRETE `SituationMentions`. See Figure 2 for

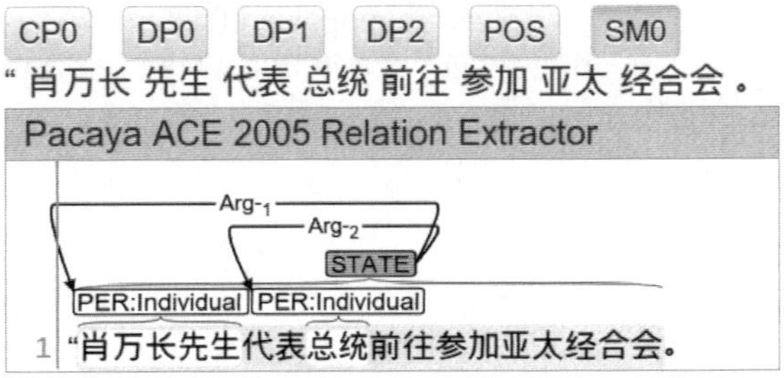

Figure 2: ACE entity relations viewed through Quicklime (Section 3.7).

an example visualization.

3.6 Cross Document Coreference Resolution

Cross document coreference resolution is performed via the phylogenetic entity clustering model of Andrews et al. (2014).[5] Since the method is fully unsupervised we did not require a Chinese specific model. We use this system to cluster `EntityMentions` and store the clustering in top level CONCRETE `Clustering` objects.

3.7 Creating Manual Annotations

Quicklime[6] is a browser-based tool for viewing and editing NLP annotations stored in a CONCRETE document. Quicklime supports a wide array of analytics, including parse trees, token taggings, entities, mentions, and "situations" (e.g. relations.) Quicklime uses the visualization layer of BRAT (Stenetorp et al., 2012) to display some annotations but does not use the BRAT annotation editing layer. BRAT annotations are stored in a standoff file format, whereas Quicklime reads and writes CONCRETE objects using the Thrift JavaScript APIs. Figure 1 shows Quicklime displaying annotations on Chinese data. In particular, Quicklime can combine and overlay multiple annotations, such as entity extraction and dependency parses, as in Figure 1b. Figure 2 shows entity relation annotations.

Acknowledgments

We would like to thank the reviewers for their helpful comments and perspectives. A National Science Foundation Graduate Research Fellowship, under

[5] https://bitbucket.org/noandrews/phyloinf

[6] https://github.com/hltcoe/quicklime

Grant No. DGE-1232825, supported the second author. Any opinions expressed in this work are those of the authors.

References

Jacqueline Aguilar, Charley Beller, Paul McNamee, and Benjamin Van Durme. 2014. A comparison of the events and relations across ace, ere, tac-kbp, and framenet annotation standards. *ACL 2014*, page 45.

Nicholas Andrews, Jason Eisner, and Mark Dredze. 2014. Robust entity clustering via phylogenetic inference. In *Association for Computational Linguistics*.

Pi-Chuan Chang, Michel Galley, and Christopher D Manning. 2008. Optimizing chinese word segmentation for machine translation performance. In *Third Workshop on Statistical Machine Translation*.

Linguistic Data Consortium. 2013. DEFT ERE annotation guidelines: Events v1.1.

Francis Ferraro, Max Thomas, Matthew R. Gormley, Travis Wolfe, Craig Harman, and Benjamin Van Durme. 2014. Concretely Annotated Corpora. In *AKBC Workshop at NIPS*.

Jenny Rose Finkel, Trond Grenager, and Christopher Manning. 2005. Incorporating non-local information into information extraction systems by gibbs sampling. In *ACL*.

Dan Klein and Christopher D Manning. 2003. Accurate unlexicalized parsing. In *ACL*.

Christopher D. Manning, Mihai Surdeanu, John Bauer, Jenny Finkel, Steven J. Bethard, and David McClosky. 2014. The Stanford CoreNLP natural language processing toolkit. In *ACL: Demos*.

Courtney Napoles, Matthew Gormley, and Benjamin Van Durme. 2012. Annotated gigaword. In *AKBC-WEKEX Workshop at NAACL 2012*.

Mark Slee, Aditya Agarwal, and Marc Kwiatkowski. 2007. Thrift: Scalable cross-language services implementation. Facebook White Paper.

Pontus Stenetorp, Sampo Pyysalo, Goran Topić, Sophia Ananiadou, and Akiko Aizawa. 2012. Normalisation with the brat rapid annotation tool. In *International Symposium on Semantic Mining in Biomedicine*.

Ang Sun, Ralph Grishman, and Satoshi Sekine. 2011. Semi-supervised relation extraction with large-scale word clustering. In *ACL*.

Kristina Toutanova, Dan Klein, Christopher D Manning, and Yoram Singer. 2003. Feature-rich part-of-speech tagging with a cyclic dependency network. In *NAACL*.

Christopher Walker, Stephanie Strassel, Julie Medero, and Kazuaki Maeda. 2006. Ace 2005 multilingual training corpus ldc2006t06. *Linguistic Data Consortium*.

Naiwen Xue, Fei Xia, Fu-Dong Chiou, and Marta Palmer. 2005. The penn chinese treebank: Phrase structure annotation of a large corpus. *Natural language engineering*, 11(02):207–238.

Mo Yu, Matthew Gormley, and Mark Dredze. 2014. Factor-based compositional embedding models. In *NIPS Workshop on Learning Semantics*.

GuoDong Zhou, Jian Su, Jie Zhang, and Min Zhang. 2005. Exploring various knowledge in relation extraction. In *ACL*, pages 427–434.

CroVeWA: Crosslingual Vector-Based Writing Assistance

Hubert Soyer[1*], **Goran Topić**[1], **Pontus Stenetorp**[2†] **and Akiko Aizawa**[1]
[1] National Institute of Informatics, 2-1-2 Hitotsubashi, Chiyoda-ku, Tokyo, Japan
[2] University of Tokyo, 7-3-1 Hongo, Bunkyo-ku, Tokyo, Japan
{soyer,goran_topic,aizawa}@nii.ac.jp pontus@stenetorp.se

Abstract

We present an interactive web-based writing assistance system that is based on recent advances in crosslingual compositional distributed semantics. Given queries in Japanese or English, our system can retrieve semantically related sentences from high quality English corpora. By employing crosslingually constrained vector space models to represent phrases, our system naturally sidesteps several difficulties that would arise from direct word-to-text matching, and is able to provide novel functionality like the visualization of semantic relationships between phrases interlingually and intralingually.

1 Introduction

Writing high quality texts in a foreign language requires years of study and a deep comprehension of the language. With a society that is becoming more and more international, the ability to express ideas in English has become the basis of fruitful communication and collaboration.

In this work, we propose a tool to provide non-native speakers of English with help in their translation or writing process. Instead of relying on manually created dictionaries, many existing tools leverage parallel bilingual corpora, using a concordancer to provide translation suggestions together with their contexts. Notable examples relevant to this demonstration are `linguee.com` and `tradooit.com`. Given a word or a phrase in a foreign language, these systems present example sentences containing the query in the source language as well as the target language, showing the correct usage of the word/phrase, and at the same time providing translation candidates.

Many applications rely on direct word-to-text matching and are therefore prone to missing semantically similar contexts that, although similar and relevant, do not share any words with the query. Instead of matching words directly, we propose a system that employs crosslingually constrained vector representations (embeddings) of words and phrases to retrieve English sentences that are similar to a given phrase or word in a different language (query). These vector representations not only allow for efficient crosslingual lookups in databases consisting of millions of sentences, but can also be employed to visualize intralingual and interlingual semantic relationships between phrases.

2 Related Work

Various types of neural network models have been proposed to induce distributed word representations and leveraging these word embeddings as features has proven viable in achieving state-of-the-art results for a variety of tasks (Baroni et al., 2014; Collobert and Weston, 2008).

Recently, methods that attempt to compose embeddings not only of words but of whole phrases (Le and Mikolov, 2014; Socher et al., 2011) have enabled vector representations to be applied for tasks that are defined over phrases, sentences, or even documents. The most relevant work for this paper are recent approaches that allow for the induction of

*Currently at Google DeepMind.
†Currently at University College London.

Proceedings of NAACL-HLT 2015, pages 91–95,
Denver, Colorado, May 31 – June 5, 2015.

word and phrase embeddings not only from monolingual text but using bilingual resources to constrain vector representations crosslingually. (Soyer et al., 2015; Hermann and Blunsom, 2014; Cho et al., 2014; Chandar A P et al., 2014). Embeddings learned using these methods not only possess meaningful properties within a language, but also interlingually.

3 Crosslingual Vector-Based Writing Assistance (CroVeWA)

Our system harnesses crosslingually constrained word and phrase representations to retrieve and visualize sentences related to given queries, using distances in the word/phrase vector space as a measure of semantic relatedness. Currently, our system supports the lookup of Japanese and English queries in English text.

Our system encourages refining retrieved results and viewing relations in different contexts by supporting multiple queries. All queries and their corresponding results are visualized together to aid a better understanding of their relationships. To illustrate the differences to phrase vector-based sentence retrieval, we also offer a retrieval option based on direct word-to-text matching using the EDICT Japanese-English dictionary (Breen, 2004) and Apache Lucene[1] for sentence retrieval.

To the best of our knowledge, our system is the first to provide writing assistance using vector representations of words and phrases.

3.1 Inducing Crosslingually Constrained Word Representations

We employ the approach presented in Soyer et al. (2015) to learn bilingually constrained representations of Japanese and English words. The method draws from sentence-parallel bilingual text to constrain word vectors crosslingually, handles text on a phrase level ensuring the compositionality of the induced word embeddings, and is agnostic to how phrase representations are assembled from word representations. In addition, unlike previously proposed models, the model can draw not only from bilingual sentence aligned data but also from arbitrary monolingual data in either language. Figure 1 depicts an overview over the method.

The method optimizes the vectors that represent each word in subject to a bilingual and a monolingual objective. These objectives operate on a phrase level, where each phrase is represented by a single vector. Composing a single vector of a given phrase means looking up the word vector for each word in a lookup table shared among all sentences of the phrase-language, and applying a composition function to collapse all word vectors of a phrase into a single phrase vector. The composition function used in this work is the arithmetic mean.

The *bilingual objective* ensures that vectors of Japanese sentences are close to the vectors of their English translations present in the sentence-parallel corpus. It minimizes the squared euclidean distance between the sentence vector of a Japanese sentence and the vector of its English translation. With the arithmetic mean as the sentence composition function, this notion of translational closeness is directly propagated back into the embeddings of the individual words that appear in each sentence. If a Japanese and an English word consistently co-occur in the translation pairs of the sentence-parallel corpus, their vectors will be moved close to each other, capturing that they are likely to be related in meaning.

The *monolingual objective* exploits the insight that sub-phrases generally tend to be closer in meaning to the phrases they are contained in, than to most other arbitrary phrases. It punishes a large euclidean distance between the vector representation of a phrase and its sub-phrase, and at the same time rewards a large distance between the vector of the phrase and the embedding of another phrase chosen at random.

Both the monolingual objective and the bilingual objective are combined to leverage monolingual and bilingual resources at the same time. Using the arithmetic mean to compose phrase vectors discards word-order as well as sentence-length information, and allows our system to handle even single words or ungrammatical sequences of words.

Currently we use Japanese and English resources to learn word embeddings, but plan to add more languages in the future. The bilingual sentence-parallel

[1] `https://lucene.apache.org/core/`

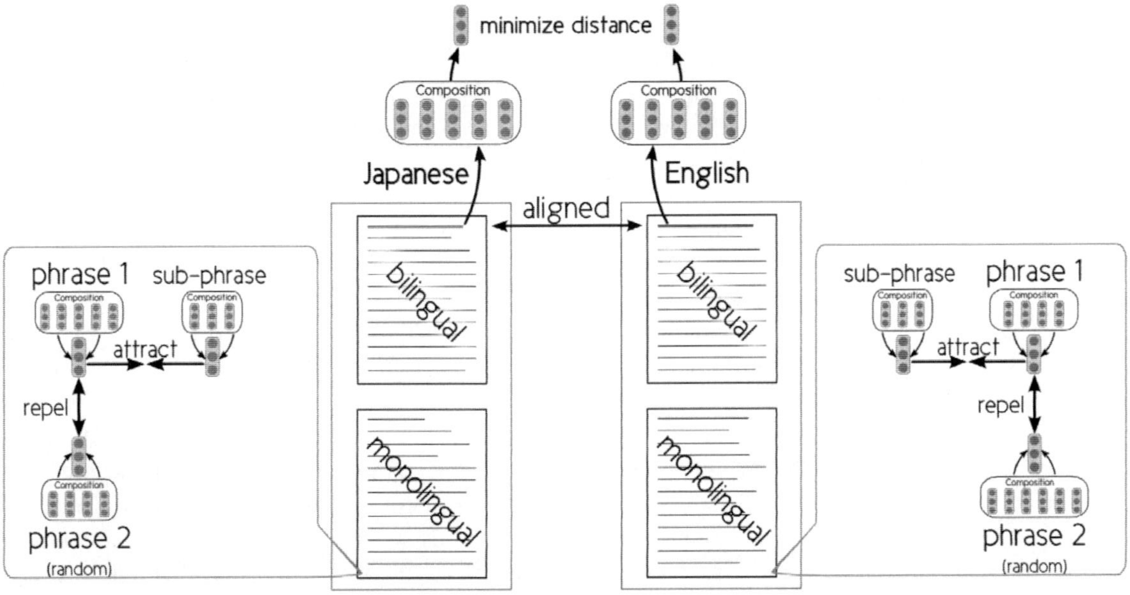

Figure 1: Overview of the method that was used to induce crosslingually constrained word representations. The method can draw from bilingual sentence-parallel data as well as monolingual data.

resource used is the ASPEC corpus[2], which features sentence-aligned text from scientific paper abstracts. For monolingual data, we use subsets of the Japanese and English Wikipedia.

3.2 Finding Related English Sentences for a Japanese Query

Inducing crosslingually constrained word representations leaves us with two sets of vectors, one corresponding to Japanese words and one to English words. Given a query in **Japanese**, we look up the vectors for each individual query word, compose them into a single query vector and find the nearest neighbors in a set of pre-computed vectors of **English** sentences. Since the word and phrase vectors are crosslingually constrained, we expect the retrieved English nearest neighbors to be semantically related to the Japanese query. In contrast to conventional word matching techniques, our vector-based approach does not require Japanese translations of the English sentences we consider during the search, nor does it require a Japanese-English dictionary.

Another difference to word matching techniques follows from the way word vectors are arranged within the same language. Generally, words that appear in similar contexts will be placed close to each other in the vector space, and so the difference between choosing a word over a closely related neighbor will be relatively small when composing a phrase vector. Interchangeability of synonyms or semantically similar words is therefore automatically supported as a property of the word representations, and the system can retrieve sentences similar in meaning regardless of the exact choice of words.

Following Mikolov et al. (2013) we use the cosine similarity as a measure of similarity between embeddings. For nearest neighbor retrieval we employ the FLANN Python module (Muja and Lowe, 2009) which exploits the clustered nature of vector representations to efficiently find an approximate set of nearest neighbors.

3.3 Visualization

In contrast to direct word matching, vector-representation-based matching retrieves not only a list of related sentences, but also a semantic vector space position for each query and result. In order to visualize the high-dimensional output vectors of the search we reduce their dimensionality to two.

Generally, reducing dimensionality involves dis-

[2] http://orchid.kuee.kyoto-u.ac.jp/ASPEC/

carding information. Commonly employed methods for this task such as, Principal Component Analysis or t-SNE (Van der Maaten and Hinton, 2008), failed to provide satisfactory results for our purposes. Instead, we apply a novel variant of multidimensional scaling (Kruskal, 1964) where we prioritize the preservation of query-to-result distances over the preservation of result-to-result distances. This yields a visually more interpretable output, with queries being the points of orientation.

An interactive plot of the resulting 2D points, illustrates the relationships between the different sentences, puts the retrieved results into context and aids the user's understanding of the meaning and relatedness of sentences. Being able to visualize these relationships is another aspect that sets our system apart from previously proposed word-to-text matching approaches.

3.4 Demonstration System

We will guide the audience through the features of our application using a set of example queries that highlight the merits and drawbacks of vector-based crosslingual sentence retrieval. Based on these query examples we will introduce novel functionality, such as our system's visualization of semantic relationships or its feature for query auto-generation. The interactive nature of our tool allows us to incorporate requests and comments into the demonstration, helping to clarify questions and to explain properties of our system.

Our system is built as a web application and therefore only requires the user to have a modern browser and an Internet connection. Figure 2 shows a screenshot of the user interface, which consists of the query input bar at the top of the screen, a result list on the left and a visualization panel on the right. For clarity, we have annotated the screenshot: annotations with white background show results and their positions in the visualization, while the ones with red background provide translations of the Japanese queries.

In the query input bar users can customize the search through a variety of options. Via the query input field a user can submit Japanese queries which can be a single word, a phrase or any sequence of words. Pushing the *Auto-Generate* button will split the entered text into semantically related groups of words and submit these groups as separate queries to visualize the relatedness of different parts of the entered text. Since not every potential user might be familiar with Japanese we provide an *English simulation mode* to input English queries and retrieve English results. We refer to this mode as *simulation* because the lookup from English to English is not crosslingual. For comparison, and as an extension to the vector-based sentence retrieval, we also provide a dictionary-based word-to-text matching search mode using the Japanese-English EDICT dictionary. Clicking the *Samples* button invokes a dialog that presents example queries to choose from. We currently provide three corpora to search, where each corpus covers a different domain. The ASPEC corpus consists of Japanese and English scientific paper abstracts related to natural sciences and engineering, the Wikipedia corpus comprises 10 million randomly selected sentences from the English Wikipedia, and the PubMed corpus features 5 million sentences from the PubMed Central collection of medical paper abstracts.

Queries make up the first entries in the result list, with fully colored backgrounds. In the visualization panel queries are represented by larger points. If two or more queries have been submitted we additionally provide a *Query Average* to retrieve results that are related to all submitted queries. Every result entry that follows the queries is colored according to the closest query from those that retrieved it. The fill level of the background of each result item indicates its similarity to the *Query Average*. Hovering the cursor over a list entry will highlight its corresponding point and vice versa. Clicking on a list entry will auto-generate queries from its text, clustering related words together to provide a visualization of the different topics the text consists of.

The annotations in Figure 2 illustrate how the system's visualization can aid a user in understanding the meaning of a sentence. The distance between a result and a query indicates their semantic closeness. Sentences located close to a query point are strongly related to the query (*canal* and *river* or *subway station* and *railway station*), phrases in between the queries feature aspects of both submitted queries (*flooding*, *subway* and *city*).

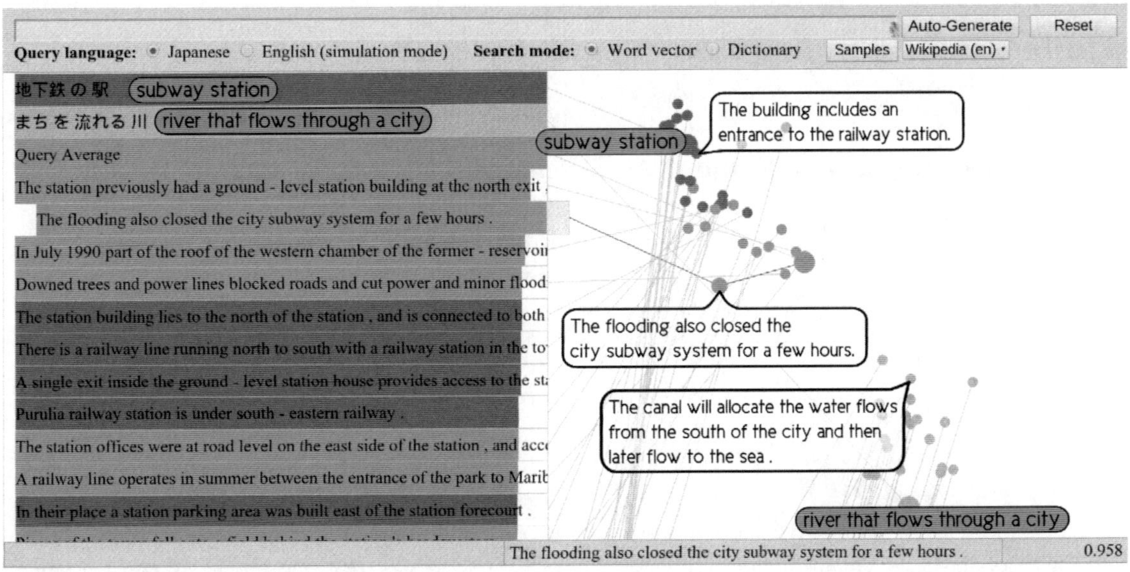

Figure 2: Annotated screenshot of CroVeWA.

Acknowledgements

This work was supported by the Data Centric Science Research Commons Project at the Research Organization of Information and Systems and by the Japan Society for the Promotion of Science KAKENHI Grant Number 13F03041.

References

Marco Baroni, Georgiana Dinu, and Germán Kruszewski. 2014. Don't count, predict! A systematic comparison of context-counting vs. context-predicting semantic vectors. In *Proceedings of the 52nd ACL*, pages 238–247.

James Breen. 2004. JMDict: a Japanese-multilingual dictionary. In *Proceedings of the Workshop on Multilingual Linguistic Ressources*, pages 71–79. ACL.

Sarath Chandar A P, Stanislas Lauly, Hugo Larochelle, Mitesh Khapra, Balaraman Ravindran, Vikas C Raykar, and Amrita Saha. 2014. An autoencoder approach to learning bilingual word representations. In Z. Ghahramani, M. Welling, C. Cortes, N.D. Lawrence, and K.Q. Weinberger, editors, *Advances in Neural Information Processing Systems 27*, pages 1853–1861. Curran Associates, Inc.

Kyunghyun Cho, Bart van Merrienboer, Caglar Gulcehre, Dzmitry Bahdanau, Fethi Bougares, Holger Schwenk, and Yoshua Bengio. 2014. Learning phrase representations using RNN encoder–decoder for statistical machine translation. In *Proceedings of EMNLP 2014*, pages 1724–1734.

Ronan Collobert and Jason Weston. 2008. A unified architecture for natural language processing: Deep neural networks with multitask learning. In *Proceedings of the 25th ICML*, pages 160–167. ACM.

Karl Moritz Hermann and Phil Blunsom. 2014. Multilingual models for compositional distributed semantics. In *Proceedings of the 52nd ACL*, pages 58–68.

Joseph B Kruskal. 1964. Multidimensional scaling by optimizing goodness of fit to a nonmetric hypothesis. *Psychometrika*, 29(1):1–27.

Quoc Le and Tomas Mikolov. 2014. Distributed representations of sentences and documents. In *Proceedings of The 31st ICML*, pages 1188–1196.

Tomas Mikolov, Kai Chen, Greg Corrado, and Jeffrey Dean. 2013. Efficient estimation of word representations in vector space. In *Proceedings of Workshop at ICLR*.

Marius Muja and David G. Lowe. 2009. Fast approximate nearest neighbors with automatic algorithm configuration. In *International Conference on Computer Vision Theory and Application VISSAPP'09)*, pages 331–340. INSTICC Press.

Richard Socher, Jeffrey Pennington, Eric H Huang, Andrew Y Ng, and Christopher D Manning. 2011. Semi-supervised recursive autoencoders for predicting sentiment distributions. In *Proceedings of EMNLP*, pages 151–161. Association for Computational Linguistics.

Hubert Soyer, Pontus Stenetorp, and Aizawa Akiko. 2015. Leveraging monolingual data for crosslingual compositional word representations. In *Proceedings of ICLR*. to appear.

Laurens Van der Maaten and Geoffrey Hinton. 2008. Visualizing data using t-SNE. *JMLR*, 9(2579-2605):85.

Online Readability and Text Complexity Analysis with *TextEvaluator*

Diane Napolitano, Kathleen M. Sheehan, and **Robert Mundkowsky**
Educational Testing Service
660 Rosedale Road, 12R
Princeton, NJ 08541, USA
{dnapolitano,ksheehan,rmundkowsky}@ets.org

Abstract

We have developed the *TextEvaluator* system for providing text complexity and Common Core-aligned readability information. Detailed text complexity information is provided by eight component scores, presented in such a way as to aid in the user's understanding of the overall readability metric, which is provided as a holistic score on a scale of 100 to 2000. The user may select a targeted US grade level and receive additional analysis relative to it. This and other capabilities are accessible via a feature-rich front-end, located at http://texteval-pilot.ets.org/TextEvaluator/.

1 Introduction

Written communication is only effective to the extent that it can be understood by its intended audience. A metric of readability, along with detailed information about aspects of the text which contribute its complexity, can be an indispensable aid to any content developer, teacher, or even reader. ETS's *TextEvaluator*[1] stands apart from similar systems (e.g.: Coh-Metrix (Graesser et al., 2011), Reading Maturity (Landauer, 2011), ATOS (Milone, 2008), Lexile (Stenner et al., 2006), and, perhaps most famously, Flesch-Kincaid (Kincaid et al., 1975)) in that it not only provides a single, holistic score of overall complexity, but also additional complexity information in the form of eight contributing components. The other systems known to us only provide one of these types of analysis. In addition to this, *TextEvaluator* will also provide the user with information on how its overall score and each of its component scores correspond to ideal values relative to a user-specified targeted grade level. All of this information is aligned with the current set of US grade school (K–12) text complexity standards outlined by the Common Core (CCSSI, 2010).

TextEvaluator's overall complexity scores are highly correlated with human grade level classifications, as shown in (Nelson et al., 2012). This study compared six systems as part of the Gates Foundation's Race to the Top initiative. Of these systems, the overall complexity scores computed by *TextEvaluator* were shown to have the highest Spearman rank correlation (0.756) between human grade level classifications on a set of 168 Common Core exemplar texts. *TextEvaluator* differs from these systems in that the computation of its overall complexity score relies on its set of eight component scores, each of which is a linear combination of four to ten fine-grained features. Most of these features are derived from information provided by part-of-speech tags and syntactic parses, unlike many competing systems which tend to only incorporate two or three basic features, such as average sentence length and average word frequency. Also unlike other systems, *TextEvaluator* differentiates between the two primary genres proposed by the Common Core: Informational texts, and their more challenging counter-parts, Literary texts. Internally, *TextEvaluator* makes use of either a model of Informational or Literary text complexity, in order to produce its final, overall score of complexity.

In this paper, we provide an overview

[1] *TextEvaluator* was previously known as *SourceRater*.

Proceedings of NAACL-HLT 2015, pages 96–100,
Denver, Colorado, May 31 – June 5, 2015.

of how one can obtain and interpret *TextEvaluator* analyses received via the web. We provide a pilot version of our system at http://texteval-pilot.ets.org/TextEvaluator/.

Additional information on the overall complexity score and the component scores, as well as validity information, can be found in Sheehan et al. (2014) and Sheehan et al. (2013). Much of this information is also provided on the website's *About TextEvaluator* page.

1.1 Limitations

At this time, text submitted to *TextEvaluator* for analysis must be plain ASCII or UTF-8 text, free of images and tables. Many of *TextEvaluator*'s features make use of paragraphs, so it is recommended that at least one hard return is inserted between each paragraph. Manual word-wrapping will be corrected, and bulleted or numbered lists will be converted into one sentence per item.

TextEvaluator was designed for short reading passages, such as news articles or short stories, the sort of material one might expect to see during an exam or classroom assignment. We are currently investigating its use with longer (greater than 5-6 pages in length) texts. It is currently not suitable for poetry, plays, or texts that contain fewer than than 2-3 sentences.

TextEvaluator was designed for use with materials that are publication-ready. Student assignments, such as essays, and transcripts of free-response monologues or dialogues, are not appropriate for *TextEvaluator*. *TextEvaluator* simply may not be able to analyze such transcripts or noisy text such as casual, online exchanges, due to its reliance on a syntactic parser (**?**). If the input contains at least one sentence that the parser cannot find a valid parse for, *TextEvaluator* cannot proceed with the analysis and will reject the text.

At this time, there is no programmatic API to *TextEvaluator* that is available to the public. However, batch-mode processing may be possible by contacting ETS via the information provided on the website.

2 Submitting a Text for Analysis

Upon visiting the *TextEvaluator* website, the user is asked to provide up to two pieces of information: a valid e-mail address and a client code. We first validate the provided e-mail address by sending an e-mail containing a link to the page described in Section 3.[2] Then, rather than have the user wait for their results to be computed, *TextEvaluator* will notify the user via e-mail when their results are ready.

An e-mail address is mandatory but a client code is not; specifying a valid client code gives the user access to some additional analyses. A client code can be obtained by purchasing a license for commercial use from ETS. However, this paper will focus primarily on the version of the website that is freely accessible for research and academic use.

Research and academic use is limited to texts that are 1600 words or less in length, and it is the responsibility of the user to truncate their texts. With a client code, the length of the text is not constrained. The user may either upload a plain text file or copy and paste such text into the larger input box. The user is then encouraged to provide a title for their submission, should they potentially have several *TextEvaluator* analyses on their screen at one time.

TextEvaluator will provide an additional set of analyses relative to a specified targeted grade level which ranges from US grades 2 to 12. At this time, the user is required to select a targeted grade. If a client code was entered, the user will be able to select additional targeted grades on the page containing their results.

3 The Results Page

The user will receive a link to their results via e-mail as soon as *TextEvaluator* has completed its analysis. Without the use of a client code, this web page will look similar to the one presented in Figure 1. Above the "Summary" tab, one can see the optional title they provided, or a title provided by *TextEvaluator*, along with two large boxes. The leftmost one will state whether or not the overall complexity of the submitted text is above, within, or below the expected range of complexity for your targeted grade

[2]This initial step is slated to be removed in a future version of the website.

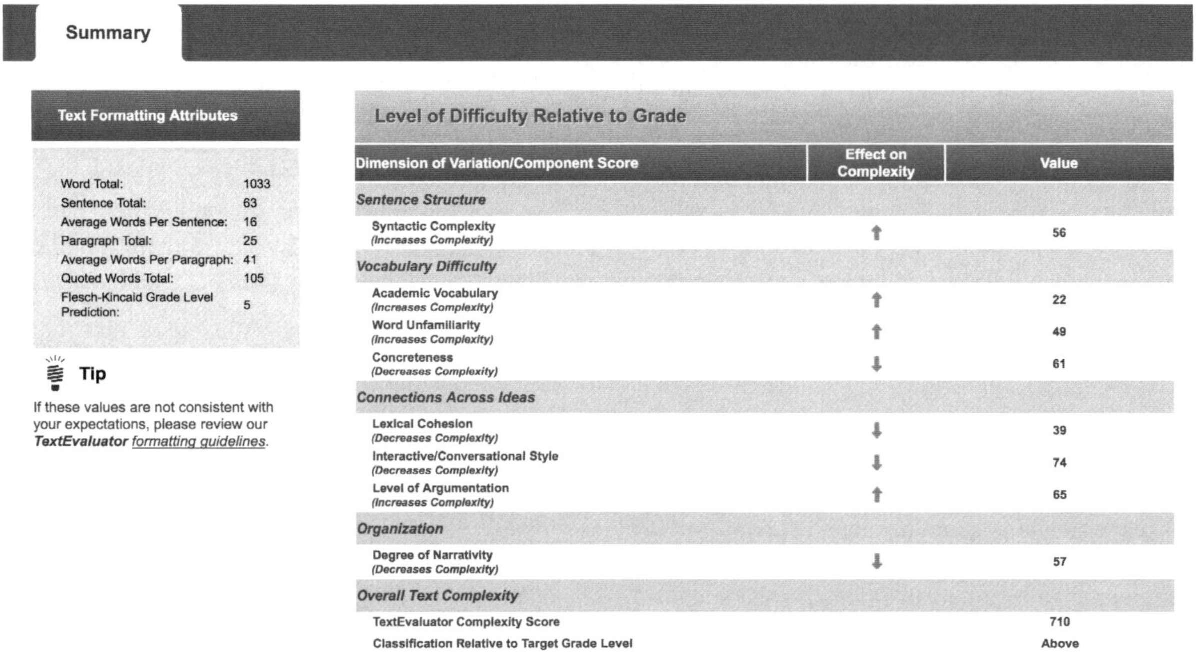

Summary

Text Formatting Attributes

Word Total:	1033
Sentence Total:	63
Average Words Per Sentence:	16
Paragraph Total:	25
Average Words Per Paragraph:	41
Quoted Words Total:	105
Flesch-Kincaid Grade Level Prediction:	5

Tip

If these values are not consistent with your expectations, please review our ***TextEvaluator*** formatting guidelines.

Level of Difficulty Relative to Grade

Dimension of Variation/Component Score	Effect on Complexity	Value
Sentence Structure		
Syntactic Complexity *(Increases Complexity)*	↑	56
Vocabulary Difficulty		
Academic Vocabulary *(Increases Complexity)*	↑	22
Word Unfamiliarity *(Increases Complexity)*	↑	49
Concreteness *(Decreases Complexity)*	↓	61
Connections Across Ideas		
Lexical Cohesion *(Decreases Complexity)*	↓	39
Interactive/Conversational Style *(Decreases Complexity)*	↓	74
Level of Argumentation *(Increases Complexity)*	↑	65
Organization		
Degree of Narrativity *(Decreases Complexity)*	↓	57
Overall Text Complexity		
TextEvaluator Complexity Score		710
Classification Relative to Target Grade Level		Above

Figure 1: The results page one will see without the use of a client code. In this example, a targeted grade level of 4 was selected.

level. This information is also presented towards the bottom of the Summary tab, and will be explained later in this section. The rightmost box displays the text's overall complexity score on a scale of 100 (appropriate for first-grade students) to 2000 (appropriate for high-proficiency college graduates). As with the above/within/below analysis, this information is also presented towards the bottom of the Summary tab.

The box in the lefthand column of the Summary tab provides information regarding the contents of your text as discovered by *TextEvaluator*. If any of this information appears incorrect to the user, they are encouraged to reformat their text and submit it again. We also provide the Flesch-Kincaid grade level (Kincaid et al., 1975) of the text, should the user be interested in comparing their Common Core-aligned complexity score to one aligned to a previous standard.

TextEvaluator's analysis of the submitted text can be found in a table in the righthand column of the page. The scores of the eight components are presented, each on a scale of 0 to 100, with information regarding whether or not a higher value for that component leads to a *more* complex or *less* complex text. This information is communicated via the arrows in the second column of this table. Each component score is the scaled result of a Principal Components Analysis which combines at least four but no more than ten distinct features per score. Provided is a brief description of each component; however, for more information, the reader is again referred to Sheehan et al. (2014), Sheehan et al. (2013), and the website's *About TextEvaluator* page.

3.1 Sentence Structure

Currently, the only component in this category, *Syntactic Complexity*, encapsulates all information regarding how complex the sentences are within the submitted text. It relies on information from syntactic parse trees[3] (Manning et al, 2014) and part-of-speech tags (Toutanova et al., 2003), as well as basic measures such as the number of extremely long sentences and the size of the longest paragraph.[4] As de-

[3] As provided by Stanford's shift-reduce parser, version 3.5.1: http://nlp.stanford.edu/software/srparser.shtml

[4] We make use of both a syntactic parser and a tagger in order to differentiate between possessives and the contractive form of "is". "'s" forms tagged as `POS` by the tagger are re-attached to

scribed in section 1.1, should the parser fail to find a valid parse for any sentence in the text, *TextEvaluator* will be unable to calculate the features necessary to compute the text's Syntactic Complexity score, and thus, unable to compute its overall complexity score.

3.2 Vocabulary Difficulty

This category's components measure the amount of:

- *Academic Vocabulary*, words that are more characteristic of academic writing than that of fiction or conversation;
- Rare words, as determined by consulting two different word frequency indices and encapsulated in the *Word Unfamiliarity* component; and
- *Concreteness*, which describes the abstractness or difficulty one might have imagining the words within the text.

The two word frequency indices were created from one containing more than 17 million word tokens focused on primary school (K–12) reading materials, and one containing more than 400 million word tokens spanning primary and post-graduate school. Features in the Concreteness component are based on values of the perceived concreteness and imageability of each content word in the text as provided by the MRC Psycholinguistic Database (Coltheart, 1981).

3.3 Connections Across Ideas

The components within this category indicate the amount of difficulty the reader may have following the concepts presented throughout the text. *Lexical Cohesion* combines several features which are computed based on the number of overlapping lemmas between pairs of sentences in each paragraph. *Interactive/Conversational Style* is concerned with the use of verbs, contractions, and casual, spoken-style discourse, common to Literary texts. By comparison, the *Level of Argumentation* component provides a measurement of more formal, argumentative discourse, much more common in Informational texts. This component encapsulates words and phrases that are commonly found in argumentative discourse, such as subordinating concessive phrases ("although", "however", "on the contrary"), synthetic negations ("nor", "neither"), "negative" adverbs ("seldom", "hardly", "barely"), and causal conjunctive phrases ("as a result", "for this reason", "under the circumstances").

the preceding noun and this modified tag structure is provided as input to the parser.

3.4 Organization

This category also only has one component, the *Degree of Narrativity*. This component differs from Interactive/Conversational Style in that it makes use of the number of words found within quotation marks, referential pronouns, and past-tense verbs, all of which are primary features of any written narrative.

3.5 The Overall Complexity Score

The determination of *TextEvaluator*'s overall complexity score is genre-dependent, relying on the idea that some features of text complexity will function differently for *Informational* and *Literary* texts. Thus, *TextEvaluator* will actually compute a different overall complexity score for each genre, each trained as a linear regression model of the component scores. Should the text actually be a combination of the two, a weighted average of the two scores is presented as the overall complexity score. The decision of which score to present to the user as the final, overall complexity score is determined by calculating the probability that the text is Informational. If that value is within a certain range, the text is said to be Informational, Literary, or Mixed. Regardless of the text's genre, the complexity score's relativity to the targeted grade level is determined the same way.

The notion of a text being above, within, or below the expected range of complexity relative to the targeted grade level is described further by the presentation of these ranges in Table 1. A text is "above" the allowable range of complexity if, for the chosen targeted grade, its complexity score is greater than the *Max* value, "below" if it is less than the *Min* value, or "within" if it is equal to, or between, the *Min* and *Max* values. The method used to establish this alignment between *TextEvaluator* complexity scores and the Common Core text complexity scale is described in (Sheehan, 2015). There, three evaluations of the proposed ranges are presented:

Target GL	Min	Max
2	100	525
3	310	590
4	405	655
5	480	720
6	550	790
7	615	860
8	685	940
9	750	1025
10	820	1125
11	890	1245
12	970	1360

Table 1: The *TextEvaluator*/Common Core alignment table, showing the expected ranges of complexity relative to a targeted grade level. Although complexity scores can be as high as 2000, only the ones presented in the ranges here have been externally validated by the Common Core (Sheehan, 2015).

one based on the 168 exemplar texts listed in Appendix B of (CCSSI, 2010); one based on a set of ten texts intended for readers who are career-ready; and one based on a set of 59 texts selected from textbooks assigned in typical college courses. In each case, results confirmed that *TextEvaluator*'s classifications of texts being above, within, or below each range of complexity are aligned with classifications provided by reading experts.

At this stage, users who provided a client code at the start of their analysis will be able to select and see analysis for a different targeted grade level. They will also receive an additional piece of information in the form of color-coding on each component score, relative to the selected targeted grade. Each score will be highlighted in red, yellow, or green, should the value for that component be either too high, a bit too high, or within or below the ideal range for a text in the same genre as the input text and at that targeted grade.

4 Conclusion

In this paper we have presented *TextEvaluator*, a tool capable of analyzing almost any written text, for which it provides in-depth information into the text's readability and complexity. This information is further summarized with a holistic score with both a high correlation to human judgement (Nelson et al., 2012) and external validity. (Sheehan, 2015) It is these characteristics that lead us to believe that *TextEvaluator* is a useful tool for educators, content-developers, researchers, and readers alike.

References

Coltheart, M. 1981. The MRC psycholinguistic database. *The Quarterly Journal of Experimental Psychology Section A*, 33(4): 497 – 505.

Common Core State Standards Initiative. (2010, June). *Common Core State Standards for English language arts and literacy in history/social studies, science and technical subjects.* Washington, DC: CCSSO and National Governors Association.

Graesser, A.C., McNamara, D.S, and Kulikowich, J.M. 2011. Coh-Metrix: Providing multilevel analyses of text characteristics. *Educational Researcher*, 40(5): 223 – 234.

Kincaid, J.P., Fishburne, R.P., Rogers, R.L., and Chissom, B.S. 1975. *Derivation of new readability formulas (automated readability index, Fog count and Flesch reading ease formula) for Navy enlisted personnel.* (Research Branch Report No. 8-75), NavalAir Station, Memphis, TN.

Landauer, T. 2011. *Pearson's text complexity measure.* White Paper, Pearson.

Manning, C.D., Surdeanu, M., Bauer, J, Finkel, J, Bethard, S.J., and McClosky, D. 2014. *The Stanford CoreNLP Natural Language Processing Toolkit.* In Proceedings of 52nd Annual Meeting of the Association for Computational Linguistics: System Demonstrations, Baltimore, MD.

Milone, M. 2008. *The development of ATOS: The Renaissance readability formula.* Wisconsin Rapids, WI: Renaissance Learning.

Nelson, J., Perfetti, C., Liben, D. and Liben, M. 2012. *Measures of text difficulty: Testing their predictive value for grade levels and student performance.* Technical Report, Washington, DC: Council of Chief State School Officers.

Sheehan, K.M. 2015. *Aligning TextEvaluator scores with the accelerated text complexity guidelines specified in the Common Core State Standards.* ETS Research Report. Princeton, NJ: Educational Testing Service.

Sheehan, K.M, Flor, M., and Napolitano, D. 2013. *A two-stage approach for generating unbiased estimates of text complexity.* In Proceedings of the 2nd Workshop on Natural Language Processing for Improving Textual Accessibility, Atlanta, GA.

Sheehan, K.M, Kostin, I., Napolitano, D., and Flor, M. 2014. The TextEvaluator Tool: Helping teachers and test developers select texts for use in instruction and assessment. *The Elementary School Journal*, 115(2): 184–209.

Stenner, A.J., Burdick, H., Sanford, E., and Burdick, D. 2006. How accurate are Lexile text measures? *Journal of Applied Measurement*, 7(3): 307 – 322.

Toutanova, K, Klein, D., and Manning, C. 2003. *Feature-Rich Part-of-Speech Tagging with a Cyclic Dependency Network.* In Proceedings of the North American Association for Computational Linguistics, Edmonton, AB, Canada.

Natural Language Question Answering and Analytics for Diverse and Interlinked Datasets

Dezhao Song **Frank Schilder** **Charese Smiley**
Research and Development, Thomson Reuters
610 Opperman Drive
Eagan, MN 55123, USA

Chris Brew
Research and Development, Thomson Reuters
1 Mark Square
London, UK

{dezhao.song, frank.schilder, charese.smiley, chris.brew}@thomsonreuters.com

Abstract

Previous systems for natural language questions over complex linked datasets require the user to enter a complete and well-formed question, and present the answers as raw lists of entities. Using a feature-based grammar with a full formal semantics, we have developed a system that is able to support rich autosuggest, and to deliver dynamically generated analytics for each result that it returns.

1 Introduction

In order to retrieve data from a knowledge base (KB), knowledge workers, such as physicians or financial analysts, often face the challenge of having to learn specific query languages (e.g., SQL and SPARQL[1]). However, the fast pace of changing query languages to different types of KBs (e.g., Relational Databases, Triple Stores, NoSQL stores, etc.) makes it difficult for users to keep up with the latest developments of such query languages that allow them to access the data they need for their work. This situation prevents users without extensive computer training from effectively utilizing the available information in the KB. Developing user-friendly natural language interfaces will make it easier for non-technical users to access the information in the KB in an intuitive way.

In this paper, we present a Natural Language Interface that allows users to query the underlying KBs with natural language questions. Unlike previous approaches, instead of asking the users to provide the entire question on their own, our system makes suggestions to help the users to complete their questions. Given a complete question, our system parses it to its First Order Logic (FOL) representation using a grammar derived from interlinked datasets; different translators are developed to further translate the FOL of a query into executable queries, including both SQL and SPARQL. Finally, our system generates dynamic analytics for the result sets in order to help users to gain a better understanding of the data.

2 Related Work

Keyword-based search (Ding et al., 2004; Tummarello et al., 2007; d'Aquin and Motta, 2011) and faceted search (Zhang et al., 2013; Zhang et al., 2014) have been frequently adopted for retrieving information from KBs. However, users have to figure out the most effective queries in order to retrieve relevant information. Furthermore, without appropriate ranking methods, users may be overwhelmed by the information available in the search results.

Early Natural Language Interfaces (NLIs) required a handcrafted interface solution for each database thereby restricting its portability (Green et al., 1961; Hendrix et al., 1978; Woods, 1973). Recent research has focused more on developing open domain systems (Kwiatkowski et al., 2013; Yao and Durme, 2014; Bordes et al., 2014), but there remains a need for specialized NLIs (Minock, 2005). One unique feature of our system is to help users to build a complete question by providing suggestions according to a partial question and a grammar.

Much of prior work translates a natural language question into SPARQL and retrieves answers from a

[1] http://www.w3.org/TR/rdf-sparql-query/

Proceedings of NAACL-HLT 2015, pages 101–105,
Denver, Colorado, May 31 – June 5, 2015.

triple store (Lopez et al., 2005; Unger et al., 2012; Lehmann et al., 2012; Yahya et al., 2013; He et al., 2014); however, SPARQL queries have been criticized to have unsatisfying query response time. In this work, we maintain flexibility by first parsing a question into First Order Logic, which is further translated into both SQL and SPARQL. This enables us to easily adapt to new query languages and allows us to choose the most appropriate query language technology for a given use case.

Finally, to the best of our knowledge, none of existing NLIs provide dynamic analytics for the results. Our system performs descriptive analytics and comparisons on various dimensions of the data, conducts sentiment analysis, and analyzes trends over time in the data. Such analytics would enable users to better conduct further analyses and derive insights from the data. This feature of our system is a clear advantage over other NLI systems that only retrieve a simple result list of documents/entities.

3 Overall Architecture

Figure 1 shows the overall architecture of our proposed NLI system. Users can input their questions

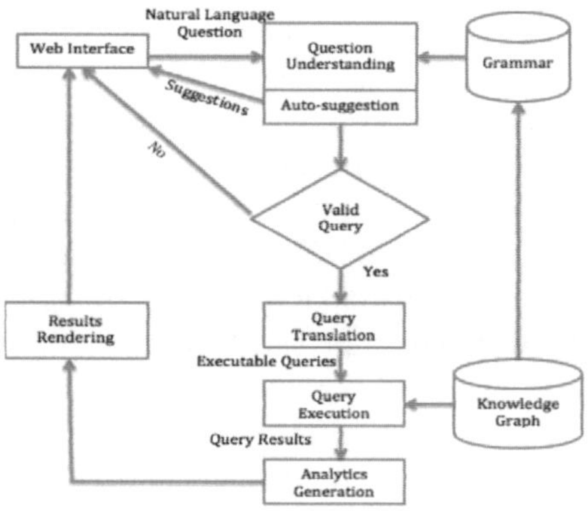

Figure 1: System Architecture

on the Web Interface and our Auto-suggestion component will guide the users in completing their questions. A complete question is then sent to the Question Understanding module again to be parsed into its first order logic representation with the grammar. As the next step, the FOL of a query is translated into an executable query with the Query Translation module. A translated query is then executed against an underlying knowledge base/graph for retrieving answers and generating corresponding analytics.

Our system currently focuses on the following domains: Drugs, Organizations, Patents, People, Finance and News. The underlying knowledge base contains about 1 million entities and 12 million relationships.

4 Question Understanding

Our system utilizes a feature-based context-free grammar (FCFG) that consists of grammar rules on non-terminal nodes and lexical rules on leaf nodes. Grammatical entries on non-terminal syntactic nodes are largely domain-independent, thus enabling our grammar to be easily adaptable to new domains. Each lexical entry to the grammar contains domain-specific features which are used to constrain the number of parses computed by the parser preferably to a single, unambiguous parse.

The following are two rules in our grammar.

1. N[TYPE=drug, NUM=pl, SEM=<λx.drug(x)>] → 'drugs'
2. V[TYPE=[org,drug],SEM=$\lambda X x.X(\lambda y$.develop_org_drug(x,y))>, TNS=prog, NUM=?n] → 'developing'

Rule 1 shows a lexical entry for the word *drugs*, indicating that its TYPE is *drug*, is *plural*, and has the following semantic: λx.drug(x). Rule 2 specifies the verb *develop*, describing its tense (TNS) and indicating that it connects an *organization* and a *drug* via the TYPE feature. By utilizing the type constraints, we can then license the query *companies developing drugs* while rejecting nonsensical queries like *rabbits develop drugs* on the basis of the mismatch in semantic type. Furthermore, our grammar also covers wh-questions, e.g., *what, which, how many, where*, and nominal phrases and imperatives.

Disambiguation relies on the presence of features on non-terminal syntactic nodes. We mark prepositional phrases (PPs) with features that determine their attachment preference. E.g., the PP *for pain* in *how many companies develop drugs for pain?* must attach to an NP rather than a VP; thus, it must attach to *drugs* rather than *develop*. Together with other features, we filter out many of the logically possible but undesired PP-attachments in queries with many modifiers. E.g., our approach is able to generate a single parse for *companies headquartered in Germany developing drugs for pain or cancer*.

5 Auto-suggestion

Our NLI provides suggestions to help users to complete their questions. Unlike Google's query autocompletion that is based on query logs (Cornea and Weininger, 2014), our auto-suggestion utilizes the linguistic constraints encoded in the grammar.

Our auto-suggestion is based on the idea of left-corner parsing. Given a query segment qs (e.g., *drugs*, *developed by*, etc.), we find all grammar rules whose left corner fe on the right side matches the left side of the lexical entry of qs. We then find all leaf nodes in the grammar that can be reached by using the adjacent element of fe. For all reachable leaf nodes (i.e., lexical entries in our grammar), if a lexical entry also satisfies all the linguistic constraints, we then treat it as a valid suggestion.

Specifically, for the query segment *Drugs*, according to our grammar, we could be looking for a verb as the next part of the question. In our lexicon, we may have many verbs, e.g., *drive* and *developed by*. Here, *developed by* is a valid suggestion because its semantic constraints match that of drugs. We continue our suggestions to the end of the user-entered query string, and never try to interpolate material either before or inside the string.

In our current system, the automatically generated suggestions are ranked by considering their popularity. We associate each lexical entry with a node in a knowledge graph. This graph contains nodes for the entities corresponding to the lexical entries, further nodes for generic types such as Drug, Company and Technology, and yet further nodes for predicates such as *developed by* and *granted to*.The edges of the graph represent relations such as *developed by* and *filed by*. For ranking, the degree of a node is as a proxy for its quality. For example, if the node "Google" filed 10 patents and is also involved in 20 lawsuits, then its popularity will be 30.

6 Query Translation and Execution

The interpreted FOL (Section 4) of a question is further analyzed by another parser (implemented with ANTLR (Bovet and Parr, 2008)) that parses FOL expressions. Figure 3 shows the parse tree of the FOL for the query *Drugs developed by Merck*. We then traverse this parse tree, and put all the atomic logical conditions and the logical connectors into a

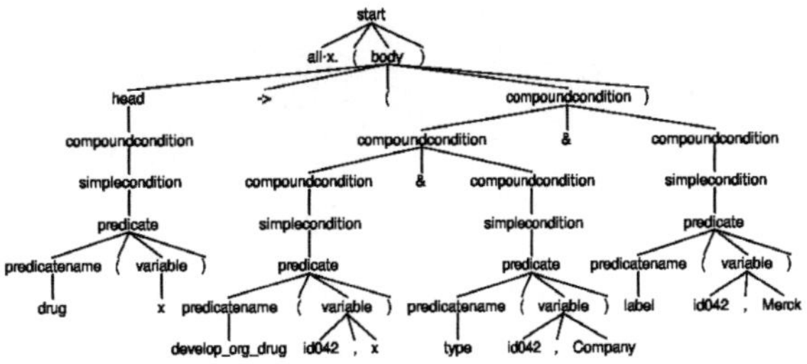

Figure 3: Parse Tree for the First Order Logic Representation of the Query "Drugs developed by Merck"

stack. When we finish traversing the entire tree, we pop the conditions out of the stack to build the query constraints; predicates in the FOL are also mapped to their corresponding attribute names (SQL) or ontology properties (SPARQL).

The following summarizes the translation from a natural language question to a SQL and SPARQL query via a FOL representation:

Natural Language: ``Drugs developed by Merck''

First Order Logic (FOL) Representation: `all x.(drug(x) → (develop(id042,x) & type(id042,Company) & label(id042,Merck)))`

SQL Query:
```
select drug.* from drug
    where drug.originator_company = 'Merck'
```

SPARQL Query (prefixes for RDF and RDFS omitted):
```
PREFIX example:  <http://www.example.com#>
select ?x ?id123 ?id042
where {
?id042 rdfs:label 'Merck'.
?id042 rdf:type example:Company .
?x rdf:type example:Drug .
?id042 example:develops ?x .  }
```

We execute the SQL queries using Apache Spark (Zaharia et al., 2010), a distributed computing environment, thus providing us the potential to handle large-scale datasets. We run SPARQL queries with Jena (Carroll et al., 2004). If a question cannot be parsed into FOL or translated to SQL or SPARQL, we then treat it as a keyword query and retrieve the results from an inverted index built out of our data.

7 Analytics

Instead of only retrieving a list of entities, our system provides several different types of analytics for different result sets. In many situations, the result is a set of records rather than one single entry. This

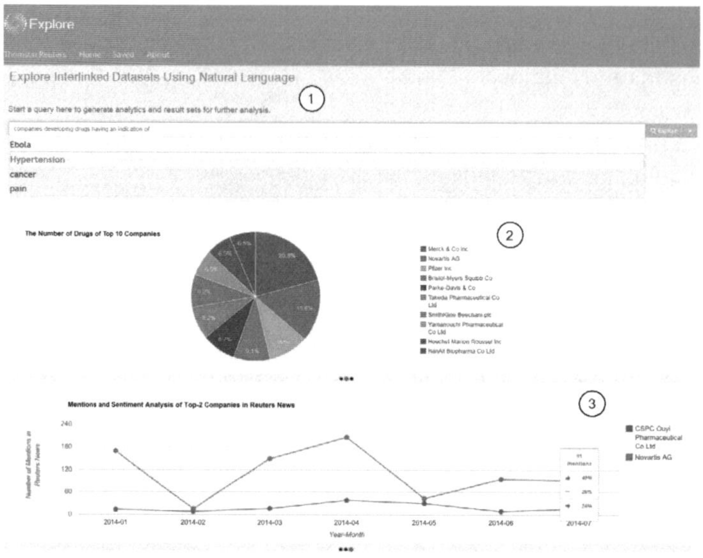

Figure 2: System Screenshot

provides us the opportunity to perform and provide further analyses of the result set for the users.

Our system provides several types of analytics. Descriptive analytics summarize the facts in the result set. For instance, for the question "show me all drugs targeting pain", our system shows the distribution of all technologies used for such drugs in the result set. We also compare the drugs in the result set on different dimensions (e.g., diseases). Moreover, we compute trends via exponential smoothing for entities that have a temporal dimension.

By linking entities from our KB to entity mentions in a large news corpus (14 million articles and 147 million sentences), we are able to perform additional analytics based on named entity recognition and sentiment analysis techniques. We adopted the Stanford CoreNLP toolkit (Manning et al., 2014) for recognizing person, organization, and location from the news corpus. Given an entity, we show its frequency count and how its sentiment may change over time. This information may provide further insights to users in order to support their own analysis.

8 Demonstration Script Outline

Figure 2 shows the beginning of the sample query: *companies developing drugs having an indication of ...?* While the user is typing, a variety of possible extensions to the query are offered, and the user selects *Hypertension* (1). Our system shows a pie chart of each company's market share for hypertension drugs (2); we also show news mentions and sentiment analysis for the most discussed companies (3).

For the demo, we will first motivate the use of natural language question answering for extracting information from complex, interlinked datasets. Next, we will demonstrate how the user can compose a variety of questions with auto-suggestion. Finally, we will walk through the generated analytics and various visualizations for different natural language questions in order to show how it allows the user to gain deeper insights into the data.

9 Conclusion and Future Work

In this paper, we presented a Natural Language Interface for answering complex questions over linked data. Our system parses natural language questions to an intermediate logical representation based on a grammar derived from multiple interlinked datasets. Different translators are developed to translate a question from its FOL representation to SQL and SPARQL queries, which are then executed against an underlying knowledge graph/base for retrieving the answers and generating corresponding analytics. In future work, we intend to cover more domains and provide more complex analytics. We will also perform a thorough evaluation of our system.

References

Antoine Bordes, Sumit Chopra, and Jason Weston. 2014. Question answering with subgraph embeddings. In *Proceedings of the 2014 Conference on Empirical Methods in Natural Language Processing*, pages 615–620.

Jean Bovet and Terence Parr. 2008. Antlrworks: an ANTLR grammar development environment. *Software: Practice and Experience*, 38(12):1305–1332.

Jeremy J. Carroll, Ian Dickinson, Chris Dollin, Dave Reynolds, Andy Seaborne, and Kevin Wilkinson. 2004. Jena: implementing the semantic web recommendations. In *Proceedings of the 13th international conference on World Wide Web - Alternate Track Papers & Posters*, pages 74–83.

Radu C Cornea and Nicholas B Weininger. 2014. Providing autocomplete suggestions, February 4. US Patent 8,645,825.

Mathieu d'Aquin and Enrico Motta. 2011. Watson, more than a semantic web search engine. *Semantic Web Journal*, 2(1):55–63.

Li Ding, Timothy W. Finin, Anupam Joshi, Rong Pan, R. Scott Cost, Yun Peng, Pavan Reddivari, Vishal Doshi, and Joel Sachs. 2004. Swoogle: a search and metadata engine for the semantic web. In *Proceedings of the 2004 ACM International Conference on Information and Knowledge Management*, pages 652–659.

Bert F. Green, Jr., Alice K. Wolf, Carol Chomsky, and Kenneth Laughery. 1961. Baseball: An automatic question-answerer. In *Papers Presented at the Western Joint IRE-AIEE-ACM Computer Conference*, pages 219–224.

Shizhu He, Kang Liu, Yuanzhe Zhang, Liheng Xu, and Jun Zhao. 2014. Question answering over linked data using first-order logic. In *Proceedings of the 2014 Conference on Empirical Methods in Natural Language Processing*, pages 1092–1103.

Gary G. Hendrix, Earl D. Sacerdoti, Daniel Sagalowicz, and Jonathan Slocum. 1978. Developing a natural language interface to complex data. *ACM Transactions on Database Systems*, 3(2):105–147.

Tom Kwiatkowski, Eunsol Choi, Yoav Artzi, and Luke S. Zettlemoyer. 2013. Scaling semantic parsers with on-the-fly ontology matching. In *Proceedings of the Conference on Empirical Methods in Natural Language Processing*, pages 1545–1556.

Jens Lehmann, Tim Furche, Giovanni Grasso, Axel-Cyrille Ngonga Ngomo, Christian Schallhart, Andrew Jon Sellers, Christina Unger, Lorenz Bühmann, Daniel Gerber, Konrad Höffner, David Liu, and Sören Auer. 2012. DEQA: Deep web extraction for question answering. In *11th International Semantic Web Conference*, pages 131–147.

Vanessa Lopez, Michele Pasin, and Enrico Motta. 2005. Aqualog: An ontology-portable question answering system for the semantic web. In *The Semantic Web: Research and Applications, Second European Semantic Web Conference*, pages 546–562.

Christopher D. Manning, Mihai Surdeanu, John Bauer, Jenny Rose Finkel, Steven Bethard, and David McClosky. 2014. The stanford corenlp natural language processing toolkit. In *Proceedings of the 52nd Annual Meeting of the Association for Computational Linguistics*, pages 55–60.

Michael Minock. 2005. Where are the killer applications of restricted domain question answering. In *Proceedings of the IJCAI Workshop on Knowledge Reasoning in Question Answering*, page 4.

Giovanni Tummarello, Renaud Delbru, and Eyal Oren. 2007. Sindice.com: Weaving the open linked data. In *The Semantic Web, 6th International Semantic Web Conference, 2nd Asian Semantic Web Conference*, pages 552–565.

Christina Unger, Lorenz Bühmann, Jens Lehmann, Axel-Cyrille Ngonga Ngomo, Daniel Gerber, and Philipp Cimiano. 2012. Template-based question answering over RDF data. In *Proceedings of the 21st World Wide Web Conference*, pages 639–648.

William A. Woods. 1973. Progress in natural language understanding: an application to lunar geology. In *American Federation of Information Processing Societies: 1973 National Computer Conference*, volume 42, pages 441–450.

Mohamed Yahya, Klaus Berberich, Shady Elbassuoni, and Gerhard Weikum. 2013. Robust question answering over the web of linked data. In *22nd ACM International Conference on Information and Knowledge Management*, pages 1107–1116.

Xuchen Yao and Benjamin Van Durme. 2014. Information extraction over structured data: Question answering with freebase. In *Proceedings of the 52nd Annual Meeting of the Association for Computational Linguistics*, pages 956–966.

Matei Zaharia, Mosharaf Chowdhury, Michael J. Franklin, Scott Shenker, and Ion Stoica. 2010. Spark: Cluster computing with working sets. In *2nd USENIX Workshop on Hot Topics in Cloud Computing*, pages 1–10.

Xingjian Zhang, Dezhao Song, Sambhawa Priya, and Jeff Heflin. 2013. Infrastructure for efficient exploration of large scale linked data via contextual tag clouds. In *12th International Semantic Web Conference*, pages 687–702.

Xingjian Zhang, Dezhao Song, Sambhawa Priya, Zachary Daniels, Kelly Reynolds, and Jeff Heflin. 2014. Exploring linked data with contextual tag clouds. *Journal of Web Semantics*, 24:33–39.

WriteAhead2: Mining Lexical Grammar Patterns for Assisted Writing

Jim Chang
Department of Computer Science,
National Tsing Hua University
101, Kuangfu Road,
Hsinchu, 300, Taiwan
jim.chang.nthu@gmail.com

Jason S. Chang
Department of Computer Science,
National Tsing Hua University
101, Kuangfu Road,
Hsinchu, 300, Taiwan
jason.jschang@gmail.com

Abstract

This paper describes *WriteAhead2*, an interactive writing environment that provides lexical and grammatical suggestions for second language learners, and helps them write fluently and avoid common writing errors. The method involves learning phrase templates from dictionary examples, and extracting grammar patterns with example phrases from an academic corpus. At run-time, as the user types word after word, the actions trigger a list after list of suggestions. Each successive list contains grammar patterns and examples, most relevant to the half-baked sentence. *WriteAhead2* facilitates steady, timely, and spot-on interactions between learner writers and relevant information for effective assisted writing. Preliminary experiments show that *WriteAhead2* has the potential to induce better writing and improve writing skills.

1 Introduction

More and more non-native speakers are writing in English as a second language for global communication, especially in academia. Unavoidably, these L2 writers encounter many problems: in form and content, in grammar, style, and discourse. Much work has been done on developing computer-assisted language reference tools to improve L2 learners' writing skills. Furthermore, many researchers have worked on providing corrective feedback and grades, by automatically detecting and correcting grammatical errors in learner writings.

Computer assisted language learning (CALL) systems typically help the users *before* and *after* writing. For example, *NetSpeak* (www.netspeak.org) uses Google Web 1T Corpus to retrieve common phrases relevant to a user query, while *Marking Mate* (www.readingandwritingtools.com) accepts an user essay and offers a grade with corrective feedback. However, learner writers sorely need concrete writing suggestions, right in the context of writing. Learners could be more effectively assisted, if CALL tools provide such suggestions as learners write away.

Consider an online writer who is composing a sentence starting with "*We propose a method ...*" The best way the system can help is probably not just dictionary-lookup, but rather in-page suggestions tailor-made for this *very* context of continuing the unfinished sentence. Furthermore, fixed-length ngrams such as (1) *method for automatic evaluation* and (2) *method for determining the* is not good enough, or *general enough*, for all writers addressing diverse issues.

Appropriate suggestions should contains *general*, *long* grammar patterns such as: (1) **method for doing something**: *method for finding a solution* (2) **method for something**: *method for grammatical error detection*. Intuitively, by extracting and displaying such patterns and examples, distilled from a very large corpus, we can guide the user towards writing fluently, and free of grammatical errors.

We present a new system, *WriteAhead2*, that proactively provides just-in-time writing suggestions to assist student writers, while they type away. *WriteAhead2* is a continuation of the work of *WriteAhead* (Liou, Yang, Chang 2012). Example *WriteAhead2* suggestions for "*We propose a method*

Proceedings of NAACL-HLT 2015, pages 106–110,
Denver, Colorado, May 31 – June 5, 2015. ©2015 Association for Computational Linguistics

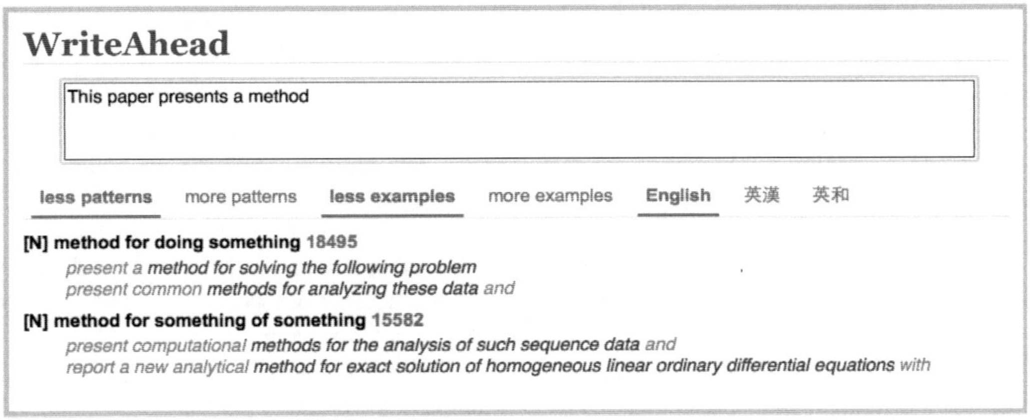

Figure 1: Example *WriteAhead2* session.

..." are shown in Figure 1. *WriteAhead2* has determined the best patterns and examples extracted from the underlying corpus. *WriteAhead2* learns these patterns and examples automatically during training by analyzing annotated dictionary examples and automatically tagged sentences in a corpus. As will be described in Section 4, we used the information on collocation and syntax (ICS) for example sentences from online *Macmillan English Dictionary*, as well as in the *Citeseer x* corpus, to develop *WriteAhead2*.

At run-time, *WriteAhead2* activate itself as the user types in yet another word (e.g., "*method*" in the prefix "*We propose a method ...*"). *WriteAhead2* then retrieves patterns related to the last word. *WriteAhead2* goes one step further and re-ranks the suggestions, in an attempt to move most relevant suggestions to the top. *WriteAhead2* can be accessed at `http://writeahead.nlpweb.org`.

In our prototype, *WriteAhead2* returns the suggestions to the user directly (see Figure 1); alternatively, the suggestions returned by *WriteAhead2* can be used as input to an automatic grammar checker or an essay rater.

2 Related Work

Using dictionaries for language learning has a long and honorable history. However, Sinclair (1991) pointed out dictionaries are limited by their narrow focus on meaning, lack in pragmatics, and insufficient genre/discipline-specific information. Therefore, Sinclair advocated corpus linguistics, corpus-based lexicography, and using a concordance in language teaching.

In the area of corpus-based language learning, Weber (2001) illustrated how combining learner writing and a concordance helped law students in writing better legal essays. Sun (2007) proposed a web-based *Scholarly Writing Template* (SWT) system for graduate students based on a small, manually-annotated corpus. In contrast, we focus on grammar, the most problematic area for learners.

In the area of automated essay rating, *Criterion* (Burstein, Chodorow and Leacock, 2003) uses statistical models to evaluate student writing and provides corrective feedback. Criterion has been used for rating 4 to 12th graders' writings, and TOFEL/GRE composition tests. *Criterion* handles essay writing, while *WriteAhead2* concentrates on helping learner with the genre of research articles.

Autocompletion has been widely used in many language production tasks (e.g., search query and translation). Examples include *Google Suggest* and *TransType*, which pioneered the interactive user interface for statistical machine translation (Langlais, Foster and Lapalme, 2002).

In contrast to the previous research in developing computer assisted writing environment, we present a system that automatically learns grammar patterns and examples from an academic written corpus, with the goal of providing relevant, in-context suggestions.

3 Method

Often, it is not sufficient to use dictionaries or lexical autocompletion to assist learner in writing. Unfortunately, very few Language tools offer compre-

Procedure ExtractPatterns(*Sent, Keywords, Corpus*)

(1) Learning phrase templates for grammar patterns of content words (Section 3.1.1)

(2) Extracting patterns for all keywords in the given corpus based on phrase templates (Section 3.1.2)

(3) Extracting exemplary instances for all patterns of all keywords (Section 3.1.3)

Figure 2: Outline of the pattern extraction process

hensive writing suggestions during writing. In this section, we address such a problem. Given a corpus in a specific genre/domain (e.g., *Citeseer x*), and an unfinished sentence, we intend to assist the user by retrieving and displaying a set of suggestions based on the corpus. For this, we extract grammar patterns with exemplary instances from the corpus. We describe the stages of our solution to this problem in the subsections that followed.

3.1 Extracting Grammar Patterns

We attempt to extract characteristic grammar patterns for keywords in a given corpus to provide writing suggestions, for L2 learners in an online writing session. The set of keywords (as will be described in Section 4) include the words academic writers use most frequently for rhetoric purposes, including stating a topic, hypothesizing, contrasting, exemplifying, explaining, evaluating and other functions. Our extraction process is shown in Figure 2.

3.1.1 *Learning Templates of Grammar Patterns* In the first stage of the extraction process (Step (1) in Figure 2), we generate a set of phrase templates for identifying grammar patterns. For example, a dictionary example with ICS—**have difficulty/problem (in) doing something**: *Six months after the accident, he still has difficulty walking*, implies that this pattern (i.e. **have difficulty in doing something**) can realize in a phrase sequences, "VP NP prep. VP NP". With such a template, we can identify potential patterns for verbs and nouns (e.g., *differ* or *difficulty*). We expand the parentheticals (e.g., **(in)**) and alternatives (e.g., **difficulty/problem**) in ICS, and keep only the most frequent templates. Finally, each of these templates is converted into a regular expression for a *RegExp* chunk parser.

3.1.2 *Extracting Patterns* In the second stage of the extraction process (Step (2) in Figure 2), we identify instances of potential pattern for all keywords. These instance are generated for each tagged and chunked sentence in the given corpus and for each chunk templates obtained in the previous stage.

We adopt the *MapReduce* framework to extract characteristic patterns. In Step (1) of the Map procedure, we perform part of speech and base phrase tagging on the sentences. We then find all pattern instances anchoring at a keyword and matching templates obtained in the first stage. Note that matching is done on the sequence of BIO phrase labels (denoting **B**eginning, **I**nside, and **O**utside of base NP, VP, PP, and ADJP). Then from each matched instance, we extract a tuple of keyword, POS, grammar pattern, collocates (of the keyword), and ngram (word sequence) in Steps (4a) through (4c). Finally, we emit all tuples extracted from the tagged sentence (Step (5)).

The Reduce procedure receives a batch of hashed and locally sorted tuples, grouped by the head word and POS. In Step (1) of the Reduce procedure, we further group the tuples by pattern. Then we count the number of tuples of each pattern (in Step (2)) as well as within-group average and standard deviation (in Step (3)). Finally, With these statistics, we filter and identify patterns more frequent than average by K standard deviation, $K = 1$ (in Step (4)), following Smadja (1993).

3.1.3 *Extracting Exemplary Phrases* In the third and final stage of extraction, we generate exemplary phrases for all patterns of all keywords of interest. The procedure is essentially the same as the Reduce procedure in the second stage (Section 3.1.2).

3.2 Retrieving and Ranking Suggestions

Once the patterns and examples are automatically extracted for each keyword in the given corpus, they are stored as suggestions for the last word the user types in. *WriteAhead2* constantly probes and gets the last written word from the writing area. With the last word as a query, *WriteAhead2* retrieves patterns and examples, and re-ranks the results to move the most relevant information toward the top.

Currently, we re-rank patterns by using word overlap between the last written sentence and the retrieved examples. When there is no word overlap, we fall back to frequency-based ranking. An exam-

Procedure Map(*Sent, AKL, Template*)
(1) *TaggedSent* = TagAndChunkParse(*Sent*)
For each *Word* $\in$ *AKL* at position *i* in *TaggedSent*
(2) *Match* = RegExpChunkParse(*TaggedSent, Template, i*)
If *Match* is found
(3) *ChunkedPhr* = CutChunk(*TaggedSent, i, Match*)
(4a) *Pat* = ExtractPattern(*ChunkedPhr*)
(4b) *Col* = ExtractCollocation(*ChunkedPhr*)
(4c) *Ng* = ExtractNgram(*ChunkedPhr*)
(5) Emit *Tuple* = (*Word, Pat, Col, Ng*)

Procedure Reduce(*Tuples* for a word)
(1) *Pats, PatTuples* = GroupTuplesByPat(*Tuple*)
(2) *Pats, Counts* = Counter(*Pats, PatTuples*)
(3) *Avg, STD* = CalStatatics(*Pats, Counts*)
For each *Pat, Count* pair in (*Pats, Counts*)
If $Count > Avg + K \times STD$
(4) Emit *Tuple* = (*Word, Pat, PatTuples*)

Fig. 3. Outline of the process used to extract CPs.

ple session is shown in Figure 1.

4 Experiments and Results

For training, we used a collection of approximately 3,000 examples for 700 headwords obtained from online Macmillan English Dictionary (Rundel 2007), to develop the templates of patterns. The headwords include nouns, verbs, adjectives, and adverbs. We then proceeded to generate writing suggestions from the *Citeseer x* corpus. First, we used Tsujii POS Tagger (Tsuruoka and Tsujii 2005) to generate tagged sentences. We applied the proposed method to generate suggestions for each of the 700 content keywords in Academic Keyword List.

4.1 Technical Architecture

WriteAhead2 was implemented in Python and Flask Web framework. We stored the suggestions in JSON format using PostgreSQL for faster access. *WriteAhead2* server obtains client input from a popular browser (Safari, Chrome, or Firefox) dynamically with AJAX techniques. For uninterrupted service and ease of scaling up, we chose to host *WriteAhead2* on Heroku, a cloud-platform-as-a-service (PaaS) site.

Table 1: Human evaluation of *WriteAhead2*

Suggestion	Count	Percent	Recall
1st suggestion	141	.53	.43
2nd suggestion	50	.19	.15
3rd suggestion	38	.14	.12
Top 3 suggestions	229	.85	.70
Not in Top 3	38	—	.12
No suggestions	62	—	.19
Not applicable	71	—	—

4.2 Evaluating *WriteAhead2*

To evaluate the performance of *WriteAhead2*, we randomly sampled sentences from conference papers. For simplicity, we tested if our system can provide proper grammar patterns for the first noun or verb in theses sentence. We randomly selected 400 sentences from ACL-2014 long papers. For each sentence, we pasted the sentence prefix up to the the first (noun or verb) keyword to the input box of *WriteAhead2*. The reason for targeting verbs and nouns is that they are considered as exhibiting regularity in local syntax (Hunston and Francis 2000) and common source of learners' writing errors (De Cock, Gilquin, Granger, Lefer, Paquot, and Ricketts 2007). Finally, we manually determined the appropriateness of suggestions for continuing part of the sentence based on the precision of the Top-3 suggestions. For example, we took a sentence:

> *There is some prior work on the related task of hierarchical clustering, or grouping together of semantically related words ...*

and identified the first noun or verb (e.g., *work*) as the anchor, and run *WriteAhead2* on the prefix ending at the anchor (e.g, "*There is some prior work*"). The Top 3 suggestions displayed by *WriteAhead2* were than examined by a human judge to evaluate for correctness in predicting what follow the prefix. For instance, if the first suggestion is:

> **work on something of something 1332:** *VoiSe is designed to work on a symbolic representation of a music score*

Then the judge would determine it is a correct prediction of *work on the related task of hierarchical clustering* and record that the first suggestion is correct. Evaluation of *WriteAhead2* showed a Top 1 precision rate of 53% and recall rate of 70% when considering the Top 3 suggestions.

5 Demo Script

In this demo, we will present a new writing assistance system, *WriteAhead2*, which makes it easy to obtain writing tips as you type away. *WriteAhead2* does two things really well. First, it examines the unfinished sentence you just typed in and then automatically gives you tips in the form of grammar patterns (accompanied with examples similar to those found in a good dictionary) for continuing your sentence. Second, *WriteAhead2* automatically ranks suggestions relevant to your writing, so you spend less time looking at tips, and focus more on writing your piece.

You might type in *This paper presents a method* and are not sure about how to continue. You will instantly receive tips on grammar as well as content as shown in Figure 1. At a quick glance, you might find a relevant pattern, **method for doing something** with examples such as *This paper presents/describes a method for generating solutions.* That could tip you off as to change the sentence into *This paper presents a method*, thus getting rid of tense and article errors, and help you continue to write something like *method for extracting information.*

Using *WriteAhead2* this way, you could at once speed up writing and avoid making common writing errors. This writing and tip-taking process repeats until you finish writing a sentence. And as you start writing a new, the process starts all over again.

Most autocompletion systems such as *Google Suggest* and *TransType* offer word-level suggestions, while *WriteAhead2* organizes, summarizes, and ranks suggestions, so you can, at a glance, grasp complex linguistic information and make quick decision. Our philosophy is that it is important to show information from general to specific to reduce the cognitive load, so while minding the form, you can still focus on the content of writing.

6 Conclusion

Many avenues exist for future research and improvement of *WriteAhead2*. For example, corpora for different language levels, genres (e.g., emails, news) could be used to make the suggestions more relevant to users with diverse proficiency levels and interests. NLP, IR, and machine learning techniques could be used to provide more relevant ranking, to pin-point grammatical errors, or to generate finer-grained semantic patterns (e.g., **assist someone in something** or **attend activity/institution**) Additionally, an interesting direction is identifying grammar patterns using a CRF sequence labeller. Yet another direction of research would be to extract and display backward-looking suggestions to complement the current forward-looking suggestions.

In summary, in an attempt to assist learner writers, we have proposed a method for providing writing suggestion as a user is typewriting. The method involves extracting, retrieving, and ranking grammar patterns and examples. We have implemented and evaluated the proposed method as applied to a scholarly corpus with promising results.

References

Jill Burstein, Martin Chodorow, and Claudia Leacock. 2003. *Criterion: Online Essay Evaluation–An Application for Automated Evaluation of Student Essays.* In Proceedings of the Fifteenth Annual Conference on Innovative Applications of Artificial Intelligence. Acapulco, Mexico.

Cornelia Caragea, Jian Wu, Alina Ciobanu, Kyle Williams, Juan Fernndez-Ramrez, Hung-Hsuan Chen, Zhaohui Wu, and Lee Giles. *CiteSeer x: A Scholarly Big Dataset.* Advances in Information Retrieval. Springer International Publishing, 2014. 311-322.

Sylvie De Cock, Gatanelle Gilquin, Sylviane Granger, Marie-Aude Lefer, Magali Paquot, and Suzanne Ricketts. 2007. *Improve Your Writing Skills.* In Rundell (2007).

Philippe Langlais, George Foster, and Guy Lapalme. 2000. *TransType: A Computer-Aided Translation Typing System.* In Workshop on Embedded Machine Translation Systems.

Hien-Chin Liou, PingChe. Yang, and Jason S. Chang. *Language supports for journal abstract writing across disciplines.* Journal of Computer Assisted Learning 28.4 (2012): 322-335.

Michael Rundell (Ed.). 2007. *Macmillan English Dictionary for Advanced Learners.* Oxford, Macmillan, 2002.

John Sinclair. 1991. *Corpus, Concordance, Collocation.* Oxford University Press, Hong Kong.

Yu-Chih Sun. 2007. *Learner Perceptions of a Concordancing Tool for Academic Writing.* Computer Assisted Language Learning 20, 323343.

Jean-Jacques Weber. 2001. *A Concordance- and Genre-informed Approach to ESP Essay Editing.* ELT Journal 55, 1420.

Question Answering System using Multiple Information Source and Open Type Answer Merge

Seonyeong Park, Soonchoul Kwon, Byungsoo Kim, Sangdo Han, Hyosup Shim, Gary Geunbae Lee
Pohang University of Science and Technology, Pohang, Republic of Korea
{sypark322, theincluder, bsmail90, hansd, hyosupshim, gblee} @postech.ac.kr

Abstract

This paper presents a multi-strategy and multi-source question answering (QA) system that can use multiple strategies to both answer natural language (NL) questions and respond to keywords. We use multiple information sources including curated knowledge base, raw text, auto-generated triples, and NL processing results. We develop open semantic answer type detector for answer merging and improve previous developed single QA modules such as knowledge base based QA, information retrieval based QA.

1 Introduction

Several massive knowledge bases such as DBpedia (Auer et al., 2007) and Freebase (Bollacker et al., 2008) have been released. To utilize these resources, various approaches to question answering (QA) on linked data have been proposed (He et al., 2014; Berant et al., 2013). QA on linked data or on a knowledge base (KB) can give very high precision, but because KBs consist of fragmentary knowledge with no contextual information and is powered by community effort, they cannot cover all information needs of users. Furthermore, QA systems achieve low precision when disambiguating question sentences in to KB concepts; this flaw reduces QAs' performance (Yih et al., 2014).

A QA system can understand a natural language (NL) question and return the answer. In some ways, perfection of QA systems is the final goal of information retrieval (IR). Early QA systems were IR-based QAs (IRQAs). However, as large KBs such as DBpedia and Freebase have been constructed, KB-based QA (KBQA) has become increasingly important (Lehmann et al., 2015; Unger et al., 2012).

These two kinds of QA systems use heterogeneous data; IRQA systems search raw text, whereas KBQA systems search KB. KBQA systems give accurate answers because they search from KBs curated by humans. However, they cannot utilize any contextual information of the answers. The answers of IRQA are relatively less accurate than those of KBQA, but IRQA systems utilize the contextual information of the answers.

We assert that a successful QA system will require appropriate cooperation between a KBQA and an IRQA. We propose a method to merge the KBQA and the IRQA systems and to exploit the information in KB ontology-based open semantic answer type to merge the answers from the two systems, unlike previous systems that use a predetermined answer type. We improve our previous system (Park et al., 2015).

Also we can answer not only complete NL sentence questions, and questions composed of only keywords, which are frequently asked in real life. We suggest strategies and methods (Figure 1) to integrate KBQA, IRQA, and keyword QA.

2 System Architecture

2.1 KB-based QA

A KBQA system takes an NL question sentence as the input and retrieves its answers from the KBs. Because the KBs (i.e., the information sources), are highly structured, the KBQA system can produce very pin-pointed answer sets.

Proceedings of NAACL-HLT 2015, pages 111–115,
Denver, Colorado, May 31 – June 5, 2015. ©2015 Association for Computational Linguistics

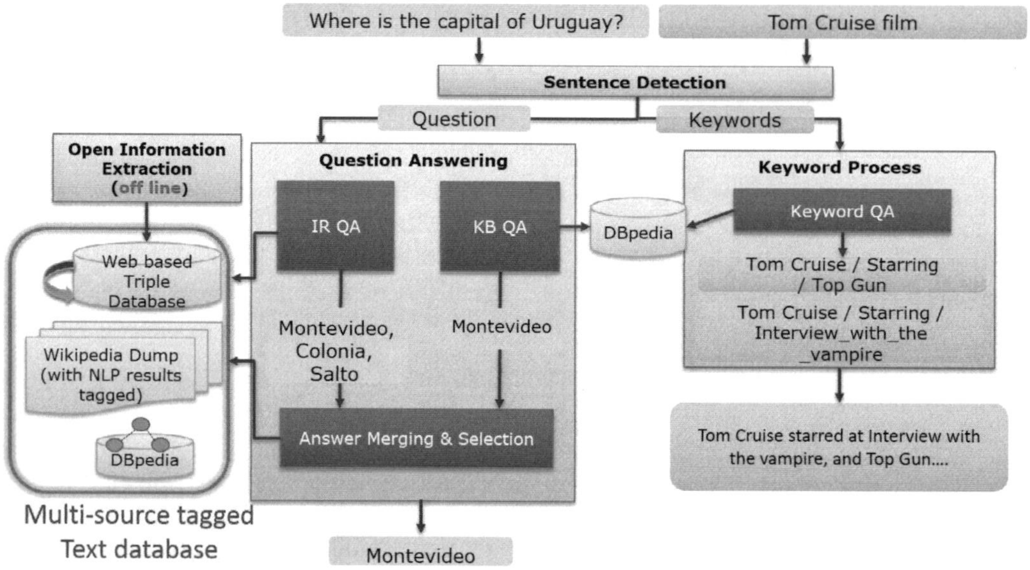

Figure 1. Proposed System Architecture

We combined two approaches to make this system possible. The first approach is based on semantic parsing (Berant et al., 2013), and the second is based on lexico-semantic pattern matching (Shim et al., 2014).

In the semantic parsing approach, the system first generates candidate segments of the question sentence and tries to match KB vocabularies to the segments by combining use of string-similarity based methods and an automatically generated dictionary that consists of pairs of NL phrase and KB predicate (Berant et al., 2013). Finally the system generates query candidates by applying the segments to a small set of hand-crafted grammar rules to generate a single formal meaning representation (Berant et al., 2013).

In the lexico-semantic pattern approach, we use simple patterns paired with a formal query template. The patterns consist of regular expression pattern that describes lexical, part-of-speech (PoS), and chunk-type patterns of a question sentence (Shim et al., 2014). Then the templates paired with these patterns are equipped with methods to extract information from the sentence and to fill the information into the template.

KBQA can assess the answers even when it has little or no additional contextual information, whereas other systems like IRQA systems can rely on the context from which it is retrieved (Schlaefer et al., 2007). Instead, type information and its hierarchy defined in the KB are good sources of contextual information that the KBQA can exploit. However, not all the entities defined in the KB have specific type information; therefore, relying only on the type information can reduce precision (Krishnamurthy and Mitchell, 2014).

When KBQA systems fail, it is usually due to incorrect disambiguation of entities, or to incorrect disambiguation of predicate. Both types of failures result in production of answers of the wrong types. For example, for a question sentence "*What sport does the Toronto Maple Leafs play?*" evoke answers about the arena in which the team plays, instead of the sport that the team plays, when the KBQA system fails in disambiguation.

2.2 IR-based QA

The system uses a multi-source tagged text database which is a combination of raw text, auto-generated triples, co-reference results, named entity disambiguation results, the types of named entities, and syntactic and semantic NLP results including semantic role label, dependency parser results, PoS tag. The system uses clearNLP[1] for syntactic and semantic NLP, Stanford Co-reference tool[2] for co-reference tagging, Spotlight (Mendes et al., 2011) for disambiguated named entity tagging, and SPARQL queries (e.g. *"SELECT*

[1] http://clearnlp.wikispaces.com/

[2] http://nlp.stanford.edu/

DISTINCT ?uri WHERE { res:Nicole_Kidman rdf:type ?uri. }") for tagging DBpedia ontology class types that correspond to entities, and triples that correspond to the sentence. As a result, from a sentence "*Kim was born in 1990 in Bucheon, Gyeonggi, and moved to Gunpo when she was six years old*", the system tags several triples such as < Kim; was born in; 1990 >, < Kim; was born in; Bucheon >, < Kim; was born in; Gyeonggi >, and < Kim; moved to; Gunpo >.

Our IRQA system consists of five parts similar to the architecture of our previous system (Park et al., 2015): the first part detects the semantic answer type of the question and analyzes the question; the second part generates the queries; the third part retrieves passages related to the user question; the fourth part extracts answer candidates using type checking and semantic similarity; and the last part ranks the answer candidates. The system analyzes questions from diverse aspects: PoS tagger, dependency parser, semantic role labeler, our proposed open Information extractor, and our semantic answer type detector. The system expands query using resources such as Wordnet[3] and dictionary.

The system uses Lucene[4] to generate an index and search from multi-source tagged text database. This is an efficient method to search triples and their corresponding sentences, instead of searching the raw text. Using Lucene, the system searches raw sentences and the auto-generated triples at the same time, but may find different sentences due to information loss during extraction of triples. These sentences are scored by measuring semantic similarity to the user query. From these sentences, the system extracts the named entities and compares the semantic answer type of the question to the types of these named entities (Figure 2.). Alongside the answer type, the system uses contextual information of the corresponding sentences of the answer candidates. By combining these two methods, the system selects answer candidates.

2.3 Keyword QA

Keyword QA takes a keyword sequence as the input and returns a NL report as the answer. The system extracts answer triples from the KB from the user input keyword sequences. The system uses previously generated NL templates to generate an NL report (Han et al., 2015).

2.4 Open Information Extraction

Despite their enormous data capacity, KBs have limitation in the amount of knowledge compared to the information on the web. To remedy this deficiency, we construct a repository of triples extracted from the web text. We apply the technique to the English Wikipedia[5] for the demo, but the technique is scalable to a web corpus such as ClueWeb[6]. Each triple is composed of the form < *argument1*; *relation*; *argument2* >, where the arguments are entities in the input sentence and the relation represents the relationship between the arguments.

The system integrates both dependency parse tree pattern and semantic role labeler (SRL) results of each input sentence when extracting the triples. The dependency parse tree patterns are used to generalize NL sentences to abstract sentence structures because the system can find unimportant word tokens can be ignored in the input sentence. We define how triples should be extracted for each dependency pattern. If a certain dependency pattern is satisfied, the word tokens in the pattern constitute the head word of each relation and argument s in the triple. We call these patterns 'extraction templates'. Since manual construction of extraction templates costs too much, we automatically construct them by bootstrapping with seed triples extracted from simple PoS tag patterns.

For each sentence, the SRL annotates the predicate and the arguments of the predicate with their specific roles in the sentence. The predicate is regarded as *relation* and the arguments are regarded as *argument1* and *argument2*, according to their roles. We manually define conversion rules for each SRL result.

3 Methods for Integration

3.1 Detecting Keywords and Sentence

Our system disambiguates whether the user input query is a sentence or a keyword sequence. To disambiguate a sentence, the system uses bi-gram PoS

[3] http://sourceforge.net/projects/jwordnet/
[4] http://lucene.apache.org/core/
[5] http://dumps.wikimedia.org/backup-index.html
[6] http://www.lemurproject.org/clueweb12.php/

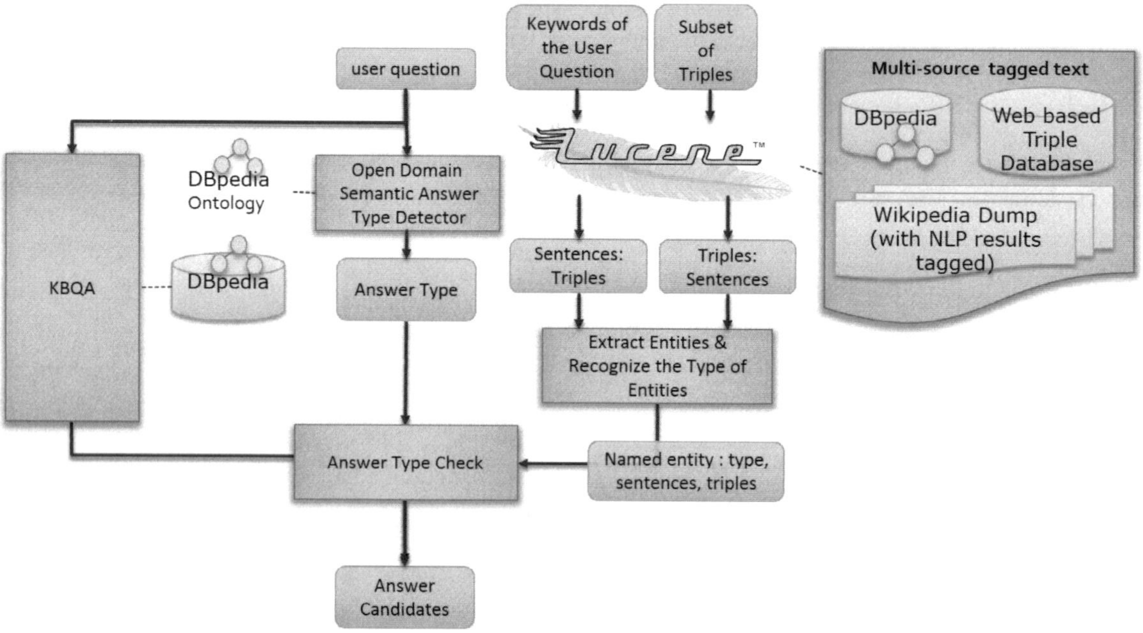

Figure 2. Semantic answer type detector used to merging answer candidates

tag features and a maximum entropy algorithm. Our dataset includes 670 keyword sequences and 4521 sentences. Based on five-fold cross validation, our system correctly detected 96.27 % of the keyword sequences and 98.12 % of the sentences.

When the user query is a sentence, the query is sent to the KBQA/IRQA system. Otherwise the query is sent to the keyword QA system.

3.2 Open Semantic Answer Type detector

The proposed system integrates the answers from the KB and the multi-source tagged text database including the auto-generated triple database. Therefore the KBQA and the IRQA must share an answer-type taxonomy. A previous answer type classification task used UIUC answer type including six coarse-grained answer types and 50 fine-grained answer types (Li et al., 2002). Instead, we use the DBpedia class type hierarchy as the open semantic answer type set. The proposed semantic answer type detector involves three steps.

1. Feature Extraction: The proposed system uses the dependency parser and PoS tagger to extract the main verb and the focus. If the question is "*Who invented Macintosh computer?,*" the main verb is *'invented'* and the focus is *'who'*. The answer sentence is constructed by replacing the focus with the answer candidate and changing to declarative sentence with period, when the focus is substituted with the answer. The system can detect also whether the focus is the subject or the object of the main verb.
2. Mapping property: The system measures the semantic similarity between '*invented*' and DBpedia properties. The system determines that the most similar DBpedia property to *'invented'* is '`patent`'.
3. Finding semantic answer type: The system can get the type of the subject and the object of the DBpedia property '`patent`'. If the focus is the object of the property, the semantic answer type is the type of the object of the property; otherwise it is the type of the subject of the property.

If the system cannot find the answer type by these steps, the system uses an answer type classifier as in Ephyra (Schlaefer et al, 2007) and uses a transformation table to map their answer type classes in the UIUC answer type (Li et al., 2002) taxonomy to DBpedia class ontology.

3.3 Answer Merging and Re-ranking

This integrated system gets the answer candidates from both the KBQA and the IRQA. The system extracts *n*-best sentences including the answer candidates from the KBQA and the keywords from the user query.

The DBpedia types of the answer candidates from both the KBQA and the IRQA can be detected and compared to the semantic answer type (Figure 2.).

Finally, the system selects the final answer list by checking the answer types of the user query and the semantic relatedness among the answer sentence substituted focus with the answer candidates, and the retrieved sentences.

4 Conclusion

We have presented a QA system that uses multiple strategies and multiple sources. The system can answer both complete sentences and sequences of keywords. To find answers, we used both a KB and multi-source tagged text data. This is our baseline system; we are currently using textual entailment technology to improve merging accuracy.

Acknowledgments

This work was supported by the ICT R&D program of MSIP/IITP [R0101-15-0176, Development of Core Technology for Human-like Self-taught Learning based on a Symbolic Approach].

References

Sören Auer, Christian Bizer, Georgi Kobilarov, Jens Lehmann, Richard Cyganiak, and Zachary Ives. 2007. *Dbpedia: A nucleus for a web of open data*. Proceedings of the Sixth international The semantic web and Second Asian conference on Asian semantic web conference (pp. 722-735).

Jonathan Berant, Andrew Chou, Roy Frostig, and Percy Liang. 2013. *Semantic Parsing on Freebase from Question-Answer Pairs*. Proceedings of the 2013 Conference on Empirical Methods in Natural Language Processing. 1533-1544.

Kurt Bollacker, Colin Evans, Praveen Paritosh, Tim Sturge, and Jamie Taylor. 2008. *Freebase: a collaboratively created graph database for structuring human knowledge*. Proceedings of the 2008 SIGMOD international conference on Management of data. 1247-1250.

Sangdo Han, Hyosup Shim, Byungsoo Kim, Seonyeong Park, Seonghan Ryu, and Gary Geunbae Lee. 2015. *Keyword Question Answering System with Report Generation for Linked Data*. Proceedings of the Second International Conference on Big Data and Smart Computing.

Shizhu He, Kang Liu, Yuanzhe Zhang, Liheng Xu, and Jun Zhao. 2014. *Question Answering over Linked Data Using First-order Logic*. Proceedings of the 2014 Conference on Empirical Methods in Natural Language Processing. 1092-1103.

Jayant Krishnamurthy and Tom M. Mitchell. 2014. *Joint Syntactic and Semantic Parsing with Combinatory Categorial Grammar*. Proceedings of 52nd Annual Meeting of the Association for Computational Linguistics. 1188-1198.

Jens Lehmann, Robert Isele, Max Jakob, Anja Jentzsch, Dimitris Kontokostas, Pablo N. Mendes, Sebastian Hellmann, Mohamed Morsey, Patrick van Kleef, Sören Auer, and Christian Bizer. 2015. *DBpedia – A large-scale, multilingual knowledge base extracted from Wikipedia*. Semantic Web: 6(2). 167-195.

Xin Li, Dan Roth, *Learning question classifiers*. 2002. Proceedings of the 19th international conference on Computational linguistics-Volume 1. 1-7.

Pablo N. Mendes, Max Jakob, Andrés García-Silva , and Christian Bizer. 2011. *DBpedia Spotlight: Shedding Light on the Web of Documents*. Proceedings of the 7th International Conference on Semantic Systems. 1-8.

Seonyeong Park, Hyosup Shim, Sangdo Han, Byungsoo Kim, and Gary Geunbae Lee. 2015. *Multi-source hybrid Question Answering system*. Proceeding of The Sixth International Workshop on Spoken Dialog System

Nico Schlaefer, Jeongwoo Ko, Justin Betteridge, Guido Sautter, Manas Pathak, and Eric Nyberg. 2007. *Semantic Extensions of the Ephyra QA System for TREC 2007*. Proceedings of the Sixteenth Text REtrieval Conference.

Hyosup Shim, Seonyeong Park, and Gary Geunbae Lee. 2014. *Assisting semantic parsing-based QA system with lexico-semantic pattern query template*. Proceedings of Human and Cognitive Language Technology. 255-258.

Christina Unger, Lorenz Bühmann, Jens Lehmann, Axel-Cyrille Ngonga Ngomo, Daniel Gerber, and Philipp Cimiano. 2012. *Template-based question answering over RDF data*. Proceedings of the 21st international conference on World Wide Web. 639-648.

Wen-tau Yih, Xiaodong He, and Christopher Meek. 2014. *Semantic parsing for single-relation question answering*. Proceedings of the 52nd Annual Meeting of the Association for Computational Linguistics. 643-648.

Using Word Semantics To Assist English as a Second Language Learners

Mahmoud Azab
University of Michigan
mazab@umich.edu

Chris Hokamp
Dublin City University
chokamp@computing.dcu.ie

Rada Mihalcea
University of Michigan
mihalcea@umich.edu

Abstract

We introduce an interactive interface that aims to help English as a Second Language (ESL) students overcome language related hindrances while reading a text. The interface allows the user to find supplementary information on selected difficult words. The interface is empowered by our lexical substitution engine that provides context-based synonyms for difficult words. We also provide a practical solution for a real-world usage scenario. We demonstrate using the lexical substitution engine – as a browser extension that can annotate and disambiguate difficult words on any webpage.

1 Introduction

According to the U.S. Department of Education, about 11% of all the students in public schools in the United States receive or have received English language learning services. The largest numbers of ESL students are in California (26% of all the students) and Texas (16%). About 70% of these students are Spanish speakers (Dep, 2004). Moreover, there is a large number of non-English speaking countries that have programs for learning English, with as many as 750 million English as a Foreign Language students in the world (Crystal, 1997).

The goal of a number of computer-based language learning tools developed to date is to provide assistance to those with limited language abilities, including students learning a second or a foreign language or people suffering from disabilities such as aphasia. These tools draw on research in education, which found that text adaptation can improve the reading comprehension skills for learners of English (Yano et al., 1994; Carlo et al., 2004). The language learning technology often consists of methods for text simplification and adaptation, which is performed either at syntactic (Carroll et al., 1999; Siddharthan et al., 2004) or lexical level (Carroll et al., 1998; Devlin et al., 2000; Canning and Tait, 1999; Burstein et al., 2007). Work has also been carried out on the prediction and simplification of difficult technical text (Elhadad, 2006a; Elhadad, 2006b) and on the use of syntactic constraints for translations in context (Grefenstette and Segond, 2003).

In this paper, we describe an interface developed with the goal of assisting ESL students in their English reading activities. The interface builds upon a lexical substitution system that we developed, which provides synonyms and definitions for target words in context. We first give a brief overview of the lexical substitution task, and then present our system SALSA (Sinha and Mihalcea, 2014) and (Sinha and Mihalcea, 2012). We then describe the functionality of the interface, and the interaction that a user can have with this interface.

2 Lexical Substitution

Lexical substitution, also known as contextual synonym expansion (McCarthy and Navigli, 2007), involves replacing a certain word in a given context with another, suitable word, such that the overall meaning of the word and the sentence are unchanged. As an example, see the four sentences in Table 1, drawn from the development data from the SEMEVAL-2007 lexical substitution task. In the first sentence, for instance, assuming we choose *bright* as

Proceedings of NAACL-HLT 2015, pages 116–120,
Denver, Colorado, May 31 – June 5, 2015.

the target word, a suitable substitute could be *brilliant*, which would both maintain the meaning of the target word and at the same time fit the context.

Sentence	Target	Synonym
The sun was **bright**.	bright	brilliant
He was **bright** and independent.	bright	intelligent
His feature **film** debut won awards.	film	movie
The market is **tight** right now.	tight	pressured

Table 1: Examples of synonym expansion in context

We perform contextual synonym expansion in two steps: *candidate synonym collection*, followed by *context-based synonym fitness scoring*.

Candidate synonym collection is the first step of our system, and refers to the sub task of collecting a set of potential synonym candidates for a given target word, starting with various resources. Note that this step does not disambiguate the meaning of the target word. Rather, all the possible synonyms are selected, and these synonyms can be further refined in the later step. For example, if we consider all the possible meanings of the word *bright*, it can be potentially replaced by *brilliant, smart, intelligent, vivid, luminous*. SALSA uses five lexical resources, as listed in Table 2, to ensure a good collection of candidate synonyms.

The second step is *context-based synonym fitness scoring*, which refers to picking the best candidates out of the several potential ones obtained as a result of the previous step. There are several ways in which fitness scoring can be performed, for example by accounting for the semantic similarity between the context and a candidate synonym, or for the substitutability of the synonym in the given context. We experimented with several unsupervised and supervised methods, and the method that was found to work best uses a set of features consisting of counts obtained from Google N-grams (Brants and Franz, 2006) for several N-grams centered around the candidate synonym when replaced in context.

The synonym selection process inside SALSA was evaluated under two different settings. The first evaluation setting consists of the lexical sample dataset made available during SEMEVAL 2007 (McCarthy and Navigli, 2007) - a set of 1,700 annotated examples for 170 open-class words. On this dataset, SALSA is able to find the synonym agreed upon by several human annotators as its best guess in 21.3% cases, and this synonym is in the top 10 candidates returned by our system in 64.7% cases. These results compare favorably with the best results reported during SEMEVAL 2007 task on Lexical Substitution.

The second evaluation setting is a dataset consisting of 550 open-class words in running text. On this set of words, SALSA finds the best manually assigned synonym in 29.9% of the cases, and this synonym is in our top ten candidates in 73.7% of the cases.

Overall, we believe SALSA is able to identify good candidate synonyms for a target word in context, and therefore can form the basis for an interface to assist English learners.

3 An Interface for English as a Second Language Learners

Our goal is to leverage lexical substitution techniques in an interface that can provide support to ESL and EFL students in their reading activities. It is often the case that students who are not proficient in English have difficulty with understanding certain words. This in turn has implications for their comprehension of the text, and consequently can negatively impact their learning and knowledge acquisition process. By having inline access to an explanation of the words they have difficulty with, we believe these students will have easier access to the knowledge in the texts that they read.

In order to support various devices and platforms, we implemented the prototype interface as a web application. Given a text, the interface allows readers to click on selected vocabulary words, and view supplementary information in a side panel. This supplementary information includes a list of in-context synonyms, as provided by our system. In addition, we also include example sentences obtained from WordNet, corresponding to the target word meaning dictated by the top synonym selected by SALSA.

The interface also includes the possibility for the user to provide feedback by upvoting or downvoting supplementary information. The goal of this component is to allow the user to indicate whether they found the information provided useful or not. In addition to providing direct feedback on the quality of the interface, this user input will also indirectly con-

Table 2: Subsets of the candidates provided by different lexical resources for the adjective *bright*

Resource	Candidates
Roget (RG)	ablaze aglow alight argent auroral beaming blazing brilliant
WordNet (WN)	burnished sunny shiny lustrous undimmed sunshiny brilliant
TransGraph (TG)	nimble ringing fine aglow keen glad light picturesque
Lin (LN)	red yellow orange pink blue brilliant green white dark
Encarta (EN)	clear optimistic smart vivid dazzling brainy lively

tribute to the construction of a "gold standard" that we can use to further improve the tool.

We evaluated an earlier static version of this interface with ESL students who read two articles from the BBC's English learning website. We manually selected difficult words from the text, and for these words provided a list of in-context synonyms and clear examples. After each reading, the students took a post-reading quiz to evaluate their reading comprehension. We then evaluated the extent to which we could predict a student's performance on the post-quiz using features of their interaction with the tool.

We also used this interface with English middle school students whose primary language is English. The students had to read short excerpts of a book that was a part of their curriculum. Students were allowed to click on only one highlighted word per excerpt. In this experiment, supplementary information was provided from WordNet. There was a post-reading quiz to evaluate the students understanding of the words. By training a regression model on the interaction features collected during the reading exercises, we were able to accurately predict students' performance on the post-quiz (Hokamp et al., 2014).

We have now enabled the SALSA interface to provide feedback on arbitrary English content from the web. By implementing the tool as a browser extension, we are able to show inline additional information about text on any web page, even when the content is dynamically generated.

The interface also collects both explicit and implicit feedback. The explicit feedback is collected via upvotes and downvotes on feedback items. The implicit feedback is based on the user interactions with the system while they are reading. Currently, we collect several kinds of interactions. These interactions include the clicked words, counts of user clicks on a given word, the difficulty of the word as measured by the inverse document frequency, and the number of syllables it contains. In the future, this data will help us to adapt the tool to individual users.

4 Demonstration

During the demonstration, we will present the use of the interface. We will allow participants to freely browse the web with our tool enabled, to view feedback on lexical items, and to provide their own feedback on the quality of the results. The system will automatically identify and highlight the difficult words during browsing, and users can then click these highlighted words to receive supplementary information, consisting of synonyms and definitions, which should assist them in reading and comprehending the content.

By hovering or clicking on an annotated word, users can access a small popup window that includes supplementary information. This supplementary information includes a list of in-context synonyms, as provided by our system, and a clear example of the word in-context. Figure 1 shows an example of the current extension interface when a user hovers over the word **film**.

Although the reading activity + quiz format described above is necessary for the empirical evaluation of our tool, it does not demonstrate a real-world usage scenario. Therefore, we designed a browser extension to show a realistic use case for the lexical substitution engine as the backend for a flexible graphical component that can add additional information to any content. We anticipate that the extension will prove useful to English language learners as they navigate the Web, especially when they encounter difficult English content.

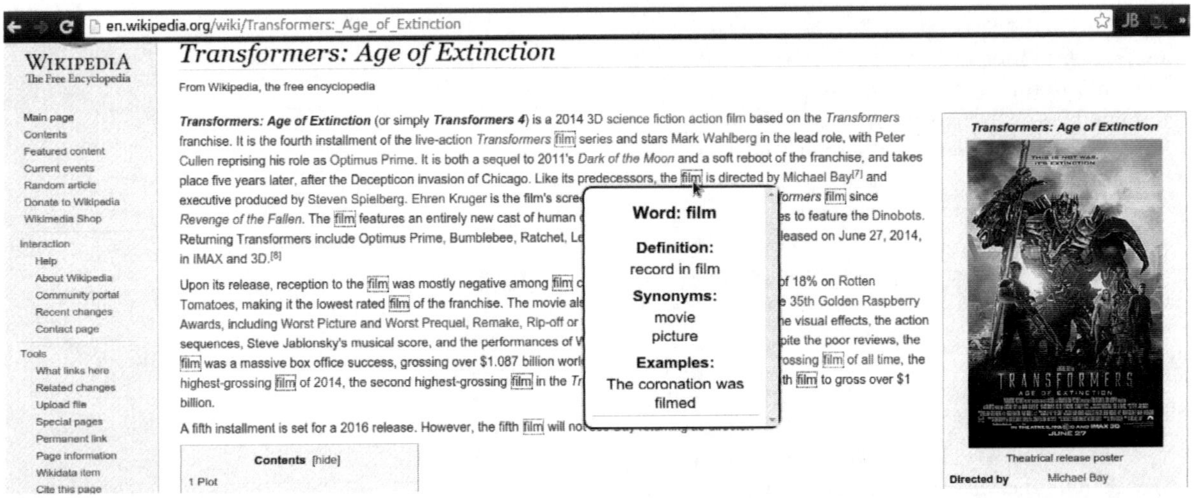

Figure 1: Example of supplementary information that the extension provides the user with when a user hovers over the word *film*.

Acknowledgments

This work was partially funded by the National Science Foundation (CAREER award #1361274) and by DARPA (DEFT grant #12475008). Any opinions, findings, and conclusions or recommendations expressed in this material are those of the authors and do not necessarily reflect the views of the National Science Foundation, DARPA, or the other sources of support.

References

T. Brants and A. Franz. 2006. Web 1T 5-gram version 1. Linguistic Data Consortium.

J. Burstein, J. Shore, J. Sabatini, and Y. Lee. 2007. Developing a reading support tool for English language learners. In *Demo proceedings of the the annual conference of the North American chapter of the Association for Computational Linguistics (NAACL-HLT 2007)*, Rochester, NY.

Y. Canning and J. Tait. 1999. Syntactic simplification of newspaper text for aphasic readers. In *Proceedings of the ACM SIGIR'99 Workshop on Customised Information Delivery*, Berkeley, California.

M.S. Carlo, D. August, B. McLaughlin, C.E. Snow, C. Dressler, D. Lippman, T. Lively, and C. White. 2004. Closing the gap: Addressing the vocabulary needs of english language learners in bilingual and mainstream classrooms. *Reading Research Quarterly*, 39(2).

J. Carroll, G. Minnen, Y. Canning, S. Devlin, and J. Tait. 1998. Practical simplification of English newspaper text to assist aphasic readers. In *Proceedings of the AAAI-98 Workshop on Integrating Artificial Intelligence and Assistive Technology*, Madison, Wisconsin.

J. Carroll, G. Minnen, D. Pearce, Y. Canning, S. Devlin, and J. Tait. 1999. Simplifying text for language-impaired readers. In *Proceedings of the Conference of the European Chapter of the ACL (EACL 1999)*, Bergen, Norway.

D. Crystal. 1997. *English as a global language*. Cambridge University Press.

2004. http://nces.ed.gov/fastfacts/display.asp?id=96.

S. Devlin, J. Tait, J. Carroll, G. Minnen, and D. Pearce. 2000. Making accessible international communication for people with language comprehension difficulties. In *Proceedings of the Conference of Computers Helping People with Special Needs*.

N. Elhadad. 2006a. Comprehending technical texts: Predicting and defining unfamiliar terms. In *Proceedings of the Annual Symposium of the American Medical Informatics Association*, Washington.

N. Elhadad. 2006b. *User-Sensitive Text Summarization: Application to the Medical Domain*. Ph.D. thesis, Columbia University.

G. Grefenstette and F. Segond, 2003. *Multilingual On-Line Natural Language Processing*, chapter 38.

C. Hokamp, R. Mihalcea, and P. Schuelke. 2014. Modeling language proficiency using implicit feedback. In *Proceedings of the Conference on Language Resources and Evaluations (LREC 2014)*, Reykjavik, Iceland, May.

D. McCarthy and R. Navigli. 2007. The semeval English lexical substitution task. In *Proceedings of the ACL Semeval workshop*.

A. Siddharthan, A. Nenkova, and K. McKeown. 2004. Syntactic simplification for improving content selection in multi-document summarization. In *Proceedings of the 20th international conference on Computational Linguistics*.

R. Sinha and R. Mihalcea. 2012. Explorations in lexical-sample and all-words lexical substitution. *Journal of Natural Language Engineering*.

Ravi Som Sinha and Rada Mihalcea. 2014. Explorations in lexical sample and all-words lexical substitution. *Natural Language Engineering*, 20(1):99–129.

Y. Yano, M. Long, and S. Ross. 1994. The effects of simplified and elaborated texts on foreign language tool's utility and effectiveness in terms of students' reading comprehension. *Language Learning*, 44.

Author Index